LEAVING a Legacy

DAVID C. BENTALL

NAVIGATING FAMILY BUSINESS SUCCESSION

LEAVING A LEGACY:
Navigating Family Business Succession

International Standard Book Number:
ISBN (hard cover): 978-1-894860-97-0
ISBN (e-book): 978-1-894860-98-7

Published by:
Castle Quay Books
1307 Wharf Street, Pickering, Ontario, L1W 1A5
Tel: (416) 573-3249
E-mail: info@castlequaybooks.com

Copy Editor: Marina Hofman Willard

Cover design by Burst Impressions
www.burstimpressions.com

Photo Credit: All colour building project photos courtesy of Anthony Fulker (except Bentall Centre, downtown, Vancouver, and TD Centre, Winnipeg, Manitoba)

Library and Archives Canada Cataloguing in Publication

Bentall, David C.
      Leaving a legacy : navigating family business
succession / David C. Bentall ; foreword by Steve McClure.

Includes bibliographical references.
Also issued in electronic format.
ISBN 978-1-894860-97-0

      1. Family-owned business enterprises--Succession--Canada.
2. Family-owned business enterprises--Canada. 3. Bentall,
David C. I. Title.

HD62.25.B45 2012   658'.045   C2012-901810-4

CASTLE QUAY BOOKS

DEDICATION

This book is dedicated to my mom, Phyllis Bentall.

She taught me about love, self-sacrifice and family.

Her gentle spirit and humility inspire me to serve others and to do my best to help other families.

I want them to discover the kind of love that she created in our home.

"When it comes to advising family businesses David's combination of intelligence, experience and integrity are unmatched. He helped our family to develop new patterns of communication and better relationships. Upon this foundation, our family's business continues to grow and expand."

Colin Bosa
CEO of Bosa Properties

"David has been uniquely gifted to help families learn to hear each other and work together. He's lived through a lot and can empathize with family members."

Nan-b de Gaspé Beaubien
Co-Chair, Business Families Foundation

"David can be trusted to genuinely seek the best for every family member. He has experienced both the best and worst a family business has to offer."

Kevin Jenkins
CEO of World Vision International
Former President and CEO of Canadian Airlines

"I think of David as the Wayne Gretzky of executive coaching and mentoring."

Stephan Luking
Managing Partner, Gramercy Developments

"David C. Bentall is a man of great integrity and depth. He's also insightful and caring."

Jimmy Pattison
Chairman, Jim Pattison Group

"I am touched by David's drive to leave a legacy in his own family, with his wife, towards his children and grandchildren. He is reaching for a legacy built upon humility, wisdom, self-discipline and love. He is a superb family business consultant, but his work with other families pales in comparison to his gift for his own."

Peter Vaughan
Principal, West Vancouver Therapy and Psychological Services

DAVID C. BENTALL

An advisor to families in business
An executive coach and mentor
A communicator and teacher

David C. Bentall is from the third generation of a Vancouver family whose members are well-known real estate developers. For 20 years, he worked in the family's business, including 7 years as president and CEO of Dominion Construction.

David is a graduate of the University of British Columbia (UBC) and the Harvard Business School. Now serving as an adjunct professor at the Sauder Business School (UBC) and founder of Next Step Advisors, he is in high demand as a presenter, family business advisor and executive coach.

A passionate water skier, David is a two-time Canadian national champion. In January 2012, he was also ranked #1 in the world in his age division. In 2004, his bestselling book *The Company You Keep* was awarded "book of the year" at the Canadian Word Guild Awards. He and his wife, Alison, have been married for 35 years, and together they have 4 children and 2 grandchildren.

TABLE OF CONTENTS

Part II: Lessons From the Bentall Family

Part III: Learning From Other Business Families

FOREWORD

Several years ago, I considered myself an athlete. I was an active full-time professional consultant, yet I worked hard at my sport and had some success. Then I met David Bentall. Friends had already warned me, "If you think you are good, he will make you think you haven't started training yet." That was, and remains, true. When David is not learning and sharing generously with family businesses or spending time with his own family, he is a passionate athlete and champion. I've known him for over a decade now and in that time have come to know him as an excellent executive coach and sought-after advisor to business families.

To David, the success of business families is personal: he comes from a respected Vancouver, British Columbia, family business. His vivid stories draw generously and respectfully from the ups and downs of his construction and real estate business family; his descriptions are at the same time meaningful and instructional. David's conclusions and insights are real and significant and emerge naturally from his fascinating and open accounts of his family and business experiences.

He draws from his own situation in a family business, yet goes well beyond the limitations of being an expert on one's own case. He understands that no two family businesses are exactly alike, yet they may share many similarities. He is acutely aware of the huge potential for bias in revealing his own rich and intense experiences, yet he transcends this limitation by presenting wise, thoughtful lessons and preserving and applying several heartfelt stories that help his readers to master the concept.

He is open, honest and humble with the story of his own family's experience. It often seems self-critical, yet through it he weaves an instructional analysis from his broad knowledge base of the family business field. He has researched and added to his toolkit the experiences of other business families, as a means of expanding his knowledge of what works and what might be applied to others' circumstances. Primarily, David believes in the advantages of families in business and that he can serve as a conduit and interpreter to assist one business family to learn from another.

David has direct experience and knowledge of family business governance: he has been both a director and a family shareholder represented by independent directors on a board. He knows the fine points of family and non-family leadership in a family firm: he started as a young family employee mentored by non-family managers and eventually became the CEO. He also knows the particular challenges of operating and non-operating shareholders who must work together: he was a business partner with siblings who did not work in the business. He can see things from the point of view of the business leader and of the most distant cousin shareholder. He understands what it takes to make a business successful, even when it must compete for the s' attention in the midst of difficult transitions within the family. He can relate vivid instructional stories from his own experience and that of others, making you think he has known you and your family for years. Then, in a completely objective way, as if he were watching from afar, he evaluates the positive and negative features of his own background, brings them into the discussion and provides a succinct summary of what you might borrow and apply to your own family business. That is a special and unique skill.

When I started my career, I had the good fortune to receive advice from a smart senior businessman who became a mentor. His advice was always in the form of stories that consistently ended with three points, no matter what the lesson. For example, the story about our firm's leader's success was based on three principles: integrity, relationships and hard work. His account of the best client service professionals he knew conveyed the values of integrity, doing one's homework and good service. At the conclusion of each story, he made his three points by holding up three fingers of his left hand. That hand only had three fingers, as he had long ago lost one in an accident. Today, I still see that imperfect hand with its missing finger, and then I remember his lessons. He presented to me a vivid example and communicated a memorable message every time while never saying, "You should do this." David Bentall has all his fingers yet has the same effect on those with whom he works.

I have come to know David ever better over the years, had the pleasure of serving as his mentor, seen his results, heard from his clients and engaged him on philosophy about how to best assist business families. If my former mentor were describing David, he would say he does three things very well: he brings integrity, he does his homework and he delivers much more than what is expected. His clients and readers are fortunate, and those who will interact with him or his writings in the future will benefit from his passionate commitment to his profession. His unique contributions, professionalism and dedication have launched him into the leadership ranks in the field of family business.

Steve McClure, PhD
Principal
The Family Business Consulting Group

ACKNOWLEDGEMENTS

I am indebted to many friends and colleagues, for without the support and guidance of a "small army" of faithful warriors this project could not have been completed.

I must begin by thanking Steve McClure, from the Family Business Consulting Group. Steve was my mentor when I was enrolled in the FFI certificate program a decade ago and when I first started working as an advisor to families in business. As part of the process, Steve encouraged me to write an article tracing all that I was learning as I transitioned from being a "family business executive" to my role as a "family business advisor." Over time, that article has grown into this book. Thank you, Steve, for all that you have taught me, as well as for all that I have learned through the journey that you inspired me to begin so long ago. Thank you, also, for so graciously agreeing to write the foreword for this project.

My roots in this field of study go back to a conference I attended just outside of Montreal. It was there that I was first encouraged by Philippe and Nan-b de Gaspé Beaubien, to think about helping other families in business. Their inspiration, dedication and guidance launched me into my career as an advisor. I will forever be in their debt. They saw potential in me and nudged me in a new direction. I want to thank them both for their wisdom and kindness.

Over the past decade, Dr. Nancy Langton has been my partner in teaching workshops for the Business Families Centre at the University of British Columbia (UBC) and for the Directors' Education Program. Her mentoring of me as a teacher and her collaboration in developing the ideas I now teach have been incredible. I want to thank Nancy for being an amazing professional partner.

During the past decade, I have had the privilege of representing the Sauder School of Business in numerous capacities, and I want to especially thank Dean Dan Muzyka for his vision in creating the Business Families Centre at UBC. It was his leadership that gave me the opportunity to become established as a teacher. I also want to thank Judi Cunningham, the executive director of the Business Families Centre, who continues to encourage and support me as an instructor and advisor for families in business and gives so much to help families in business as well as their advisors.

When I wondered if I could ever become a competent advisor, Dr. John Davis, Dr. John Ward and Ivan Lansberg each encouraged me to "roll up my sleeves" and start helping families. They were my first instructors, and they not only trained me but also gave me the confidence necessary to start a new career. Thank you all from the bottom of my heart.

As I have been working on this project, there have been many colleagues who have kindly read initial drafts and offered their insights. I wish to gratefully acknowledge John Weston, Jim Murphy, Jonathan Michael, Ruth Steverlynck and Luke VanEekeren for taking the time to help refine and in some cases re-direct me, so that this project would be more useful to our readers. Your friendship and assistance have been wonderful gifts to me.

Susan Martinuk, who also edited my first book, has been patient and long-suffering, as we have worked on this manuscript for far too long. Thank you, Susan, for never growing weary and for always keeping me on my toes, requiring me to condense things, and for pointing me in the right direction. Adriana Torellini has been responsible for typing and retyping the manuscript, collecting photos, correcting footnotes and organizing a myriad of details. Without her assistance, I would have never made it through.

My research assistant, Emma Su, generously volunteered her time and expertise to help search the latest articles, books and research materials to give the book substance and credibility. Thank you for playing such an important role and for doing so in spite of your other many commitments.

For the past 20 years, I have had the professional support of Carolyn Langton as my executive assistant. She knows what I need even before I ask or think, and she has been an outstanding partner in establishing my new career as an advisor to families in business. I actually think that Carolyn must be an angel, because she is heavenly to work with.

I also want to thank my publisher, Larry Willard, for believing in this project from the very beginning and for being willing to compress the schedule to make it possible to get the finished product completed in time for me to meet some of my commitments. I also want to thank Marina Hofman Willard for her tireless efforts and good spirit while finalizing the manuscript.

I also wish to acknowledge that this book would have been far from complete if it were only about our family and the lessons that can be learned from our experiences. Therefore, I want to thank the individuals and families who have so graciously allowed me to share something of their experience with my readers. You have taught me a lot, and as a result, many other families will learn as well. I am profoundly grateful to the following individuals who have so generously shared their wisdom and experience with me for inclusion in this book:

Peter Armstrong, Vic Bachechi, Keith Beedie, Ryan Beedie, Jay Bornstein, DJ DeVries, Ashleigh Everett, Ken Finch, Charles Flavelle, Karen Flavelle, Robert Foord, Michael Higgins, Paul Higgins, Richard Ivey, Greg Kuykendall, Peter Legge, Stuart McLaughlin, Brenda McLean, David McLean, Jason McLean, Sacha McLean, Jack McMillan, Paul Melnuk, Dave Miller, Larry Rosen, Greg Simpson, Jane Tidball and Bill Yeargin.

In addition, Murray Berstein and his three sons, Ben Berstein, Dan Berstein and Jason Berstein, not only allowed me to share their story, but in addition, they have assisted me in summarizing, for the benefit of my readers, what "best practices for families in business" actually looks like. Thank you for your generosity and insights. Each of you has helped me enormously, and I am confident that by sharing your experiences you will help many others as well.

Finally, I want to thank my family for their support and assistance along the way, and especially my wife, Alison, for patiently enduring the months of late nights and other occasions when I was distracted by this project. As a consequence I was not always "there" for her in the way I would have liked to have been, but she never complained and even took a turn with some of the typing. No man has ever had a better life partner than I have in Alison.

PREFACE

Over the past decade, it has been my privilege to teach countless workshops, seminars and courses on family business, most notably in my capacity as an adjunct professor at UBC. In these contexts, I have been delighted to witness how helpful it has been for others to learn from our family's story.

In addition, it has been my privilege to advise and learn from many other family businesses. From these, I have chosen nearly two dozen whose experiences, I believe, are exemplary and worth emulating. It is my hope that they will serve as an inspiration regarding what families should do just as powerfully as our family's story should serve as a warning regarding what not to do.

Part I examines, retrospectively, what occurred in our family business as we navigated through succession three separate times. Amazing as it sounds, I was in the middle of the process each time.

Part II explores the powerful lessons that can be learned from the mistakes we made, as well as from the things we did well.

Part III moves beyond our family as we profile 23 business families who have done exemplary things. These profiles are both instructive and inspiring.

Part IV offers tools and resources to aid families in their journey towards excellence.

Part V contains a few of the heartfelt lessons I have learned through both the painful disappointments and the exhilarating successes I have experienced.

In the end, this book is not about what our family did wrong; nor is it about what we or anyone else did right. Instead, it is intended to be a guidebook and a resource, designed to help families in business learn how to integrate family and business effectively.

MAJOR RESTRUCTURING PLANNED FOR THE BENTALL FAMILY EMPIRE

DATELINE: VANCOUVER, BC, Wednesday, August 17, 1988.

The Bentall family development and construction empire has announced it will undergo a major restructuring. One branch of the family will take over the construction and the other the real estate and development side of the 77-year-old private company, one of the largest in Western Canada.

Bob Bentall, President and Chief Executive Officer of The Bentall Group Ltd, acknowledged there was a difference of opinion over the strategy for the company, but added there were no serious disagreements between family members. He stated that "Clark's family (Brother Clark, Chairman of The Bentall Group) wanted to concentrate on construction."

Under the new structure, Bob's side of the family will get out of the construction business. He will lead a new company, Bentree Holdings Ltd., which will concentrate on real estate development. He will also remain head of The Bentall Group.

Clark's side will purchase the Canadian construction operations and certain land holdings of Dominion Construction Co. Ltd., the group's construction arm. His son, David, will become Senior Vice President of the operation.

When the above words appeared in *The Globe and Mail*, I had just recently celebrated my 33rd birthday. I felt like someone had kicked me in the stomach.

Ever since I was a little boy, my father (Clark) had cultivated a dream that one day I would head up our family real estate and construction business. Now, almost overnight, all our dreams were evaporating.

Earlier that year, Dad had celebrated his 50th year with the business. After an illustrious career, he said his only remaining professional aspiration was to see me become president of The Bentall Group. Instead, the business he had helped build was being dismantled. Tragically, the seismic shift caused by these traumatic events irreparably tore our family apart.

Now, almost 25 years later, I am writing this book in order to help other families avoid the kind of pain and disappointment we endured. I want to share my perspective on all that has happened, both to me and to others in our family.

I am not writing this book in order to explain or justify my position or to criticize others. Instead, I have tried to be as even-handed as I can, in order to assist others in learning from our circumstances.

It is my intention to use our experience as a canvas upon which to paint a portrait regarding what "best practices in family business" look like. As a family, there is no denying that we made many mistakes. However, we actually also did many things right.

I want to share openly and honestly what I have learned from our experiences, both good and bad. In the process, it is my desire that families in business, the world over, will be helped in their quest for success in both their family relationships and in their businesses. In other words, my purpose is to help others to fulfill their desires for LEAVING A LEGACY.

PART I

THE
Bentall
FAMILY STORY

The World Newspaper Building, Vancouver 1911.
Structural steel, designed by Charles Bentall.

CHAPTER 1

A STRONG FOUNDATION

In 1908, Charles Bentall, a 26-year-old British structural engineer, stepped off a Canadian Pacific passenger train in the rapidly developing city of Vancouver. He had completed a long journey from England, crossing the Atlantic by steamship and then travelling coast to coast across Canada by rail. Charles first gained significant public attention in 1911 when he designed the structural frame for Vancouver's World Newspaper Building. At the time, it was the tallest building in the British Empire. Now known as The Sun Tower, it still stands proudly on the skyline of downtown Vancouver, a reminder of a bygone era.

In 1912, Charles, whom we all called Granddad, joined a well-known local business called Dominion Construction (Dominion). He started as assistant general manager but soon entered into an agreement to acquire the firm. It was a risky venture since the owners insisted on a formal contract where the interest rate would increase as he paid down the principle. With such tight financial constraints, it is no wonder that his first decision as owner was to sell the company owned car, a Cadillac. He obviously wanted to shed expenses and run a tight ship, but Granddad also believed it was inappropriate for management to be driving fancy company cars while construction crews, carrying out the real work of the company, did not.

When he acquired Dominion, he likely had no idea of the powerful impact that his leadership in the business would have on his family heritage over the next century.

A MAN AMONG MEN

Granddad was, quite simply, a "man among men." He built his business on a threefold foundation: i) integrity, ii) hard work and iii) respect for his employees. He became known as a man of exemplary character who conducted his business affairs—and his life—with impeccable honesty. His word was his bond, and major projects that would today require a cohort of lawyers and negotiators were often settled with a mere handshake. While growing up, the only negative thing I ever heard

Charles Bentall on site.

said about him was that, at times, he could be stubborn. Frankly, for a man developing a growing business, I suspect that trait likely came in handy on more than one occasion.

BUILDING THE BUSINESS

From 1915 to 1955, Granddad served as the company's president and beloved leader. As an engineer, he brought both a new level of expertise and an innovative approach to the construction business. Most significantly, he decided Dominion could provide greater service and value to its clients by designing as well as building their projects. By centring the company on this idea, he transformed Dominion into a design builder, a full-service enterprise that offered design, engineering and construction services. This approach was unique at that time and soon became one of the firm's hallmarks.

> *Integrity, hard work, and respect for your employees are a strong foundation for any business.*

During this time, the business helped establish the industrial base of Western Canada by building numerous pulp mills and sugar refineries. Notable Dominion projects also included the Stanley Theatre and the original Georgia Viaduct, both of which are still well-known Vancouver landmarks. When Safeway first came to British Columbia, Dominion was awarded the contract to build 26 of their stores. The company moved construction crews from one site to the next, finishing one

Charles Bentall assisting final pour at completion of Bentall I.

Knole Mansion, 2206, SW Marine, Vancouver, BC.

Bulk storage facility for sugar factory, Taber, Alberta, September 1947.

Canadian sugar refinery, Alberta, May 1933.

25

Dominion Construction, pioneers of tilt-up construction in Western Canada.

new store per month over a 26-month period. This contract eventually launched Dominion into the development and ownership of shopping centres.

Dominion built numerous fine homes in the pre-war period, many of which still remain today, in some of Vancouver's finest neighbourhoods. Always innovative, Dominion became a pioneer of tilt-up concrete construction. As a result, Dominion became the leading design builder of industrial and warehouse distribution facilities in Western Canada. By acquiring land and then reselling it as a package deal (including land, design and construction), Dominion soon became a leader in the development of industrial parks. Early branch offices were soon established in Calgary, Edmonton and Kelowna.

A HEART ATTACK BRINGS CHANGE

Granddad was at the helm of Dominion Construction for 40 years as the company prospered and expanded beyond his wildest dreams. But his life was irrevocably changed by a sudden heart attack in June 1955. As he lay in his hospital bed, he was, perhaps for the first time, forced to come face-to-face with his own mortality. Suddenly he had to think about the future of the business if he was unable to continue as its leader. Approaching his 70th birthday, and given his circumstances, he must have come to the conclusion that it was time for a changing of the guard in the family enterprise.[1]

As Granddad lay in the critical care ward of Vancouver General Hospital, in the maternity ward of the same hospital my mom welcomed me into the world. My father, Clark, would visit his dad and then take the elevator to another floor to visit my mother (Phyllis) and me. I can only imagine how my dad's emotions must have been running in overdrive. One day his father almost dies and the next day he has a new son. Before too long, he would also have a new job.

Clark and Charles Bentall reviewing the plans.

---

[1] Thankfully, he recovered fully and lived another 20 years, until he was well into his 90s.

Primogeniture (the centuries-old common-law right of the firstborn son to inherit the family wealth or business) was still a common business practice in the 1950s. However, Granddad's first-born son, Howard, chose to pursue a career as a minister rather than join the family firm. That meant the natural choice to head the company was my dad, who was the second-born son. He was a professional engineer who had already accumulated 15 years of experience working in the family business. Dad and his younger brother, Bob, also an engineer, had both joined the business right after graduation and were now vice-presidents of Dominion. However, in keeping with tradition, Granddad determined his elder son would be promoted to president and his younger son would be promoted to executive vice-president. Thus, when Dad came to the hospital to visit his father, Granddad passed him the reins of leadership with the simple words, "I guess the business is yours now, Son."

Dad knew what was expected of him. So he simply went to the corner office that was home to the company president and made it his own. With that, the first management succession in our family business was accomplished. There was no fanfare, no fuss, no lawyers and no paperwork.

SMOOTH MANAGEMENT SUCCESSION

There were several positive implications evident in how Granddad handled the issue of management succession:

1) A leader with appropriate education and 15 years of experience in the business was chosen. These factors contributed to broad acceptance of Dad as the top executive and his ultimate success in that role.
2) A clear leader for the next generation was chosen and given appropriate authority to lead.
3) The uncertainty and anxiety related to Granddad's health were quieted with the appointment of someone who could provide decisive leadership.
4) The new president was selected while the elder generation was still available to provide guidance and support.

OWNERSHIP SUCCESSION

Granddad wanted to treat all three of his boys equally when it came to his estate planning. He felt that by doing this each of them would feel loved, included and treated fairly. Many years before he died, he gifted to each of them one-third of his shares in Dominion.

He was comfortable giving shares to his sons who were working in the business because he was confident that this would give them an incentive to steward the company for the future. Additionally, he wanted to make sure that Howard received his own reward for choosing to serve as a full-time pastor. Granddad actually felt that Howard had the more important job and that he shouldn't be disadvantaged by choosing to serve God and the

Left to right: Clark, Howard, Bob and Charles Bentall (seated).

church over the family business. Both Dad and Uncle Bob were in general agreement with this view, and therefore everyone was fine with the equal division of shares. In essence, given that the boys were all treated the same, ownership succession was accomplished quietly and without any controversy.

OWNERSHIP TRANSFERRED WHILE THE ELDER GENERATION IS ALIVE

Many family business owners set up the formal transfer of the voting control of their business to the next generation to occur after they die. However, in our case, voting control was transferred from one generation (G1) to the next (G2) well before the first generation passed away. This permitted G2 to gain a significant amount of experience and learn the responsibilities of ownership while its members still had the mentorship of the elder generation. This was a definite plus and certainly contributed to the ongoing success of the business.

Notwithstanding this, if Granddad had been able to anticipate some of the challenges that lay ahead, he might have used this time to help his boys develop agreement on a shared vision for the future.

CREATING A SHAREHOLDERS' AGREEMENT

To formalize the new ownership arrangements, Granddad asked Paul Daniels, a senior partner at the law firm of Lawrence and Shaw, to draft a shareholders' agreement that would "make sure the boys always remain together." He wanted to ensure that their co-ownership could not be dissolved, as sometimes happens in a family business after the founder passes away. Mr. Daniels did an

> *Transferring ownership while the elder generation is still alive permits them to mentor their successors. This is much wiser than leaving successors to "learn to be owners" without any support or guidance.*

excellent job with his assignment (perhaps even too good a job). His legal work cemented the three brothers together in an agreement that would be impossible to break. Unfortunately, because Granddad assumed the boys would always remain together and collaborative, there was no mechanism in the documents to deal with potential disputes should they arise.

DAD AND BOB WERE A GOOD TEAM

For over 40 years, my dad and his brother worked together as they led Dominion and its related companies. They each excelled in their complementary leadership roles. Dad was gregarious and outgoing, acting as "the outside guy," networking and bringing in new business. Bob was more studious and methodical, serving as "the inside guy," carefully tending to the myriad of details required in a growing organization. Two or more days a week they would have lunch together, usually with prospective clients or senior staff. In addition, they had a daily ritual of meeting in Dad's office around 5:00 p.m. They would review the day's activities and typically had a roll of drawings laid out before them, analyzing the latest design challenge on one of the company's projects.

In addition to the two brothers, a strong management team developed around them as they expanded across Canada. The family company grew steadily and by the 1980s had developed into a fully integrated real estate enterprise known as The Bentall Group. The firm owned an impressive list of subsidiary companies:

Dominion Construction – now one of the ten largest construction firms in Canada, boasted offices in Vancouver, Calgary, Edmonton, Regina and Winnipeg.

Domco Engineering – had structural, electrical and mechanical engineers on staff and had developed the capacity to complete both conceptual designs and working drawings for major office and retail projects.

Dominion Management – offered leasing and property management services for several million square feet of commercial space across Western Canada.

Bentall Properties – had ownership in numerous completed projects, including office buildings, industrial parks and shopping centres, with a total leasable area in excess of two million square feet.

Smaller subsidiaries contributed to the fully-integrated services of The Bentall Group, including an interior design firm, a custom millwork manufacturing operation, an equipment leasing company, and an electrical and mechanical contractor.

A NAME YOU COULD TRUST

Just as early customers trusted our granddad to seal a deal with a handshake, companies like Scott Paper, Northern Telecom (now Nortel), BC Tel (now Telus), Sauder Industries and Home Depot trusted the "Dominion Way." Each of these firms decided, over many decades, to award to our firm virtually every project they built in Western Canada. Dominion Construction had such relationships of mutual trust with these clients that it could have served as a poster boy for author and motivational speaker Stephen M.R. Covey, who explains that virtually everything takes less time and costs less when there is a high level of trust.[2] The company became recognized as a leader in both construction and real estate development. It was also known across Canada for the way it conducted business, the way it treated its employees and the quality of its projects. In time, this reputation delivered real strategic advantages to the company. For example, a Dominion-built building typically sold for a 5% premium above prevailing prices in the market (maintenance and repair costs of these buildings were lower and consequently provided significant savings for their owners).

A VISIONARY LEADER

Dad never studied business at university, but he was a keen reader, and his success was a reflection of the many business leaders he was able to meet through the pages of their biographies. He also had a particular interest in the development of office buildings. Several biographies about the Rockefeller family so intrigued him that he travelled to New York in the late 1950s just to view the Rockefeller Center. This amazing multi-building complex, with simple architecture, beautiful plazas and soothing fountains, inspired his vision for a similar project in Vancouver. As a result, land was acquired at the corner of Burrard and Pender, in the heart of downtown, and Bentall One was soon under construction. Boasting 21 stories, the building was completed in 1967.

The development of office towers remained Dad's primary focus for the next 20 years, and the completion of The Bentall Centre was perhaps the crowning

---

[2.] Stephen M.R. Covey and Rebecca R. Merrill, *The Speed of Trust* (New York: New York Free Press, 2006), 13.

achievement of his remarkable career. Named after my grandfather, Charles, it now consists of five office towers, underground retail space and beautifully landscaped plazas, all in the heart of Vancouver's business district. Today, The Bentall Centre is one of the largest integrated office complexes in Western Canada.

By 1988, as Dad completed his 50th year with the family business, Dominion Construction had developed, and The Bentall Group now owned a portfolio of properties that comprised $500 million in assets. With five regional offices across Western Canada, the company was voted one of the 100 best companies to work for in Canada.

CONCLUSION

When Granddad disembarked from the train in Vancouver in 1908, he could never have predicted how successful his career as a builder would be. The company he would establish over the next 40 years would be a testament to his character and his drive. When many years later he transferred ownership of the business to his three sons, family relationships were strong, as was the company. On the surface, at least, things in the Bentall family seemed about as good as it gets.

From left to right: Bob, Howard and Charles Bentall, George
Tsutakawa (sculptor of fountain for Bentall II Plaza)
and Clark Bentall.

Dominion Construction crew, Alberta sugar plant,
Calgary, 1933.

Dominion Construction Co. Ltd, Barge
and dredging equipment.

Yorkshire Trust Building, Vancouver,
April 1913.

Capital Theatre, Vancouver,
October 1920.

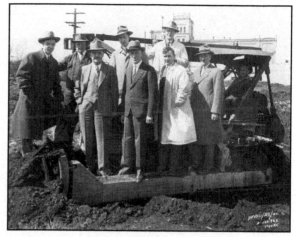

*St. Regis Paper Co., Vancouver,
April 1946.*

*Imperial Oil
service station.*

*General Motors building, Calgary,
1931 (Dominion's first real
estate development,
midst of Great Depression).*

Bob and Charles Bentall ,1953.

*Keats Island summer cottage, 1946 (Charles Bentall smiles
celebrating the completion of construction in one day!).*

Bob, Clark and Charles Bentall enjoying the latter's 90th birthday celebration.

Topping off ceremony, Bentall I (Frank Musson - architect, Bob, Clark and Charles Bentall), 1968.

Bentall II fountain unveiling (Charles Bentall and sculptor George Tsutakawa), 1969.

Sod turning ceremony for Bentall III (Bob Bentall on far left, Clark Bentall on far right), 1971.

CHAPTER 2

PROBLEMS BENEATH THE SURFACE

TURN OFF THE TV AND DO YOUR HOMEWORK

When I was a little boy, I remember one evening, just after our family finished eating dinner, I was sitting quietly in the den watching *Casper the Friendly Ghost*. My dad suddenly walked into the room and abruptly said to me: "Turn off the TV and do your homework." When I didn't immediately obey, he warned me with the words "David, you can't be president if you don't do your homework." From that day on, Dad made it clear that he saw me as the heir apparent and that his wish was for me to follow in his footsteps and lead the family company. In many ways you could say that I didn't choose my career so much as my career—or should I say my dad—chose me. It seemed that my path was pretty much set from the time I was just 10 years old.

> *Share your passion!*
> *A positive, creative and inviting introduction to the family business can create both interest and excitement in a young person.*

Some have said that Dad was cruel to put this kind of burden on me at such a young age. But I chose to see it as a great gift. The exciting vision that my father held for my future and my career didn't make me feel constrained or obligated. Rather, as I grew older, it gave me a tremendous sense of confidence and security, knowing that my father believed in me and that, if I wanted to, I could have the opportunity of extending the reputation of success that he and my grandfather had so ably forged over the years.

Some have asked why I was "chosen" by my dad, given that I was the youngest of four children. Dad had originally hoped that my elder brother. Chuck.

would work in the business. He is almost 13 years older than I am, but by the time I was in grade five, he had already decided to pursue a career in architecture, independent of the company. Furthermore, given our Dad's belief that the construction industry was no place for women, neither of my sisters had ever been encouraged to pursue a career in the family firm. Consequently, I think that Dad simply saw me as his last hope.

My initial orientation to the business involved a Vancouver city map (mounted on a corkboard) and a box of pins with pink plastic heads. Every night after dinner, Dad would describe for me one of the many buildings our company had completed during the industrialization of our city. Together we would locate that particular project on the map and use a pin to mark its precise location. I learned about our industrial developments in Richmond and along Vancouver's Clark Drive as well as our office buildings in the downtown core. As a young lad I was eager to learn and treasured this special time with my dad. However we had built so many buildings in the city that my youthful exuberance and genuine interest eventually waned and the routine lost its appeal, long before we ran out of projects or pink pins.

Dad also helped to spur my interest in the company by talking to me about business and engaging my services as an assistant as we were driving together in the car. Invariably he would think of something he needed to remember and hand me his pen and a three-by-five inch notepad with the instruction to jot down things like "Call Frank regarding the new property" or "Invite Walter to lunch." Now that I look back on it, I realize that it was a great exposure to the business, even though at the time I didn't realize how much I was learning.

I also have fond recollections of my father holding court at the dinner table after a day's work, sharing his experiences and interactions with the people he had met that day. He'd tell us about lunches with prominent business people like Jimmy Pattison and Gordon McFarland[3] or report on what the mayor had said during a meeting to discuss the park that Dad was determined to build across the street from Tower Four of The Bentall Centre. Demonstrating enormous perseverance, Dad worked for over a decade and with four successive mayors in an effort to establish his dream of a new urban green space. I'm proud to say that this eventually happened in 1980. When I stood before the crowd to speak at the park's opening celebration, I had to marvel at his persistence. His efforts had produced the first new park in downtown Vancouver in over 50 years.

[3.] Jimmy Pattison is a billionaire and one of Canada's most highly respected business leaders. Gordon McFarland was the chairman and CEO of BC Tel (our provincial telephone company and, at that time, our company's largest and most important client).

A SENSE OF HUMOUR CAN BE A GREAT ASSET IN BUSINESS

Dad was also known to bring home jokes that he had heard over lunch that day at the Kiwanis Club. Frankly, he wasn't a very good joke teller, but he did have a wonderful sense of humour and always loved to share a laugh with others. In fact, I still recall the response of George O'Leary, the former chairman of the board of Scott Paper, when I asked him what my dad contributed to their board. (After all, he was just a dad to me, and I couldn't understand why anyone would want him as a director.) George explained, much to my surprise, that in addition to his gifts as a businessperson and as a leader Dad had a reputation as someone who could always diffuse a tense situation with an apt word or through the injection of some light humour. He said that he appreciated how Dad was something of a "tonic" for the board.

With this combination of wit and wisdom, it is no wonder that people liked having Dad around, and no surprise that he had the privilege of serving on many prestigious boards during the twilight years of his career. Over time, he served on such elite boards as the TD Bank, Finning Tractor, BC Forest Products, Cominco and Expo 86, as well as non-business boards such as The Vancouver Foundation and The Vancouver Club. These responsibilities also provided a natural incentive for Dad to transition more leadership authority to his younger brother, Bob. Partly because of these outside activities, Dad in time agreed to transfer the roles of president and CEO to Bob.

Surprisingly, in spite of all his positive attributes as a business leader Dad found it difficult to teach me business principles. I recall once when I was a young boy asking him to explain to me what a mortgage was and he very unhelpfully replied that it was "a charge against a piece of property." When I asked him what a "charge against a piece of property" was, he replied that it would be called "a mortgage." I realized later on that rather than making fun of me with his circular logic, he was simply incapable of explaining it to me in language that I could understand.

> *Serving on outside boards can be a terrific way to extend your career, while making room for others in the family to grow into leadership.*

Some of these recollections may seem to be of little consequence to raising a child to have an interest in the family business. But, years later, I still recall those conversations fondly. The fact that I never forgot them shows the powerful impact Dad had on my development. If you are leading a family company, you don't need to hold an orientation seminar or develop a formal mentorship program for

Cominco LTD board of directors (Clark Bentall standing 4th from the right).

Scott Paper LTD Board (chairman George O'Leary seated in centre; Clark Bentall standing 4th from right).

TD Bank Group board (chairman Richard Thompson, seated 6th from right; Clark Bentall, standing 6th from right).

your children in an effort to generate an interest in the family business. Rather, valuable business lessons can be communicated effectively through the smallest and most seemingly insignificant interactions that you share with your children each day.

As I entered university, Dad still maintained his dream that one day I would become president of the family company. In fact, he often told me that if it wasn't for me and my potential to lead the firm, he would want to sell it. The message was clear: he was counting on me.

PREPARING TO JOIN THE FAMILY FIRM

Joining the family business was always "Option A" for my career. However, even as late as my final year of university, I had questions about the idea. Up to that point, virtually all senior executives at our family firm (including my grandfather, father and uncle) had been professional engineers. Obviously, there was a reasonable assumption that I would follow a similar path if I wanted to lead the business. But, to be frank, math and physics weren't my thing, and so I doubted engineering would be either. This fact fuelled my doubts about whether I was cut out to lead our construction business. Instead of studying engineering, I obtained a commerce degree, majoring in urban land economics (real estate) at the Sauder School of Business. In hindsight, it is now easy to see that there were several educational options that I could have taken to gain appropriate academic credentials.[4] As a result, I now encourage family business successors to feel free to choose a different path than their predecessors so they can develop a plan that suits their own uniqueness.

As I approached graduation, it became apparent that none of my siblings and none of my cousins were interested in joining the family firm. As each member of my generation took up roles outside of the family business, it became quite clear that I was the only one who could continue the family connection to our business. Engineer or not, it seemed to me that there was a clear path to the top, if I wanted it. I was excited by the prospect, although admittedly naive.

As part of my preparations for a career in the family firm, my dad encouraged me to take a position there each summer while I attended university. I worked several summers as a labourer on construction sites and later on moved into the office, working in accounts payable. Prior to my final year of university, one of our divisional managers offered me a job, effective September 1979.

[4.] I could have chosen a degree in economics or finance; I could have specialized in marketing or human resources, or possibly taken an MBA.

OPPORTUNITIES TO LEARN AND GROW

I accepted the offer and worked at BC Millwork that summer. After I graduated, I accepted a full-time job in the same part of the firm. It is fair to say that I didn't start out pushing a broom, but I didn't exactly start at the top either. Our millwork operation (which also included an interior contracting and millwork manufacturing plant) was our smallest division. Working as the assistant to our general manager there, I thoroughly enjoyed my early experiences with the business.

During my first year, I had plenty of opportunities to learn and grow. I was asked to help create our division's first strategic plan, first marketing plan and first human resources plan. I also assisted our production manager in developing a new scheduling system for our custom millwork shop and helped to resolve start-up problems in our new overhead garage door plant. It was extremely rewarding to witness the management team jell into a unified team and to witness a successful resolution to our production and scheduling problems. Overall, it proved to be an ideal first assignment.

Starting at the bottom enables family members to learn the business and, more importantly, to earn credibility and the respect of others.

Following this initial year, I moved to head office and was given the responsibility for all strategic planning within The Bentall Group. Seeking to broaden my experience and develop my resumé, I was subsequently able to secure opportunities to work in Calgary (two years), Toronto (two years) and California (one year). As a young father, this was an ideal time for me to travel and gain experience, because none of our three children were of school age yet. I learned so much during those five years that I now passionately advocate that would-be successors follow a similar strategy in their own careers, especially before putting down roots.

In 1986, when I returned to the head office in Vancouver, I had achieved one of my key career goals; I had essentially worked in every division and every geographic region in which our company operated.

To further enhance my credentials, I had also managed to squeeze in a meaningful work experience outside the family business, working for Cadillac Fairview (while living in Toronto). At that time, this corporation was one of the largest real estate development firms in North America.

My dad was initially "dead set" against me working outside the family firm. He reasoned that there was so much to learn within the company that I could work there for my entire life and still not know everything about our enterprise. But by the end of my two-year apprenticeship at Cadillac Fairview, he'd seen how much I had grown and matured by being out of the "family nest." He also realized that I had proven myself, independent of the family firm, and I could potentially bring new ideas and insights back to the business. A man who rarely needed to admit his mistakes, he took me aside and said, "Son, you were dead right and I was dead wrong. That was the best thing you could have ever done for your career." That day, for the first time in my life, my dad accepted me as a man.

I was so thankful that I had resisted the temptation, compelling as it was, to work only for our family firm. My dad and I both agreed that my apprenticeship period had taught me a lot, and at the time, we thought it had helped to prepare me to potentially be my Uncle Bob's successor.

PROMOTED THROUGH THE RANKS

In 1986, my Uncle Bob appointed me at the age of 30, as a corporate vice-president, responsible for all real estate development activities in Canada. That year, we were exploring the development of a retail mall in Saskatoon and an office tower in downtown Winnipeg. I was enthusiastic about both of these ventures, and we were successful in finding ways to make both projects happen. During the previous years, I had begun to focus on real estate development and become quite passionate about this area of business. I saw it as a key strategic priority for our firm's future success and therefore recognized that this particular focus would allow me to make a significant contribution to the firm.

Working outside the family firm gave me confidence. At the same time, I developed skills that I could bring back with me to help our company.

Things went very well, and soon some of the senior executive team were recommending that I be made a senior vice-president. I assumed that this would position me perfectly as the heir apparent, with the next logical step being a promotion to president. By now I had become committed to this goal and had worked hard to prepare myself for the reins of leadership. It seemed like my father's dream, birthed so long ago, was about to become a reality.

THE LEADERSHIP TEAM

By this time, Uncle Bob and Dad had worked side by side to lead the company for several decades. For most of this time, Dad had carried the title of president, and Bob was executive vice-president. They had the support of a very effective core management team that also included Frank Worster (VP of finance), Don MacIntosh (VP of engineering) and Ole Pederson (director of construction). Dad served as the "rainmaker," Bob was the "detail guy," Frank was the "money guy" and Don was, quite simply, "a genius" (at least according to Dad).

Don was also a bit of a character who was merciless in his teasing and wouldn't hesitate to point out anyone's faults in front of others. Dad said it was often hard to take and he felt the sting of Don's criticism. He said that Don was usually right and so he would "take the good with the bad" and put up with it. Unfortunately for Bob, he was more often the brunt of Don's jokes. As the youngest on the team, it must have hurt to have Don "give him the gears" on a regular basis. Bob probably wished his older brother would put a stop to the emotional abuse. The fact that he didn't likely undermined Bob's faith in Dad's leadership.

TWO DIFFERENT VIEWS OF SUCCESSION

When Granddad transferred the president's title to my dad, years earlier, the event in some ways seemed beautiful in its simplicity. However, the circumstances surrounding the simple transfer of power contributed to problems that would surface later. Dad came to believe that succession in a family business is the responsibility of the incumbent leader, who has the power and authority to appoint his successor when he is ready to step aside. He also believed that succession is an easy decision that takes little forethought or planning. On the other hand, Uncle Bob was left out of the succession discussions completely and probably felt that there might have been a better way of handling things.

NO DISCUSSIONS ABOUT WHO WOULD LEAD

Perhaps the emotions at the time (Granddad being hospitalized) played into how events played out, but I would venture a guess that it would never have occurred to Granddad or Dad that they should include Bob in discussions about the proposed management succession. To be more precise, they didn't think about including Bob in the discussion in which it was determined that Dad—and not Bob—would be president. Compounding things, the men of the 1950s were of necessity a stoic lot. The tragedies of war and the cultural norms at the time did not permit much room for men to share their feelings. Therefore, it would have been highly unusual in that era to ask Bob how he felt about the plan for his elder brother to be president. The decision was made, and Bob was just expected to carry on doing his job.

SEEDS OF DISCONTENT

Looking back, it is regrettable that other members of the family were not consulted regarding the choice of Dad as president. It is also unfortunate that there was no consideration given to how long he would have this role. Both these factors contributed to hard feelings between the brothers that would surface many years later.

I'm certain that neither Granddad nor Dad had even the slightest hint of how much Bob must have been hurting during all those years playing second fiddle. The two brothers actually had the same salary, the same size office and the same car. So, in effect, Bob was treated as an equal in every way, except in terms of authority. But Bob was only a few years younger than Dad, and he likely realized that if his turn to lead ever came, it might be short-lived. Understandably, he didn't want to get stuck spending virtually his entire career without ever having an opportunity to serve as president.

Forty years later, I asked Bob if it had bothered him that he had been required to work under my dad's authority for all those years. He explained that he had made peace with the idea years ago. Yet even a casual observer could see from his body language that, four decades later, the pain of that experience was still very real.

NO ACCOUNTABILITY

Throughout this time, the company had a board of directors, at least on paper, but there were no formal meetings and no independent members on the board. Consequently, Dad had no practical accountability as president. He was a good leader who solicited input and advice from his team, but like his father before him, he felt that the ultimate burden of leadership rested on his shoulders. Rather than regarding his brothers as equal, Dad believed that it was his job to lead the company on behalf of the family. Over time, he would demonstrate that he was a competent and strong leader. However, he would also gradually alienate his brothers by his relatively autocratic style. In some ways, he was imitating Granddad's leadership style, the only one he had experienced first-hand. Unwittingly, he was making a common mistake made by second-generation family leaders, who seldom appreciate how important it is to take into account the needs and desires of their sibling partners. Unfortunately, when a sole owner transitions the leadership of a company to a sibling partnership, the successor generation typically has no model for shared leadership.

OWNERSHIP SUCCESSION

When Granddad transitioned ownership to my dad's generation, he gave his three boys equal shares. Howard, the eldest brother, worked for the business during the summers while at university, but upon graduation, instead of joining the company, he pursued a full-time career as a pastor. In time, as the business expanded into Alberta, a new company was established to facilitate this growth. Our VP of finance, Frank Worster, was given one-quarter of the shares in this new business (equal with the three brothers). Years later, when that new company was merged back to the main business, Dad acquired some additional shares, and the shareholders of The Bentall Group became Frank (18%), Bob, (24%), Howard (24%) and Clark (34%).

> *When a sole owner transitions the leadership of a company to a sibling partnership, the successor generation typically has no model for shared leadership.*

In the 1970s, in order to accommodate his brothers obtaining more favourable tax treatment, Dad sold each of them an additional 1.01% of the company. This resulted in Dad having just under 32% and Howard and Bob each holding 25.01%. Between them, Bob and Howard now held 50.02% of voting shares of the company. For the next decade, no one paid any attention to the fact that they now had effective control of the company.

CONCLUSION

When I joined the family firm, I was excited about the prospect of one day following my grandfather, my father and my uncle and to become the future leader of our family firm. As I worked there over the years, I did my best to prepare myself for this responsibility. I knew that my dad and my Uncle Bob didn't agree on everything, but that seemed normal. Little did I know how much trouble was brewing beneath the surface or that I was about to be caught in a raging storm.

Bentall Centre, downtown, Vancouver.

CHAPTER 3

A FAMILY TORN APART

PROBLEMS ARISE

It was a prosperous time for The Bentall Group in 1986 when my Uncle Bob promoted me to the position of corporate vice-president. About ten years earlier, Bob had been appointed president and CEO, roughly coinciding with Dad's 30th anniversary in that role. Dad agreed to assume the role of non-executive chair so that Bob could assume the top executive post in the company (and therefore be responsible for effectively directing and leading the company).

However, it didn't take long to realize that underneath the veneer of success something was very wrong inside the corporate offices. A cool distance had now developed between Dad and Bob. They managed day-to-day matters well, but more often than not, they were no longer in alignment.

As an example, Bob saw the need for the company to adopt professional management techniques, including job descriptions, goal setting and clear lines of authority. Dad, the entrepreneur, didn't like to be constrained by such practices, which he viewed as a waste of time and energy. I could feel the ground begin to shift in 1986, as we were about to celebrate the firm's 75th birthday. As this milestone neared, it was clearly evident that Dad and Uncle Bob had radically different visions for the future of the rapidly expanding Bentall Group. Worse still, those divergent views included the following four critical areas: ownership, strategy, leadership and purpose.

1. **Ownership**. Dad wanted the company to remain privately owned, while Uncle Bob felt there would be benefits to the company going public.

2. **Strategy.** Dad wanted the company to stay in both real estate and construction, while Uncle Bob wanted to focus solely on real estate.
3. **Leadership.** Dad wanted me to run the company, while Uncle Bob felt a more experienced professional manager would likely be better for the business.
4. **Purpose.** Dad wanted to continue to build the company so it would remain a legacy for future generations of our family, while Uncle Bob wanted to sell the company and donate the proceeds to charity.

Looking back, it's hard to imagine how their respective visions could have been more different or more foundational in nature. As the opposing visions surfaced, I think that Bob legitimately became frustrated by his inability to get Dad to talk about future plans. Bob had begun studying family business succession and knew the importance of strategic planning and having an independent board of directors. It was exhaustingly painful for him as he tried to communicate with Dad and to convince him of the importance of these activities. But Dad was reluctant to even discuss these matters. He continued to reason that the company had already enjoyed enormous success—and it had been accomplished without the time, expense and bureaucracy implied by these initiatives. In short, Dad thought, "Why bother?"

EVERYTHING COMES UNRAVELLED

Dad had long ago relinquished the corner office to Bob, yet the leadership struggle continued as Dad exhibited a trait that is common in family business—a reluctance to let go. His Bentall Group business card carried the title "Chairman of the Board" and this unfortunately reinforced his view that he was still the ultimate authority for the business. As chair, he was now in a governing role and should have deferred to Bob's authority to run the company. Instead Dad's continued influence became a major problem. Uncle Bob felt that Dad's presence was undermining his leadership, and as long as Dad was around, it was impossible for him to lead.

In retrospect, it seems that Bob's leadership challenges were not limited to Dad's reluctance to relinquish control. Another impediment may have been Bob's lack of confidence in his own ability. He had been in Dad's shadow for so many years, how could he have developed an appropriate self-confidence? Perhaps this is why he struggled to create an independent leadership style that could accommodate Dad's continued presence. Eventually their escalating conflict and the ongoing tension over different visions of the future conspired to create an untenable situation for the two brothers.

A decision regarding the appointment of a new corporate VP of real estate became the "straw that broke the camel's back." For many years, Dad had been the driving force behind The Bentall Group's real estate success. As Dad transitioned himself out of day-to-day management, the company would need to replace him in this critical role. Following much deliberation, Bob selected Robert Flitton, who had worked for The Bentall Group for many years and achieved notable success with a difficult project in Kamloops, BC. Bob told Robert of his decision to promote him to this new position, and they made plans for an official announcement.

Dad was unaware of this development when an old business associate named Wally Pierce told him that he had left his previous employer and was looking for a job. Dad felt he would be perfect for the real estate role and offered him the job on the spot. He then advised Bob that he had found a perfect candidate to lead the company's real estate efforts. This action effectively undermined Bob as CEO and confirmed that his older brother would probably never be able to let him lead. One can only imagine the humiliation he suffered, being told that he would simply need to tell Mr. Flitton that he wouldn't be getting his promotion after all.

A LAST DITCH EFFORT TO AVOID DISASTER

Things were quickly escalating out of control, and, in a last ditch attempt to avert a disaster, both Dad and Bob agreed to bring in an independent facilitator to determine if a mutually satisfactory solution could be found. The facilitator would first meet with Dad and our family (including my siblings and our spouses) and then meet separately with Bob and his family. It was also agreed that my Uncle Howard's family would be invited to participate in this process, given that they owned essentially the same number of shares as Bob and his family. Finally, it was agreed that the goal for the facilitator was to ask each family to consider the future and provide a response to the question "What do you really want?"

> *It's a common challenge for patriarchs and leaders to struggle with letting go of their authority in the family business. If this cannot be accomplished, disaster is often the result.*

One of our senior executives (our "trusted executive") volunteered to attend these meetings, suggesting that he had factual information that the families might need to aid in their deliberations, such as valuations of the businesses and assets. Naively we agreed that he should attend and, at the suggestion of our independent facilitator, it was agreed that our trusted executive would chair the proposed family meetings. This seemed like a logical course of action. (After all, we didn't need two facilitators, and this particular executive was a long-term employee who was trusted by all of us.) We weren't holding our breath, but we were optimistic as we met to discuss what we could do to avert a crisis.

THE MERIDIAN HOTEL

So, my parents, their four children and our respective spouses gathered together at the Meridian Hotel in downtown Vancouver to discuss the company's future and our options to remain a part of the business. We gathered in a spacious boardroom and were pampered by hotel staff that offered us coffee, tea and a catered lunch. It was a difficult discussion, and frankly, by the time lunch came around, we were no longer in the mood to eat.

We had assumed that our neutral hotel boardroom provided an environment of trust and confidentiality. As such, we each shared our deepest desires and hopes for each of our futures and for the future of the business. Throughout the day, we also considered what we would do if it proved untenable for the three families to continue as partners in the family business. Our facilitator seemed focused on the assumption that we were incompatible for the long term, and, based on that assumption, he asked us each to consider what we would want in return if the company was divided. Did we want operating companies? Land? Buildings? Cash? Or did we want some combination of these options?

After eight hours of deliberations, I am proud to say that our family came to the decision that none of these options would be satisfactory. For us, relationships in the family were the most important priority, and by comparison, nothing in the business was as important. We agreed unanimously that all we really wanted was the "restoration of relationships in the family." It was a heartfelt conclusion, and we were hopeful that this clear priority and our open-handed approach would be welcomed by everyone. Howard and Bob's families were scheduled to subsequently meet with our trusted executive. In the days that followed, we eagerly awaited news of their discussions.

"MISSING" EACH OTHER

Much to our astonishment, we never heard what the others wanted. Instead, everything just fell apart! Relationships that previously had been genial, at least in terms of everyday business, now turned icy cold. Lawsuits were threatened, ultimatums were put on the table, and we were left bewildered as to what had caused the turmoil. Eventually, my father and I were invited to attend a meeting with my two uncles and their lawyers. My brother-in-law, Phil George, and my brother, Chuck, also attended.

During the meeting, we were told that, as 32% owners of the business, our family had only two options if we wanted to stay in the family business. Either we could buy everybody else out or we could endorse Bob's plans for the future.

In hindsight, it is tragic that Dad and Bob "missed" each other so fundamentally. As president and CEO, Bob had tried for almost ten years to obtain Dad's support for the creation of a shared vision and a strategic plan for the future. However, Dad was unable to adapt to this new way of approaching business. In addition, Dad found it difficult not to interfere with Bob's leadership and was reluctant to accept his judgment that we needed more experienced management for the future. These were such fundamental issues that they were too difficult for Bob to simply sweep them all under the carpet, though Dad would have probably been happy to.

In an attempt to provide a way for the family to remain together, Bob proposed a plan that would address each of these essential areas of concern. He suggested the following four steps be implemented:

1) Dad would commit to not interfere with Bob's leadership as president and CEO.
2) To help with this, a suitable executive office for Dad, as chairman of the board, would be created separate from The Bentall Group offices.
3) We would agree to sell the company's "non-core" assets and focus on the more profitable activities of real estate development and property management.
4) We would seek to find a capable, experienced real estate professional to become the company's next CEO, someone who could mentor me, in my role.

Unfortunately, by this time emotions were running so high that Dad and I couldn't see how reasonable and wise these suggestions were and instead we were reactive rather than responsive.

Dad and I could only see the curtailment of our authority and a departure from our historic roots of construction. Now, with the benefit of hindsight, I can see that we had actually missed an opportunity. We didn't realize it at that time, but something of an olive branch had just been extended to us.

> *A formalized strategic planning process enables the family, shareholders, board and management to collectively build a shared vision for the company's future.*

In our view, even if we agreed to Bob's recommendations, the new situation would prove to be untenable, and we wouldn't be able to work together with Bob productively. Consequently, we concluded that it must be time to end the partnership. However, we were reluctant simply to sell out. Perhaps because I was by far the youngest in the room, I thought we should at least investigate ways for the minority shareholders to acquire the rest of the business.

Dad and I decided to meet with our trusted executive to obtain his assistance in creating a financial scenario to make this happen. I was very disappointed in his response, as he discouraged our efforts to buy the company, stating that it was too risky for such a small minority to purchase the balance of the company.

Shortly thereafter, our trusted executive organized a meeting that was attended by my three siblings and me. There were just the five of us, meeting in a spacious 31st floor office overlooking the beautiful Vancouver harbour. There was just one item on the agenda. Much to the surprise of everyone, we were informed that I was to be removed from my role as a vice-president of The Bentall Group. The meeting didn't last long, but the consequences of that encounter permanently changed the course of my life.

SOLD OUT

About two years later, I had a casual conversation with my cousin Rob as we sat on a dock by his cottage, overlooking the Pacific Ocean. I told him that I still didn't understand why things fell apart in the family so suddenly after we had indicated "all we wanted was restoration of relationships in the family." You can imagine my surprise when Rob told me that they had never been told that we wanted to mend family relationships. Instead, he revealed that our trusted executive had reported that all we wanted was cash.

Tragically, because of this miscommunication, our hopes for reconciliation had been scuttled. In spite of our noble ambitions and our genuine love, relationships never had been given a chance to be restored. In spite of our clear resolve, our wishes had never been passed along to the other members of the family.

Much later we were advised that our trusted executive had been paid a seven figure bonus for creating a plan to reduce my father to a line on the balance sheet that simply read, "minority interest." No one ever disclosed who made this payment, or if in fact it was ever made. Regardless, by the time this news was reported it would have been impossible to rectify the situation, either by legal or other means.

Sadly, the potential for restoration of relationships within our family was never even explored. Instead, the other shareholders of the company were able to consolidate voting control of the company and establish a permanent control block through the creation of a holding company known as Bentree. They each transferred their shares into this company, thus creating a voting block that owned 68% of the company. This transaction not only solidified their control of the company, but it also effectively reduced the value of Dad's estate by 50%. To make matters worse, our trusted executive then offered Dad the opportunity to sell his interest in the business, on the provision that he accept an additional liquidity discount of 15%.

HOW DID THIS REDUCE THE VALUE OF DAD'S ESTATE?

At that time, the net equity in The Bentall Group was now worth a substantial amount of money. If the company's assets were sold and the equity distributed, my dad's share would have been more than he had ever hoped for during his lifetime. Following Granddad's example, the shareholders had plowed the vast majority of company earnings back into the business, on the assumption that the growth in equity would accrue to the shareholders.

In 1988, publicly traded real estate companies were trading at a price that was 50% of the underlying equity value of the business. So, if we had been a publicly-traded company, the market value of our company's shares would have been 50% of what they were as a private company. (This is because shareholders in a public company do not have access to the cash flow or assets of the business but instead must trust the management of the company to determine what will be done with the assets and the equity under their management.)

By creating a control block, through the establishment of Bentree, my dad's shares were now worth no more than if they were shares of a public real estate company. Our trusted executive had effectively cut my dad's wealth in half.

Some people have asked me why Dad didn't mount a legal challenge, based on "oppression" of a minority shareholder. Our legal advisors explained that these actions were not oppressive for two reasons: 1) Dad was not required to sell his shares, and 2) all shareholders were being paid the same dividends (which were negligible). As a result, our lawyers were persuaded that we would have had difficulty proving our case.

This sad situation didn't seem fair to me, but it reminded me of something I learned on the first day of business school, in my introductory law class. Professor Dave McPhillips told us, "That which is fair, that which is just, that which is moral and that which is legal are all different concepts. Don't ever get them mixed up." Back then, his words were merely knowledge; now they had become my experience. I believe that what happened to my dad was both unfair and unjust. Unfortunately, in Canada it was also legal.

Even if there had been a legal case, my dad told me that he would never initiate legal action against his brothers. Such was the depth of my dad's commitment to family.

A BROKEN HEART

I loved my dad for many reasons, but his commitment to acting in a principled way—even in the midst of pain and betrayal—was truly inspiring. He was a man of principle and always sought to take the high road. He also believed in the importance of turning the other cheek, and his faith in doing things God's way was unshakable.

> "That which is fair, that which is just, that which is moral and that which is legal are all different concepts. Don't ever get them mixed up."
> Dave McPhillips

For my part, I sought to encourage my father by making a list of all that he was able to leave his children as a result of his success. In spite of all he had just lost, I tried to convince him that everything was all right. I added up the value of our shares, the cash payments we had been given earlier, the small family foundation we were able to steward, the homes we each owned, the acreage on Keats Island, the one company we would acquire and the few buildings we owned collectively. In total, our dad was still able to leave his kids a lot, by any measure. He had succeeded enormously in his 50-year career and he had provided us with an amazing legacy. Sadly, no tangible evidence of his success seemed to mean much to him in the midst of the fractured family dynamics and the broken relationships with his brothers.

Until 1988, my father had been both the chairman of the Board and The Bentall Group's largest shareholder. He had worked for the family business for five decades and served as its devoted leader for much of that time. Yet, as he approached his 75th birthday, and due to a series of events that he never could have imagined, he literally found himself "on the outside looking in." He and his brothers never reconciled, and the pain of rejection and separation from his brothers was almost more than he could bear. Fourteen years later, when Dad died, he did so with a broken heart. He had lived an exceptional life, one that had been devoted to his family and the family business. But in the end, I think he deserved better.

WHAT WENT WRONG?

In retrospect, it is relatively easy to see both how this situation developed and how it might have been avoided had things been handled differently by all members of our family. The following points summarize some of the key mistakes we committed that devastated our family and destroyed our family business:

1. **ABSENCE OF A SHARED VISION.** My dad and uncle were both focused on the day-to-day priorities of building a successful business. In fact, they were so exclusively focused on those issues that they seldom, if ever, talked about why they were doing it or what they were working towards. In other words, they never discussed a long-term vision for the company, and by the time that all-important conversation took place, each man already had very different ideas of where the company was headed.

2. **AVOIDERS AND ACCOMMODATORS.** On a more personal level, these discussions didn't happen because my dad and my uncle were experts in the art of avoidance and accommodation, respectively. Dad was an "avoider," ignoring longer-term issues in the hope that they would eventually resolve themselves or, better still, just go away. On the other hand, Bob had spent most of his professional career "accommodating" the preferences of his elder brother. Eventually he got tired of this and decided to seek a different solution.

In his excellent workbook on conflict management, Alexander Hiam explains that there are five basic ways of handling conflict or a difference of opinion: accommodation, avoidance, competition, compromise and collaboration.[5] It is a tragic reality for our family and the business that Dad and Bob never learned how to compromise and collaborate, at least not regarding major issues related to the future. Instead, after 40 years of working together, Bob felt he had no choice but to "compete."

[5.] Alexander Hiam, *Dealing with Conflict Instrument* (Amherst: HRD Press, 1999), 5.

Figure 1. Five Different Ways of Handling Conflict (Source: Alexander Hiam)

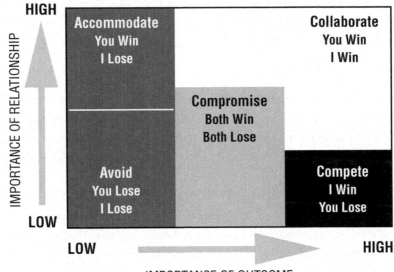

3. **NO CONFLICT RESOLUTION MECHANISM.** This unfortunate scenario might also have been avoided had my father been more familiar with the company's shareholders' agreement and its implications. Not being litigious by nature, Dad didn't consider consulting this agreement to determine what options were available to him once things started to turn sour with his brothers. He naively assumed that if the trouble continued, they would eventually work it out together. Amazing as it may seem, The Bentall Group's shareholders' agreement failed to provide a mechanism for conflict resolution, and, as a result, there was no pre-agreed method for them to amicably resolve the impasse that eventually developed between them. Once things deteriorated, they had no way to address the problem.

4. **THE ABSENCE OF INDEPENDENT ADVICE.** Our family failed to take advantage of the opportunity to have truly independent advice. This was particularly ironic, given that we had access to an experienced, knowledgeable advisor who was willing to assist us; we just didn't use him. Instead, we trusted our future to one of our senior executives. It is clear that we were unwise to trust our family's future to someone who had a vested interest in the outcome.

LEARNING FROM OUR MISTAKES

This was my first intimate experience with succession in a family business. As an advisor to family businesses, I can now look back on what happened and see what went wrong—and what could have been done differently. In retrospect, the following are two of the lessons from our experience that are potentially applicable to virtually any family enterprise.

1. **AGREE ON A LONG-TERM VISION FOR THE FAMILY ENTERPRISE.** Three of the most important responsibilities of the shareholders of a family firm are to determine its vision, clarify its values, and define its metric of success. Unfortunately, these tasks are often regarded by family business owners as too academic to deserve their time and attention. My dad was one of those owners who couldn't see the value in these things, and as a result he and Bob were never able to develop an agreed-upon long-term vision.

2. **DECIDE HOW YOU WILL RESOLVE CONFLICTS.** It is essential for family firms to deal with minor disputes as they arise—before they become major problems. This rule should cover the joint ownership of any family asset, including non-business items such as the summer cottage.[6] If partners can't agree on how to end their working relationship before they begin, then they should probably postpone working together.

CONCLUSION

Although there was relative harmony and financial success for years in our family business, we had many foundational issues that were left unaddressed for far too long. As a result, both the business and the family were torn apart. The falling out between brothers threw the whole extended family into turmoil. Spouses and cousins inevitably ended up choosing sides. Instead of enjoying casual visits or even spending holidays together, many of us became separated by a wall of distrust and hurt.

It was tragic to watch as our family, once characterized by mutual respect, deteriorated into a fractured wasteland of broken relationships. Some branches

---

[6.] It is commonly agreed that one of the most contentious issues between siblings following the death of a parent is the summer cottage. Without a plan to settle disagreements, the ownership, use and maintenance of this typically prized possession can be a source of great conflict.

of the family remained close but most of us retreated into safer, more comfortable relationships that did not include extended family.

Had we known then what we know now, we might have been able to write a different ending to our story, but, tragically, we lacked the wisdom and foresight to deal with our challenges before they became unmanageable.

CHAPTER 4
SELLING THE FLAGSHIP COMPANY

Around this time, my two uncles, Bob and Howard, determined that it was time to sell the construction company that had been synonymous with the Bentall name for more than 75 years. Their priority had become real estate development, and since the construction business did not fit with their plans for the future, they had no use for what they regarded to be a tired old enterprise.

WHY WOULD ANYONE SELL THE GOLDEN GOOSE?
Dad was shocked by their decision to get rid of the company. He reasoned that it was still worth keeping because Dominion:
- Employed a capable and substantial workforce (150 staff and 150 tradesmen)
- Enjoyed 75 years of business success
- Built all the real estate assets we owned
- Essentially provided all the projects that had funded all our real estate development activities
- Enjoyed a sterling reputation for quality in construction
- Had a management team that was well-known for integrity

Yet, despite all these positives, Bob saw many reasons to sell the company, including:
- In more recent years, an increasing proportion of The Bentall Group's profits were coming from real estate operations.

- The construction business was no longer needed to fund future growth.
- The management time and energy associated with the construction business and its significant number of employees sometimes prevented senior management from focusing on the more lucrative real estate development activities.
- Over time, the construction business had become dependent on its real estate parent for work, and it was no longer a hungry, competitive enterprise.
- Construction work in BC was increasingly being awarded to non-union companies, and Dominion was locked into collective agreements that made it increasingly difficult to remain competitive.

As a result, even though my dad believed it was sacrilegious even to consider selling Dominion, it would be hard to argue that there weren't solid business reasons to do so. When Dad realized that the other shareholders were intent on the disposition of the firm, he asked his brothers if he could buy the business and keep it in the family.

Wanting to handle things professionally, Bob advised that if Clark was serious, he should hire a lawyer and an accountant and make a formal offer. Dad just wanted to discuss matters "as brothers" and was hurt when the others insisted on the involvement of third parties. Dad believed that family was more important than business, and family was his priority. For his brothers, the priorities somehow seemed to be different.

PRESERVING A LEGACY

Dad decided that something had to be done to preserve his father's legacy. That's when he convened our second-ever family meeting. My wife, Alison, and I joined Mom and Dad, my three older siblings and their spouses in a meeting at my sister's home. As with our family meeting at the Meridian Hotel, it was a rather sombre gathering. But Dad was determined, and so he gathered his brood around him once again to consider the future of the family business.

Families in business are wise to avoid waiting until a crisis to hold their first family meeting.

An estate freeze, accomplished 15 years earlier, had provided my siblings and me with shares in the family business, although Dad and Mom had retained the voting shares. Practically speaking, they had the power to make the decision to buy the business, but out of respect for us and in recognition of Dad's advanced age, they wanted to obtain our input regarding the purchase of Dominion Construction. It was an awkward meeting because Dad was still struggling with having lost control of the family company and now he was out of his comfort zone again, as he asked his children for their input into a major business decision. To be honest, I think he wanted to just "get on with it" and buy the company but realized that if we bought the company, it was going to be up to his children to make it successful, and so he felt obliged to seek our concurrence. He was so used to being in charge, both at the business and family level, that I think the whole situation really threw him for a loop.

To add tension to the situation, none of us had ever been included in discussions of this nature or magnitude before. As a family business advisor, I obviously never recommend that families wait until a crisis like this to start having formal family meetings.

> *Families can build unity and develop knowledge by making decisions by consensus, even if Mom and Dad still "technically" hold all the voting shares.*

My eldest sister, Helen, initially seemed uncertain about the prospects of buying Dominion. But when my father pressed her to say exactly what she thought, she squirmed and said, "I think it would be a good idea." Rather than accept her agreement as a *fait accompli*, Dad pushed us all to think further about what we really wanted by asking her "Why?"

Searching for something solid upon which to construct a rationale, my sister began to reminisce. She reminded us that she began collecting the coats at the company Christmas party when she was 12 years old and had spent her Saturday mornings having picnics on various job sites. In other words, the company had really been a huge part of her life and she felt, "It just wouldn't be right for some other family to own Dominion."

Personally, I thought back to a time when I was a young boy and the company built a large antique brick deck for our home. The project lasted several months, and each day my mom would pack me a lunch box so I could sit with the construction crew during their coffee and lunch breaks. I often sat beside Eddie Leck, project manager and "bricklayer extraordinaire." To a five-year-old boy, it was just like I was part of the crew. That special relationship was re-established 11 years later when I undertook my first summer job as a labourer for Dominion Construction and was assigned to work for Eddie on the expansion to the Safeway milk plant in Burnaby. (Thirty years later, at the age of 70, Eddie would come out of retirement to build a rock stairway connecting the hot tub and pool in our backyard.)

As we considered our family's strong attachment to the company over the years, each of us recognized that we felt a deep sense of allegiance to our employees. Many had been with the firm for over 25 years and had faithfully worked to help make our business a success. It was relationships with people like Eddie that made us want to ensure that the employees were looked after now, just as they had helped to look after us for so many years. Clearly, we were all reluctant to see the business sold to someone outside the family.

Beyond the emotional ties, the deal made sense financially. My brother-in-law, Phil George, pointed out that the company had a nearly unbroken record of profitability for 75 years. In fact, the business had been profitable every year except for one year in the Great Depression when it had recorded a loss of just over $100. Phil sealed the deal by reminding us that if we wanted to be in the real estate business, we could use the construction company as a springboard to get back into real estate development, just as my father had done so successfully, many years earlier.

In summary, we decided to retain the company for five key reasons:
• We wanted to preserve our heritage.
• We wanted to maintain an allegiance to our employees.
• The company was consistently profitable.
• We had an emotional attachment to its legacy.
• It could assist us in developing future real estate projects.

SIBLINGS BECOME PARTNERS

Thus, in 1988, the members of my generation (Helen, Mary, Chuck and I) agreed to become co-owners and partners in Dominion Construction. We bought the firm though a tax effective process called a "butterfly of assets" (see part IV for a full explanation). The transaction essentially allowed us to acquire the construction business from The Bentall Group with very little debt through the transfer of some real estate assets (in this case, mostly buildings) to the other shareholders.

An emotional allegiance to a family business can give rise to pride, dedication and a commitment to making the company thrive.

In our case, my uncles and their partner (the Worster family) together owned just under 70% of The Bentall Group, while my dad (and our family) owned just over 30%.[7] By electing to use the mechanism of a butterfly of assets, our family was able to acquire 100% ownership of Dominion Construction while the other owners of The Bentall Group acquired 100% ownership of some real estate assets in California. Technically, The Bentall Group declared a dividend, but instead of receiving cash, we received a company, and the other shareholders received some buildings in California, which, incidentally, Dad was happy to divest of anyway.

When the butterfly transaction was completed, my siblings and I were each able to become 25% owners of Dominion Construction.

ACCOMMODATING EVERYONE'S NEEDS

Although we agreed to act collaboratively in buying Dominion, each sibling had radically differing objectives in doing so. My eldest sister, Helen, had a genuine interest in the business, and she wanted to be active on the board in addition to becoming a shareholder. As the eldest, she was also interested in getting some cash out of the transaction since she had lived much of her life with paper wealth but little discretionary cash.

On the other hand, my brother Chuck, an architect, preferred more independence. He agreed to participate in the purchase on the condition that the rest of us would purchase his interests in the business over a five-year period. In other words, he participated in the acquisition of Dominion even though he wanted no ongoing involvement with the company.

My sister Mary was interested in the long-term potential of the business, partly because she had no near-term need for cash. Unlike Helen, she had no desire to be involved on the board and appointed her husband, Phil George, to take her place at the table.

As for me, I didn't need cash at the time of the purchase so I was quite willing to use the company's cash flow to buy out Chuck over time and, subsequently, pay Helen for half of her shares. This would free Chuck to pursue his own business interests and allow Helen to become an active owner while at the same time providing her with some liquidity. In the end, all of these interfamily agreements resulted in Mary and me each acquiring 40% of Dominion Construction, while Helen held the remaining 20%.

[7.] The Worsters were the children of Frank Worster, who had served as VP of finance of the company for several decades. As a valued and trusted employee, he had acquired 18% of the company many years earlier. When he passed away, shortly after his retirement, his children inherited his shares.

DAVID C. BENTALL

Figure 2. Ownership Options for Families in Business

	MANAGEMENT	BOARD	SHAREHOLDER
CHUCK BENTALL not an owner	X	X	X
MARY GEORGE investing owner	X	X	✓
HELEN BURNHAM governing owner	X	✓	✓
DAVID BENTALL managing owner	✓	✓	✓

The above diagram illustrates the four different ownership roles adopted by members of the Bentall family shortly after they acquired Dominion Construction in 1988.

There were several positives to this transaction. My siblings and I were happy because we were each able to participate in the purchase of the business on terms that suited our individual priorities. However, more importantly, our dad was relieved to be able to retain the construction business within the family. In doing so, he was able to preserve the heritage that had been passed down to him by his father and to continue his association with the company that he had built up for the past five decades.

INDIVIDUAL GOALS AND OBJECTIVES

Finding a customized solution that was tailor-made to each of our needs was not easy to visualize. Thankfully, this was accomplished through the facilitation skills of our brother-in-law, Phil, who held individual meetings with each of us. He listened carefully to what we each wanted and then acted to ensure that those individual interests were met.

Typically, in an emotional situation like this, it is difficult to uncover the individual needs of all members of the family and then create a solution that will satisfy everyone's desires. Usually an independent professional will be required to facilitate discussions aimed at creating a genuine win-win solution for everyone. We were very fortunate to have a wise family member who was willing to play this role for us.

Families in business must learn to compromise and collaborate. In order to find win-win solutions, family members need to really listen to each other.

66

DO OTHER FAMILIES PLAN TO SELL THEIR BUSINESSES?

Most families have no intention to sell their business. A recent survey suggests that 96% of surveyed firms want the business to remain in the family for at least the next five years.[8] Another similar study found that 90% of family firms want to keep the business in the family, while only 10% of firms have considered or would consider selling their business.[9]

CONCLUSION

Thankfully, an innovative agreement was reached to permit us to keep the business. However, there was no excitement as we closed on the purchase. Instead, the pain and hurt of broken relationships hung over us like a cloud. We had reached a business solution, but the fractured relationships and the gulf between our Dad and his brothers were now permanently cemented by a formal division of assets. We were determined to make the best of a stressful situation, but it was still a very sad and painful time.

[8.] Laird Norton Tyee, *Northwest Family Business Survey* (Seattle: 2008).
[9.] Barclays Wealth, *Barclays Wealth Insights, vol. 8, Family Business: In Safe Hands?* (London: Barclay Wealth, 2009).

CHAPTER 5
LEADERSHIP TRANSITIONS

AN INTERIM NON-FAMILY PRESIDENT

At the time we purchased the business, Dominion Construction was under the capable leadership of a professional engineer by the name of Dick Meyers. This 63-year-old businessman had been company president for nearly a decade. He was also the first non-family leader of the company in over 60 years. He was recruited from outside the company in 1980 because, at the time, no one in the family or the existing executive team had the experience or knowledge to take on that role. It is a testament to my uncle's farsightedness that he had specifically sought someone who was of an age that he would not be in conflict with me or other aspiring successors to the role of president. He recognized that, ideally, senior non-family executives should be seen as potential mentors rather than competitors. (I will always be grateful to my Uncle Bob for graciously considering my career aspirations when he recruited Dick.) But now it was 1998, and Dick let it be known that he was planning to retire within the next few years. Nonetheless, he agreed to help us in our transitional planning.

If a family member is to have a legitimate chance of succeeding as president, he or she must have both the support of the family owners and the senior business leadership.

Since Dick's retirement loomed in the near future, it was obvious that we needed to choose and prepare his successor. I was no longer an employee of The Bentall Group, and given my nearly ten years of related industry experience, the new shareholders agreed that I would be the official "heir apparent" and that Dick would mentor and guide me in that role over the next few years.

We anticipated that this plan would enable us to maintain a strong family involvement in the day-to-day running of the company and help to ensure the preservation of our cherished values and heritage.

A FORMAL, WRITTEN TRANSITION PLAN

As a board member, I was given the responsibility to draft a proposed employment agreement for Dick that formally outlined his responsibility to "transfer leadership and authority to David and the rest of the management team over a two to five year period." Although it was unusual that I was the one to draft this particular letter of understanding, it should be noted that I did so on behalf of the board and with support of all shareholders. It also made sense on a practical level since I would also need to live with the terms of the agreement.

OUR CEO WAS AGGRESSIVE IN TRANSITIONING AUTHORITY

After we acquired the business, my initial management appointment was as a vice-president, with responsibility for overseeing human resources. Not long after, my management duties expanded to include Dominion's Calgary and Edmonton divisions. The next year, I was promoted to senior vice-president, with the added responsibility of overseeing our Regina and Winnipeg offices. In 1989, our board appointed me to the office of executive vice-president, with all functions reporting to me except our CFO. The next promotion added the title of president. Finally, three years after purchasing Dominion, I was honoured to be given full leadership over the company as both president and CEO.

> *If the CEO's planned retirement date is published years in advance, the family, board and senior management can all help to prepare for a smooth leadership transition.*

Much to my surprise, the whole process actually moved much faster than I would have predicted. Yet, as impatient as I was, it was Dick who set the pace for each transition, and he often surprised me by how much authority he was willing to thrust upon me. Dick was extremely disciplined and was a

> *I realized I had made many mistakes, and this helped me to be thankful for the privilege of leading our family firm.*

model of consistency and stability. He had a clear management philosophy that was worth emulating, and he was, by nature, an encourager and developer of people. It was a gift, to have Dick believe in me and my abilities, but that gift also came with high expectations for performance. Mediocrity simply wasn't accepted.

HARD HITTING PERFORMANCE EVALUATIONS

Twice per year, Dick would ask our 11 vice-presidents for specific examples as to how I could do better in my role. Then, almost in a fatherly way, he would explain to me how I should improve my performance or change my behaviour. I couldn't have asked for a better mentor in our time of transition; nor could I have asked for a better man to help me to achieve my dream of being the president of our family firm. I will always be thankful for his positive influence as a mentor and a friend.

> *"You can't achieve anything unless someone else wants you to succeed."*
> *Peter Legge, CEO of family-owned Canada Wide Media Group*

It would be ideal if all would-be successors had the mentorship, guidance and emotional support that I enjoyed. Sometimes this isn't available from executives within a family enterprise. When that is the case, a similar role may be played by a well-respected business leader or executive coach.

Much has been said in business academic circles about the significance and wisdom of family members *not* reporting to other family members in a family company. Instead, it is virtually always best for an aspiring family business successor to be mentored by a non-family executive. As Aronoff and Ward state, "One of the major advantages of hiring non-family executives is that they can mentor your children and help prepare them for leadership roles in your business."[10] Their objectivity in providing career coaching and performance evaluations is virtually irreplaceable. Yet, according to a survey conducted in 2007 on New Zealand family businesses, 74% of family firms do not have a performance appraisal system for family members and 43% of family firms indicated that they don't carry out regular performance appraisals for

> *All family business successors should have the mentorship of a supportive and experienced non-family executive.*

---

[10] Craig E. Aronoff and John L. Ward, *More than Family: Non-Family Executives in the Family Business* (Marietta: Family Enterprise Publishers, 2000), 32.

their employees.[11] Although this may not be surprising, it is nonetheless a gross disservice to would-be successors. Sadly, it often becomes the missing link in their development.

EXPANSION AND SUCCESS FOR THE NEXT GENERATION

During the ten years that Dick and I worked together, he helped me grow and develop as an executive. From 1988 to 1998, Dominion Construction experienced notable growth and success. We secured a number of prestigious government projects, such as the design and construction of new city halls for the British Columbia cities of Delta, Port Moody and Coquitlam. We completed the new Pacific Press printing plant in Surrey, BC, where the *Vancouver Sun* and *Province* newspapers are now both published. Our most public success was the design and construction of GM Place (now Rogers Arena), the 20,000-seat facility that is home to the NHL's Vancouver Canucks. It has hosted many other major entertainment events and served as the prime hockey venue for the 2010 Olympics. For five years, it was also home to the Vancouver Grizzlies, an NBA team that later relocated to Memphis, TN. At a total cost of just over $100 million it was, at the time, the largest project in our company's history.

To secure this opportunity, Dominion had to compete against four larger construction companies, each with strong credentials and experience. As a result, we decided to share our bid with the Phoenix office of Hubert, Hunt and Nichols (HHN), an American firm that had already built over 30 stadiums and arenas across North America and had unparalleled expertise in this field. We needed their size and expertise, but they needed us, too. They had never done a design-build project, didn't know the local trades and had no relationship with our prospective client. In addition to bringing strengths in these three areas, Dominion also brought the capacity to complete the concrete work that would be critical to completing the project on time.

LANDING THE ARENA CONTRACT

At that time, Arthur Griffiths was the well-known president of Orca Bay Sports and Entertainment and the owner of the Vancouver Canucks and Vancouver Grizzlies. He and I met shortly after he made the announcement about building a downtown arena that would house both teams. I have to admit my first thoughts were that the idea was a bit frivolous since the city already had what

---

[11] Kosmos Smyrnios and Lucio Dana, *The MGI New Zealand Family and Private Business Survey* (New Zealand: 2009), 7, 19.

I considered to be a perfectly good hockey arena (even though it was 30 years old). However, it didn't take long for me to see how out of touch I was with what the people of our city wanted. In our first meeting, I explained to Arthur that the worst thing he could experience in this process was to complete the design and then, after tendering the project to contractors, find that he was way over budget. Because we had a design-build team at Dominion, I offered our services to assist in managing the design and ensuring that it met his $75 million budget. Arthur didn't initially elect to have our help, and when the five major builders (including Dominion/HHN) submitted prices for the construction of the arena, the results were exactly what I had warned him about. The lowest bid was in excess of one hundred million dollars.

Unfortunately, we were not the lowest bidder and were advised that Orca Bay had asked the company with the lowest price to see if they could come up with cost savings of $25 million, in order to bring the project back on budget. They were given three weeks to accomplish this task.

At that point, I asked for a private meeting with Arthur. At Dominion, we had 80 design professionals on staff, including numerous award-winning engineers, and we requested the opportunity to review the plans to see if we could identify the savings he was looking for. We offered to do this work at no cost, provided that Arthur and his company would be prepared to at least review our revised submission.

Our team worked tirelessly, and I am proud to say that we identified $18 million worth of legitimate cost-saving. Unfortunately, this was exactly the number that the other contractor also found. We were very disheartened when Orca Bay advised they would be proceeding to negotiate a contract with the other company. Discouraged, we rolled up the drawings and went on with other things.

However, it wasn't long before we were advised that our competitors were unwilling to sign a contract at the revised price they had submitted. Kevin Murphy, the vice-chairman of Orca Bay, called me to discuss whether we were still interested in the project. He revealed the fact that, in spite of three weeks of negotiations, a contract had still not been finalized with the other party. He asked whether we would be willing to invest a weekend working with our respective lawyers to see if we could come up with a contract prior to his Monday morning meeting with the board of directors. We worked day and night for three days, ordering in pizza and sandwiches so we could stay on task. On Monday morning, Kevin presented our signed contract to the board for approval.[12] When we presented the board with a completed agreement, after just three days, the firm that had been dragging its feet for three weeks was set aside. We were now on our way!

A MAJOR CULTURAL SHIFT

Gaining the contract to build GM Place was a most gratifying achievement for me, and I feel very privileged to have been a part of the team that put this deal together. But, even more significantly, it was symbolic of a major cultural shift in our company, as the business transitioned from an engineering-dominated culture to one dominated by sales and marketing. A few years earlier, when I was initially asked about buying the business, I recall feeling a sense of reluctance because I felt that the company's firmly established "culture" was antithetical to what I felt it should be. I didn't know whether we could effect the kind of cultural transformation that would be required. The problem stemmed in part from the reality that as The Bentall Group grew and became more actively involved in real estate development, Dominion Construction became a captive contractor that was largely building for its parent company. Over time, Dominion lost the need to be lean and competitive in order to secure business, and this contributed to a general sense of over-confidence and a lack of hunger to compete. To make matters worse, our family's concern for our employees over the years inadvertently contributed to a sense of entitlement within the company ranks. Our generosity fostered a strong sense of loyalty, but some mistook it as a sign that our family should and would look after them, no matter what events transpired. This kind of dependence undermined the growth of strong, self-reliant individuals who would be able to contribute to the company and help it compete effectively in the marketplace.

Although I initially had my doubts about whether or not we could change the corporate culture, over time we were successful in making momentous changes in the way the company operated. The following is a partial list of the key initiatives that we undertook.

Strategic Planning. Within the first months of purchasing the company, we invited senior management to attend a four-day strategic retreat wherein we created a new vision and strategy for the company. This not only set the tone for the major changes that we wanted to implement, but also let employees know that their ideas and leadership mattered, and we expected them to help us build

---

[12.] Although our original contract was for much less, our contract scope was increased to $102 million when the NBA franchise was awarded to Vancouver.

a different kind of company. The strategic plan gave rise to annual operating plans that became the basis for all performance measures, including management bonuses.

Annual Profit-Sharing Plan. We expanded the annual profit-sharing plan (that had previously applied to only a portion of the company) to include all salaried employees. The plan tied the following elements together:

- Individual goal setting
- Regular performance appraisals
- Divisional profitability
- Corporate performance

This plan was instrumental in communicating to all employees that we expected them to make a contribution to the company's future and, most importantly, that we were prepared to reward them for doing so. Giving all staff a financial incentive to help ensure the success of their own business unit and the company as a whole also served to remind them that profits at both the divisional and corporate level were important.

Cultural Goals. Together with our senior management team, we created a list of ten goals that outlined the new reality we wanted to create in terms of employee culture. These enabled us to formally communicate to all our employees regarding how we wanted things to be different.

Long-Term Incentive Plan. We invited the company vice-presidents to begin thinking like owners by rewarding them like owners. As a private company, we realized that offering stock options would not be a practical solution. Instead, we created a sophisticated long-term incentive plan that was essentially in the form of "phantom equity." Through these arrangements and on a tax-deferred basis, all our vice-presidents were awarded the opportunity to participate in the growth of the company provided we met our equity growth targets. Under this plan, the shareholders agreed to share 15% of the increase in equity above an agreed upon floor with our senior team. (We reasoned that as shareholders we were entitled to 85% of any increase, given that it was our money at risk.)

Sales and Marketing Training. We also invested heavily in business development and created a customized sales training program that was introduced to the company via numerous workshops over a several-year period. Ultimately, I think, this was the key to creating our new culture that looked to the marketplace for opportunities, rather than to our family for handouts. Initially I was pretty naive about what was required to bring about these changes. I started by asking a sales trainer to do a $2,500 sales seminar for us on a Saturday, thinking this would be sufficient. He helped me to realize that the kind of cultural transformation we were after couldn't be accomplished in one day. He did a great job for us, and in the process his contract grew from a $2,500 assignment to $80,000 spread over several years. However, the payback was definitely there. We only needed to land an additional two construction projects per year to recover this investment (e.g., two jobs worth $4 million, each having a net fee [or profit] of 1%, would enable us to fully recover the $80,000). Thereafter, each year we could anticipate the prospect of greater profits on a sustained basis.

New Divisional Leadership. This was the most difficult initiative related to our senior management talent and the need to make some very tough choices about our leadership team. However, if we were going to change the culture, we needed to be decisive. In the end, we felt that we could only change the business trajectory by changing virtually every vice-president in the company. We accomplished this by:

- Offering early retirement to a 32-year veteran
- Relocating an operational winner to another office so a salesperson could lead
- Promoting a draftsman without a university education because he could sell
- Offering a divisional leadership role to a man who we were told couldn't manage people but who could sell
- Supporting a renegade leader because he was committed to selling
- Removing an engineering star because he was not committed to the new culture we were creating

All of these changes were made in an effort to support our shift away from an entitlement mentality and towards the sales-driven enterprise we wanted to create. It was a bold strategy, but others would later observe this and help us to create an outstanding marketing machine.

PROFESSIONALIZATION OF MANAGEMENT

Integrated with the cultural shift that was underway, Dick also brought a professionalized management approach to the company. He ensured that everyone's role in the company was clearly defined and that we operated with carefully developed plans, budgets and goals. Dick was not an expert in family business, per se, yet in his roles as CEO and chairman of the board he provided excellent leadership regarding governance and succession planning. Family business expert Don Hershman would have given Dick high marks because he believes,

"Two critical focus areas for professionalizing a family firm are instituting effective corporate governance practices and managing family dynamics by carefully defining roles and planning for succession."[13] Clearly, Dick was focusing on the right things to help us effectively transition the leadership of our firm. (Ironically, these were precisely some of the things Bob had wanted to do years earlier. Yet these had contributed to his falling out with my dad.)

REWARDING RESULTS

Over the next several years, these many changes bore fruit, and the following are some of the positive results we enjoyed.

- The company prospered during a difficult economic period while many reputable real estate companies were failing.
- Each regional office developed a strong market presence and some even became market leaders in their area.
- The corporation developed a sustainable and consistent approach to marketing and sales.
- We successfully penetrated new markets, including the government sector.[14]

As any company ages certain cultural norms—both good and bad—become entrenched. However, in a family company it is typical for old patterns to last much longer and become far more-deeply rooted, since family leadership can extend for decades (in contrast to the more typical five-year lifespan for the CEO of a public company). As a consequence, inheritors of a family company or successors coming up through the ranks are often confronted with the need to initiate a cultural trans-

A shift in a corporation's culture is possible, but it requires determination, dedication and patience.

formation to move the company forward and to shed old patterns that are no longer suited to current market realities. In our experience, accomplishing a cultural revolution was a multi-year process that required dedication, determination and a multi-faceted approach, as described previously.

[13.] Don Hershman, "Professionalizing Your Firm Helps To Ensure Continuity," in *Hershman Family Business Magazine* (2008),
http://www.hershco.com/pdf/Hershman_Family_Business_Magazine_Summer2008.pdf.
[14.] In our largest region, the new market reality was that virtually all new construction was going "non-union," and, as a union contractor, we were no longer able to compete. The exception to this rule was government construction projects. Although we had not previously done work in this sector, we developed a strategy to compete and were successful in obtaining contracts to build city halls for Port Moody, Delta and Coquitlam.

CONCLUSION

In a family business, one of the most critical challenges is mentoring the next generation for leadership. In our situation, I was fortunate to have an experienced, capable non-family executive who served as my mentor. He encouraged my growth, believed in me and instilled in me the confidence I needed. At the same time, he provided me with unvarnished, challenging performance feedback, requiring me to learn and grow before being awarded increased responsibility. He brought professional management techniques to the company and helped to shape not only my leadership but that of the whole management team. His strong, supportive guidance was instrumental in ensuring a smooth management succession. In addition, the stability he provided also made it possible for me to successfully execute the cultural transformation we needed.

CHAPTER 6

TRANSITIONING OWNERSHIP

As a teenager, I was asked to sign some documents related to our family business. When I asked what they meant, I was simply advised, "They make you an owner of the company." When I asked if I should read the papers before signing, I was told that it wasn't necessary and that I wouldn't understand them anyway. I felt uneasy about all this, but becoming an owner didn't sound like a bad thing and so I closed my eyes and signed.

Sometime later, I was again asked to put my signature on an agreement. This time, when I inquired about the paperwork, I was informed that the intent was to sign over corporate dividends that had been declared in my name and the money was to be transferred to my dad. When I asked why I should do this, it was explained to me, "The money is really your dad's anyway." There was no need to read the documents. Again, I closed my eyes and signed.

If my experience were unique or rare, it wouldn't be worth commenting on. However, as family business expert Ruth Steverlynck observed, "The distressing phenomenon of adult children signing documents that they neither understand and in some cases have not even read, is unfortunately much more common than we want to admit."[15] When asked why they would sign a legally binding document that they have not read or understood, successors say, "I had no choice, because if I didn't sign, I would be communicating that I didn't trust my parent or their advisor."

[15.] Ruth Steverlynk, 2012 interview with David Bentall. Ruth is a lawyer, mediator and family business advisor for RES Consulting. (ruth@resconsultinggroup.com.)

Unfortunately, this ritual of blind indoctrination is repeated over and over again across our country. This is partly because many family business professionals have as their primary focus the minimization of taxes. Consequently, although they may be doing a good job with respect to tax planning, they and their clients usually spend little time thinking about how to prepare the succeeding generation for their responsibilities as owners.

AN ESTATE FREEZE AS A MEANS OF TRANSFER

The most common strategy for minimizing taxes and transferring ownership between generations in Canada is an "estate freeze."[16] It is without a doubt an effective planning tool. Similar estate planning structures are employed in other countries, where the goal is to defer taxes related to the transfer of the company or family assets to the next generation. Although an estate freeze is effective in accomplishing this, it can also have unintended consequences that families would be wise to recognize before they begin.

For example, the "growth shares" that are created by an estate freeze and may be given to the next generation are of little or no value at the time of transfer. Therefore, family members often view the transfer of these shares as a non-event, and the inheritors of a business are rarely given any training or orientation regarding what these growth shares mean. In addition, they are seldom given any training regarding what will be involved in eventually owning the business that in time will create value in these shares. In addition, an estate freeze will usually place siblings into co-ownership arrangements without any prior conversation or consideration of alternatives. This type of arrangement is usually motivated by generosity on the part of the elder generation and a desire to treat all offspring equally. However, given that becoming a co-owner in a business is much like getting married, the long-term consequences and the compatibility of the parties ought to be considered very carefully.

Another problem with this kind of planning is that members of the elder generation typically are encouraged to retain all the voting shares until their demise in order to avoid the risk of them being cut off from the wealth that they have created. This is an effective mechanism for protecting the parents' interests, but it is an unnatural arrangement for several reasons:

> *Simply transferring assets to the next generation, in a tax effective way, is not a succession plan. Successors need to also be prepared to become competent owners.*

[16.] See section IV for a complete explanation of what an estate freeze is.

1) It creates a situation where the elder generation's control may be perpetuated well beyond what would be wise for the business. I know of many situations where founders in their 80s and 90s are still calling all the shots.
2) It arbitrarily perpetuates the next generation's status as "children" well into their adult years. This erodes their self-esteem and can result in them never growing into maturity. As a result, some have trouble learning to live independently or productively.
3) Instead of creating a healthy environment in which the next generation is encouraged to become wise and knowledgeable owners, the members of the next generation are often instructed to accept their parents' generosity without understanding what the arrangements are or what it means to be an owner.
4) Eventually, when control is ultimately transferred to members of the next generation, they are ill equipped for the responsibilities of ownership.

OPTIONAL SOLUTIONS FOR TRANSFERRING OWNERSHIP

Instead of waiting until they die to transfer shares to the next generation, wise family business owners may decide while alive to give voting control to the members of the next generation who are running the company.[17] When this is done the elders can provide guidance and direction to their offspring.

If not all members of the next generation want to be involved in ownership of the business, they can be given non-voting shares or other assets instead, such as real estate.[18]

If the elder generation is not ready to transfer voting control to the next generation, an interim arrangement may be considered whereby the two generations share ownership; for example, by transferring anywhere from 25-50% of the shares to the succeeding generation, they can become substantial partners without yet having control. Customers, suppliers and financiers will rapidly recognize this as more than token involvement, and hence credibility will accrue to the successors.[19]

In a recent study, 57% of surveyed family firms reported that they have a formal estate plan, but 43% of firms don't.[20] Unfortunately, even for those who have

[17] Barbara Spector, *The Family Business Succession Handbook* (Philadelphia: Family Business Publishing Company, 1997).

[18] Ibid.

[19] Ibid.

[20] Mark Fischetti, *The MassMutual Family Entrepreneurship Study: What Every Entrepreneur Wants to Know About Being in Business with a Family Member* (Philadelphia: Family Business Publishing Company, 2010), 9.

an estate plan or a strategy to minimize taxes, very few have anything that would constitute an effective plan for ownership succession. For example, a commercial lawyer recently told me that most of his practice was devoted to "succession planning" and "estate planning." He said he typically assists his clients in structuring their business affairs so as "to effect a tax effective transfer of assets to the next generation." I am all for minimizing taxes, but I also believe that a successful transition in ownership involves much more than this. Many advisors are just focused on tax planning, and the existing owners are typically focused on running the company, so no one is paying attention to the training of the next generation regarding their role as owners.

STRUCTURE AND FAIR PROCESS

Typically, when transitioning ownership to the next generation there will be multiple owners. In order to create a healthy environment for shared ownership, there are two key principles that should always be kept in mind. One is the need for suitable structure, and the other is the need for fair process. As family business expert Ruth Steverlynck states, "Both are critical for creating a safe environment to raise topics and discuss issues that are causing concern." To achieve this, families ought to develop a pattern of meeting regularly. Moreover, if they are able to agree upon a set of principles to govern their interactions when they are together, they can create space for difficult conversations and should be able to work through most challenges productively. In this kind of environment, expectations of "just trust me and sign" will be replaced by mature adult conversations.

BECOMING COMPETENT OWNERS

As a family, we didn't have either appropriate structures or fair processes. Nor did we have a road map for developing as good owners. We were actually offered no training or orientation at all. However, having seen G2 fail badly in their relationships as co-owners, our generation worked hard to do things differently. The following paragraphs explore some of the things we did that proved to be very effective. They also reveal some of the most important priorities that need to be addressed by any business family in order to accomplish a successful intergenerational transition of ownership.

1. CREATE A SHARED VISION

Having seen the pain that resulted when Dad and his brothers failed to discuss or develop a shared vision, my siblings and I realized that we needed to invest the time to create a shared vision as owners. To this end, even prior to buying the company, we agreed on five key priorities:

- Continue in the commercial construction business.
- Focus on Western Canada and close our Eastern Canadian office.
- Prioritize the reduction of debt by eliminating dividends for the first five years, so cash could go to debt reduction.
- Add shopping centre development activities (for resale, not to build a portfolio).
- Expand into California after a few years of success and profitability.

To confirm these priorities, one of the first things we did was to hold a strategic retreat to develop a corporate mission statement and a five-year plan. This was a new exercise for management, yet it enabled us to communicate our priorities and obtain "buy-in" from the whole senior management group. It was invaluable and gave us a solid foundation upon which to build the company for the future.

2. CLARIFY YOUR VALUES

As a foundation for our working relationship, all three shareholders agreed that we would fully endorse the values of our father and grandfather. Both men had reputations for integrity in their business dealings and both had an unwavering commitment to quality workmanship on all projects. They also were committed to caring for their employees, treating them fairly and with dignity. If you were to summarize their values in three words, they would be integrity, quality and caring.

In hindsight, we probably could have been more rigorous in how we articulated these three core values. However, through our cultural goal setting process, we did communicate to all employees our expectations regarding how employees would treat one another. The following excerpts for our cultural goals are statements that reflect our primary values. These were developed by our leadership team as part of our strategic planning process, and they served as powerful tools for change management:

- We confront issues and concerns openly and honestly to avoid corporate politics.
- We involve individuals in decisions that impact them and to which they can contribute.

3. DEFINE SUCCESS

The shareholders of a corporation have the privilege of determining what success looks like for the enterprise. For some companies, success may be measured by growth in assets; for others, earnings may be the top priority. At Dominion, our primary measure for success was return on equity. This was a new way of measuring success for our employees. Consequently we had a challenge to define, explain and even defend our new expectations. Prior to our acquisition of the company, the full financial picture of the company had never been disclosed, not even to senior management. To help create understanding, motivation and commitment, we decided to bring the employee group into our confidence and share complete financial information with all of them. This helped us all to work collaboratively towards clearly understood targets and provided an environment where the criteria for success could be well understood.

4. CREATE A REAL BOARD, WITH REAL AUTHORITY

Many experts say that the most important duty of the shareholders is to elect a competent board of directors. However, in many family companies there is no attention given to the role of the board. In contrast, when my sisters and I bought the company, we decided to invest the time and effort required to constitute a formal functioning board.[21] Our intention was not only to provide for good governance, but also to position the board as the primary vehicle for corporate decision-making, rather than the shareholders or management.

While the idea of having a "real" board was new to our management team, it wasn't difficult to convince them that this wasn't just a paper board. The board was chaired by our dad, and Dick Meyers served as vice-chair. In addition, each of us as sibling owners appointed one board member. Consequently, it was readily apparent to our senior executives that this group would be the ultimate decision-making authority for the business. Although the board was

> *"EVERY BOARD MEMBER SHOULD BE A STRATEGY:*
> *In other words, they should each have a specific strategic reason for being on the board. Then everyone will know what is expected of them."*
> *Marjorie Engle*

not involved in day-to-day operations, we were responsible to approve all major

---

[21.] We wanted a board of intelligent, experienced individuals who could provide guidance, support and oversight for management.

capital expenditures, our strategic plan, our annual budgets, as well as executive compensation.

As a shareholder, Helen decided to appoint herself to the board and was happy to fulfill a lifelong dream by being more personally involved with the firm. She brought to the table a strong focus on preserving the family legacy and a particular interest in human resource management. Mary was a busy full-time mom, and so she asked her husband, Phil, to sit on the board in her place. His entrepreneurial orientation and successful record of accomplishment in business made him well suited to represent her interests. I also decided to join the board. As someone who had worked in the real estate industry for ten years and who was now working full-time for the company, I think I offered a relevant perspective.

Our five-person board worked very productively during the first few years. I think Dad was particularly pleased having a role to play, especially given that he had now retired from his full-time executive responsibilities. For Phil, Helen and I, the board provided an ideal forum for us to begin getting acquainted with the new enterprise we had purchased and to come together as an ownership group. We initially met monthly, but, as Phil said, in the construction industry that was a little bit like "watching the grass grow." For a while we met every other month, before ultimately settling on a pattern of quarterly meetings.

Having a formal board required us, as shareholders, to take a strategic approach to the business and helped us to avoid any temptation we might have had to interfere in the day-to-day operations. The board also provided accountability for our management team and induced them to be more professional in their approach and more disciplined in their planning. (For a more complete examination of the critical role of a board in a family business, please see chapter 14 and Peter Armstrong's experience in Section III, regarding the board of Rocky Mountaineer).

5. ESTABLISH REGULAR COMMUNICATION

During his career, Dad never intended to exclude or alienate the other shareholders of the company. However, over time they all felt various levels of dissatisfaction, and they had no forum within which to discuss their issues. Having seen the pain that was eventually caused by their feelings of being "disenfranchised," I was determined not to make the same mistake. With this in mind, I decided it was critical for me to establish regular and open communication among all shareholders. The board was a beginning, but I didn't think it was enough. Besides, Mary had elected not to serve on the board, and she owned 40% of the company.

Because there was nothing formal in place for us as a shareholder group, I took it upon myself to adopt an informal communications strategy. Wearing my hat as a co-owner, I made it a point of personal discipline to call each of my sisters at least once per week. I did this typically while driving home from work. I maintained this routine weekly for ten years; that's over 1,000 phone calls! Looking back, this may seem like a lot of time to invest, but this was a small price to pay to keep in touch and maintain good relations. It also provided me an opportunity to keep my co-owners informed regarding company priorities.

6. PLAN HOW TO DEAL WITH DECISION-MAKING AND CONFLICT

As witnesses to the deterioration of relationships in our parents' generation, my siblings and I sought a means to ensure that any of our business dealings included ample provisions for differences of opinion—and that meant conflict resolution strategies that would help act to preserve family relationships. To this end, we did three things:

- We created a 12-person management committee responsible for day-to-day operations and then agreed upon its limits of authority.
- Similarly, we clarified limits of authority and decision-making rules for the board of directors.
- Finally, we created a mechanism in our shareholders' agreement that would enable any one of us to end our co-ownership of the company, if the need arose. (See Section IV for a complete explanation regarding the auction agreement and how it could be triggered.)

CONCLUSION

Most family business experts agree that the owners of a company have numerous key responsibilities, such as determining the vision, values and goals for the company and electing a competent board. In our family, we didn't know that these were our responsibilities because, like many successors, we had not been trained for our responsibilities as owners. However, having observed the mistakes of our father's generation, we were highly motivated to avoid the pitfalls that we had witnessed. As a result, we became proactive as owners.

Looking back now, it is gratifying to see that we did a pretty good job regarding what I now realize are the main duties of a shareholder group. In essence, G1's mistakes had provided motivation as well as a training ground that helped foster our success.

DOMINION CONSTRUCTION PROJECTS COMPLETED DURING G3'S SIBLING PARTNERSHIP YEARS (1988-1998).

BCAA building, Burnaby, British Columbia.

Broadway Church, Vancouver, British Columbia.

Delta Municipal Hall, Delta, British Columbia.

Rogers Arena, Vancouver, British Columbia.

Meadow Gardens Golf Club, Pitt Meadows, British Columbia.

United Way Building, Burnaby, British Columbia.

TD Centre, Winnipeg, Manitoba.

TELUS Mobility Building, Burnaby, British Columbia.

TELUS Mobility (reception), Burnaby, British Columbia.

CHAPTER 7

BUYING AND SELLING THE FAMILY BUSINESS

PAYING OFF DEBTS

From 1988 to 1998, Helen, Mary and I enjoyed a ten year G3 sibling partnership. During that time our company's annual sales grew from $150 million to just under $300 million. In spite of some recessionary challenges we faced during this time, the business was profitable most years, and we were able to see it move steadily forward. At the same time, a more cohesive culture began to emerge. The five different divisions of the company, which had previously been fiercely independent, began to share information and become more interdependent. As a result, market opportunities and operational "best practices" were shared across the company, for everyone's benefit.

As a result of these operational changes and our focus on marketing, we enjoyed consistent financial success and were able to repay all debts associated with the purchase of the company. This included the timely repayment of the corporate debts we owed to The Bentall Group (within three years), my brother (within five years) and my sister (within seven years). By 1995, we were essentially debt-free. We did have a small operating line of credit, but the company was on a strong financial footing as we headed towards the company's 85th anniversary.

All shareholders enjoy it when their business is able to pay dividends. This can be particularly true of successor shareholders, and often they become accustomed to this income and the support it provides for their living expenses. We were no different. However, when my sisters and I bought Dominion we agreed, as part of our shared vision, that there would be no dividends until we repaid the loans we obtained to finance the purchase.

> *Family firms typically carry less debt and as a result may experience less volatility in their earnings.*

Some people might think that we didn't need to pay off these debts so aggressively or that we might have been wise to put more funds into growth initiatives. The truth is, we had obligated ourselves to make these payments, and so we had little leeway. More importantly, we were conservative investors and wanted to reduce our debt as quickly as possible so we could enjoy more peace of mind.

We were not alone in this approach. Family businesses, as a general rule, tend to carry less debt and are more conservative. Many comparative studies have demonstrated this, but one interesting study showed that family firms had a ratio of total debt to total assets of only 20%, compared to 25.9% for non-family firms.[22]

Our early success and focus on debt reduction enabled us to fulfill our purchase obligations in a timely fashion. We were very fortunate to have done this while business was strong because, almost immediately after we completed our final payments, the markets softened, and we were grateful that we had put our financial house in order.

CONFLICTING NEEDS FOR CAPITAL

Like every family in business, we had to determine our priorities in spite of conflicting demands for capital. First and foremost, virtually every business needs capital to grow and expand. Second, the owners of the business want dividends for their own personal use. These two competing needs are essentially in direct opposition to each other. Adding to this tension, during the transition from one generation to the next most families have a requirement for capital to be paid out to fund the retirement needs of the elder generation. Finally, as we experienced, there may be some members of the family who would rather have cash than shares, and their exit from the business may need to be accommodated.

Yet, despite these realities, most families don't anticipate or plan for these competing capital needs. They are often overlooked for the following reasons:

- As the business prospers, family members can grow accustomed to dividends being paid out of the business to fund ever-growing family and lifestyle needs.

[22.] Daniel McConaughy and Michael Phillips, "Founder versus Descendants: The Profitability, Efficiency, Growth Characteristics and Financing in Large, Public, Founding-Family-Controlled Firms," *Family Business Review* (1999), 12.

- The elder generation typically sees the business as their "retirement fund" and seldom thinks about withdrawing capital for this purpose.
- The inheritors are usually more accustomed to thinking about their parents giving them money, rather than the other way around.
- The elder generation often doesn't want any of their offspring to "opt out of ownership," and as a result, parents fail to discuss or plan for this possibility.

Fortunately, we were able to agree on a plan that addressed each of these areas without too much difficulty. However, in most cases, working through these conflicting needs can be a very challenging process for a family, and once a plan is developed, it may take 10-20 years to fund, in order to prevent placing an undue burden on the company.

> *Begin planning for ownership succession when the family CEO turns 40. It may take up to 20 years to fully fund an appropriate retirement plan.*

BROTHER-IN-LAW WANTS TO SELL SHARES

About the time we completed paying all our debts, my brother-in-law, Phil George, approached me for a private conversation. He indicated that he was 55 years old and, ten years hence didn't want to leave his three children financial interests that were "linked" with others in the family. He therefore asked if I might be interested in buying my sister's 40% stake in the business. As he pointed out, I was the most logical person to control the company, given that I was already president, CEO, a 40% owner and the only family member working in the firm.

Many people would have been ecstatic about an opportunity like this. But I was initially uninterested. When I got home from the office that night, I reminded my wife that I had decided in grade 10 that "I didn't want to be in construction!" Yet here I was, facing the prospect of going into debt to buy a company in that very industry. The real irony was that although I was the head of the company, in many ways I realized that this business just didn't suit me. I didn't want to get in "any deeper" than I already was.

Other factors that influenced my thinking were my conservative nature and my desire to avoid debt. Having just spent seven years paying off debts related to our acquisition of the firm, I was enjoying the easing of some financial pressure; I didn't relish the idea of going to the bank and signing up for a new loan.

As the summer of 1997 approached, I decided that the kids were at a perfect age for me to build a tree fort for them near our summer cottage. I was looking forward to this summer diversion and recall reasoning to myself that I would be foolish to voluntarily take on a debt that might prevent me from feeling at liberty to take the time off to do this.

ARE YOU A STEWARD OF CAPITAL OR AN ENTREPRENEUR?

As I look back on this season of my life, I have come to recognize that I had the mentality of a steward rather than that of an entrepreneur. Frankly, I think this is quite typical of the offspring of successful entrepreneurs. For individuals like me, preserving capital is the priority. Given Dad's substantial business success, I grew up thinking that "the only significant thing I could do in life was to lose everything!" As a result, my preoccupation was to be a good steward of the resources I have been blessed with, and hence retention of capital became "Job One." In contrast, an entrepreneur is someone who pursues opportunity without regard to whether they have the resources necessary to capture the opportunity.[23]

Whether family members tend to be stewards who focus on preserving capital or entrepreneurs who focus on creating wealth is something for all family business inheritors to consider. I finally came to terms with this choice in my own life while away for a week, cruising with my wife. Early on the morning of my 50th birthday, we took the dog for a walk around Tugboat Island. It was a beautiful day, and the sound of the waves breaking on the shore and the wonder of the half-dozen bald eagles soaring overhead put me in a contemplative mood. I thought about my own life and began comparing it with the lives of Dad and Granddad. What had been the secret to their financial success, I wondered. In that moment, I realized that not only had they been outstanding salesmen, capable businessmen and solid leaders, but they had also been terrific entrepreneurs. As a successor, I realized that I had been tutored in the science of management, but not the art of an entrepreneur. Throughout my career, I had sought to follow their example in the first three areas, without realizing that the last characteristic (being an entrepreneur) was at the core of their respective successes. It remains remarkable to me that I had spent three decades trying to follow their example without realizing the true hallmark of their success. I'm sure this situation is common, as family business successors seek to learn from their elders without ever realizing what lies at the root of their achievements.

> *As a successor, I was tutored in the science of management but not in the art of entrepreneurship.*

[23.] Sue Birley and Daniel Muzyka, *Mastering Entrepreneurship: Your Single Source Guide to Becoming a Master of Entrepreneurship* (Harlow: FT Prentice Hall, 2000), 8.

MAKING AN OFFER

Phil and I spent most of a year in discussions regarding my potential purchase of Dominion. At the same time, my older sister Helen indicated that she would want to sell her shares if Mary sold her 40% in the company. Helen explained that she did not want to remain a minority owner of 20% if I owned 80%. As I contemplated these matters, I kept coming back to the words from a little sign that used to hang on my office door, "Let's consider at least one reason why it CAN be done." Eventually I decided that if I could find some partners who would join me in buying the business, I would not need to borrow as much money and maybe we could find a way to make a deal happen. As a result, I proposed to Phil that I would be willing to buy the business based on the following conditions:

- Our management team would agree, as a group, to acquire 10% of the company.
- I could find a partner willing to acquire a 25% stake in the business and who would be able to bring operational expertise and design-build experience to the table.
- We could agree on a price.

After several months of discussions, the management team agreed "in principle" to participate in the purchase. In addition, I had found a Florida-based construction company that appeared to be a perfect candidate to partner with me.

- They were a design-build construction company operating almost exclusively in the commercial and institutional markets, as we were. They did more institutional work than we did, and I felt we could learn from them.
- Like us, they had an in-house design and engineering staff, but in addition they had figured out how to be profitable in this part of the business, and therefore they would be able to assist us in this area.
- Our companies were of similar size. Their annual sales volume was about $400 million and ours was just shy of $300 million.
- Both were family-owned companies that had been successful doing some real estate development, in addition to their core construction businesses.
- Their founder, like ours, was well-known and well-respected in the community, and the company cultures were similarly dedicated to quality craftsmanship and ethical business practices.
- They operated in 40 states, but not in the Western USA. We were headquartered in Vancouver and operated across Canada and into California.

Between us, we could easily service all of North America. Together we would have sales of $700 million, and the goal of creating a one billion dollar enterprise seemed well within reach.

• If our partnership didn't work out long-term, I could see this firm being a potential purchaser for my shares or, alternatively, I might end up being the "exit strategy" for their family CEO and owner.

I was thrilled when this potential partner expressed enough interest to have one of their senior management visit our operations in California, Vancouver and Regina. I travelled with their chief operating officer as he met our people and got to know a little more about us. At the end of his trip, I was very pleased that his perceptions about our company's strengths and weaknesses were nearly perfectly aligned with my own. Specifically, he agreed that we needed to improve our operational efficiencies and accountabilities.

Unfortunately, after his trip to visit our operations he concluded that the help we needed would require the dedication of more management time and talent than they could spare at that time. Consequently, the deal fell apart.

TRYING AN ALTERNATE APPROACH

Not one to give up easily, I decided to try another tack with Phil. Instead of buying the business with the support and help of a partner, I proposed that we structure the buyout so that I would be allowed to pay for the business over time, out of earnings. In this strategy, the "sellers" would essentially be financing the transaction and we would not need to incur third party debt. In addition, since Phil wanted out within ten years, I proposed that we complete the buyout within that time period. I made a formal offer and named a price that I was willing to pay for the business. My brother-in-law received the proposal gratefully but soon advised me that he believed the company was worth more than I had offered. What were we going to do now?

THE AUCTION CLAUSE

As mentioned previously, when my dad and his brothers decided they could no longer work together, there was no conflict resolution mechanism or buy-sell clause in their shareholders' agreement; nor was there an agreed-upon formula for resolving disagreements should they arise. Having witnessed this problem in their generation,

> *An auction clause is a more appropriate solution for a family business than a shotgun clause.*

my sisters and I had realized the need to have a section in our Dominion share-holders' agreement to help us deal with this kind of situation.

Consequently, we had put in our shareholders' agreement an auction provision that could serve as a conflict resolution mechanism. This arrangement was designed to allow any of the shareholders to trigger a bidding process for the company. In the end, the shareholder who valued the company the most would be committed to buying the others out.

We had decided that this clause could not be invoked during the first five years to allow us time to pay down our debt to The Bentall Group and my brother Chuck. In addition, this "stand still period" would give the new co-ownership group a minimum of five years to see if we could make "a go of it" together.

MECHANICS OF THE AUCTION AGREEMENT

Our internal auction specified both minimum bid increments and time frames for the process. The following guidelines provided a framework for reaching a legally binding agreement:

1. The initial bidder must put an offer in writing and formally deliver it to the other shareholders.
2. The other shareholders would have 60 days to accept the offer and agree to sell at the offered price or counter, in writing, with a higher bid.
3. If a counter offer was made, the other shareholders would have five days to accept or respond with an increased bid.
4. If the matter was not settled after the first counter offer, then counter offers would continue with five-day time limits for acceptance, until an agreement was reached.
5. During this process, the initial counter offer would need to be at least 5% higher than the original offer. Subsequent offers were required to be higher than the immediately preceding counter offer by at least 2.5%, then 1.25%, then 0.75% and finally 0.5 %. After this threshold was reached, all bids would need to be at least 0.5% higher than any previous ones.
6. In order to avoid confusion, all counter offers would be required to match the terms and conditions of the initial offer except price.

This arrangement is a creative option for resolving conflicts among share-holders within a family business, and I now enthusiastically recommend it to all my clients for potential incorporation in their shareholders' agreements.

As president of the company, I had confidence that I would be able to continue to own and run the business indefinitely because of this auction clause, unless I was offered a price at which I would be happy to sell. For my sisters, this arrangement gave them the assurance that they could either buy or sell the company whenever they wanted to, with confidence that they would also get a fair price. We were all very grateful that we had this mechanism as our conflict resolution strategy instead of the more common shotgun clause. It gave us considerable peace of mind.

SHOTGUN CLAUSES

Simply put, a shotgun clause provides a mechanism for any party to a shareholders' agreement to end the co-ownership. This can be done by one party formally providing written notice of his or her desire to do so. When triggering the shotgun clause, the initiator is obliged to state the price at which he or she would be willing to buy their partner's, shares or be bought out. Such a clause can be a very effective mechanism for arriving at a fair price. It is not unlike the classic situation where two youngsters are squabbling over a piece of pie. Wisely, Mom may simply ask one of the kids to cut the pie into two equal pieces, while the other child gets to choose which one he would prefer. Obviously, this arrangement is designed to force one party to be fair in choosing where to draw the line down the middle of the pie.

Similarly, a shotgun clause forces the party who triggers it to be fair because, once the initiator establishes a fair price for the business, the other party gets to choose whether to be a buyer or a seller.

PROBLEMS WITH A SHOTGUN CLAUSE

Because of its intrinsic fairness, this mechanism is virtually ubiquitous in shareholders' agreements in Canada.

But while a shotgun clause may be a good way to arrive at a fair price, I don't believe that it is the best way to determine which family member will own the company. Often, with a shotgun clause, the most logical owner may not be the one who ends up with the company. For example, if a competent manager who is running the family business and has capacity to buy the business from his partner(s) decides to trigger the shotgun at a fair price, there is nothing to stop less-competent partners from buying the business.

Furthermore, and perhaps more troubling, a shotgun clause is definitely not a good way to build and maintain family harmony. This is especially true if one family member is forced, by a shareholders' agreement, to metaphorically load a gun and point it at the other partner's head. This is hardly the best environment for building rapport among siblings or other relatives and can create negative consequences for family relations that will reverberate for generations to come. For this reason, I recommend that other, more creative, solutions be considered by business families.

> *71% of family firms haven't adopted any procedures for resolving conflicts between family members.*[24]

Owners have many options that may enable them to sleep better at night and give them a better chance of preserving relationships in the family. (See the part IV for additional options worth considering for resolving conflicts.)

REACHING AN AGREEMENT

In our situation, Phil and I agreed to invoke the auction clause as a means to finding an agreement on price. Having made the first offer, I asked Phil and Mary to make the first formal counter offer under the terms of our shareholders' agreement. They responded by offering to buy my shares for essentially the same price as I had offered, but with more favourable terms. They offered to pay one-third down, with the balance (including interest) due over three years. I had 60 days in which to accept this offer or counter the bid with a price at least 5% more.

During the following two months, I carefully considered the possibility of countering their offer. On the one hand, I was reluctant to sell the business because my grandfather and father had worked in and led the company for 40 and 50 years, respectively. By now, I had been employed there for nearly 20 years myself. As I thought about all this, I began to realize that our family business represented not only my legacy and my heritage, but also my identity.

It is not uncommon for people to find their identity in their careers. Others may find it in the car they drive, the house they own or even the clothes they wear. But as I reflect on it now, I can see that my identity was a composite of Dominion Construction, its prominent place in the community and my family heritage all rolled into one. If I left Dominion, I feared the loss of my identity. This was very unsettling.

However, before the two months were up, Helen and I agreed on a price at which we were willing to sell the business to our sister, Mary. All of us were satisfied with the agreed-upon price, and we were all thankful that these arrangements had at least spared us the stress and uncertainty that might have been created if our shareholders' agreement contained a shotgun clause.

[24.] "Kin In the Game," PwC Family Business Survey, 2010/2011.

WHY HAD I DECIDED TO SELL?

In hindsight, it is now clear to me that my heart was never in the construction business. I enjoyed certain aspects of it, but not the core business itself. While Dad had loved to tour construction projects on weekends, I found job sites of little interest. I was dedicated to my job and committed to doing my part to continue our family's success, but I was more passionate about extending and protecting the legacy of our family than I was about building buildings.

CONFIRMING THE DECISION

I will always remember the day that the decision to sell was made final. I was wearing a light grey suit, which seemed to suit my mood. I left my spacious corner office in the Bentall Centre and drove to Phil's office. I had seldom visited his place of business, and I was uneasy.

I didn't like what was happening, but I had made a decision and I needed to follow through with it. I handed Phil a one-page letter formally accepting his offer to buy my shares. I explained that I was willing to stay on as company president for an interim or transition period. I estimated that it might take him 18 months to find my replacement. Beyond that, I don't think either of us knew what to say. After an awkward silence, I picked up my briefcase and left the building. A few days later Phil convinced me to stay on as president, retaining a 10% stake in the business. I liked the idea, since I had no immediate plans to do anything else. As well, we were enjoying good success with our new marketing initiatives, and I enjoyed the management team that we had assembled. However, I also remember thinking that Phil and I were so different that this arrangement was not likely to last for long. My staying on provided a time of stability while the employees got used to the new ownership. It also gave me time to get used to the idea that I might not be there long-term. This transition, being incremental in nature resulted in a smooth transition for everyone.

CONCLUSION

Buying and selling a family company can be a complicated process. One of the biggest challenges is the competing needs for capital. However, if families plan ahead and take into consideration the various stakeholders, a plan can usually be developed. That's why families in business are wise to start planning in earnest over 20 years prior to the elder generation's retirement. It may take that long to satisfy all the families' needs without putting undue financial pressure on the business.

In addition, families are wise to plan ahead regarding how they will "exit" if one or more shareholders want to sell their shares. In our family, we were fortunate to have an auction process that served us very well when two of us decided to sell.

CHAPTER 8

FINDING YOUR PASSION

During the 1970s and 1980s, the NFL's Dallas Cowboys became known as "America's team." Today, with a market value well in excess of 1.8 billion dollars, they are one of the most valuable franchises in professional sport. Some fans are attracted by their high profile players, while others are attracted by the famous Dallas Cowboy cheerleaders. However, the single most important reason why this team has generated such a loyal fan base is that it has enjoyed a strong tradition of winning. In fact, between 1966 and 1885, the team enjoyed 20 championship seasons and appeared in five Super Bowls, winning twice.

This success was orchestrated in large part by Tom Landry, their legendary coach from 1960 to 1988. During that time, he established the successful culture and innovative systems that still undergird the team today—over 20 years later. Year after year, his team was amongst the elite of the league, and as one who also aspired to excellence, I was curious to know his secret.

When I was 31, I took it upon myself to write Landry a letter, telling him that I had been a Cowboys fan for years and now, as a young executive and as a "student of management," I was eager to learn his secret to success. He wrote me back, advising me that training camp for the next season was about to begin and if I could be at his office at 3:20 p.m. on the following Thursday, he would give me 20 minutes of his time. We were living in Southern California then, and the Cowboys training camp was only three hours away by car, and so I agreed.

While we were together, Tom Landry shared numerous thoughts about the team's success. His main point was that it takes a shared philosophy to build a strong team. He explained that unless all the players and all the coaches believe in the same philosophy, goals and objectives, people won't be "pulling in the same direction" and the effort will be wasted. This is why, from time to time, Landry had passed up opportunities to draft Heisman Trophy winners or to sign assistant coaches who had been extremely successful elsewhere. He reasoned that if they didn't share the same philosophy as he did, then they would be better off joining another club. That afternoon, he provided me with an important insight into success and what it takes to build a perennial winner. However, as I drove back to our home in Villa Park, I couldn't help but think that there must be something beyond a "shared philosophy" that had made him successful as a coach. Why was he was so dedicated to the game? Why had he introduced computers to the world of sport long before most of corporate America could even spell the word? What had inspired him to revolutionize the college draft through the use of computers? Why had he pioneered a sophisticated play-calling approach that is now commonplace?

Then it occurred to me: Tom Landry loved football! It was his passion. The "what" behind his success was a shared philosophy, but the "why" was his passion for the game.

Michael Jordan is a legendary superstar who associates passion with excellence. He was once asked what he would do if he could design the ideal basketball training program for young boys. How would he ensure that their skills were developed to the highest level possible? What kind of training would optimize their chances for future success? His answer was simple: "I would make it fun." He reasoned that excellence begins with desire, and that desire stems from a love (or passion) for the game. If the practices were fun, the boys would be willing to work hard, and this would lead to excellence.

PASSION IS THE KEY

Similarly, family business scholars have identified passion for business as a critical success factor in the succession process of family business.[25] Both my grandfather and my dad were passionate about construction, and when all is said and done, I truly believe their successes can be traced to their love for the business and their resulting drive for excellence. Their shared passion made it very natural for my father to follow in his father's footsteps by joining the family firm, and this resulted in, at least partially, a very smooth and seamless intergeneration succession.

[25.] P. Sharma, J.J. Chrisman and J.H. Chua, "Predictors of Satisfaction with the Succession Process in Family Firms," *Journal of Business Venturing* (2003), 5.

My mother's passions were music and her garden. As a young woman she won awards as a soprano singer, and throughout her entire life she loved to play the piano. It was therefore natural that our home was always full of music and that the flowerbeds surrounding the house were stunningly beautiful. Mom was also passionately devoted to her four children and sixteen grandchildren. Her love and concern for all of us was the glue that held the family together. In addition, she was a great support for Dad, enabling him to focus on his passion.

THE PASSION IS MISSING!

Unfortunately, the vast majority of successors in family businesses don't appear to share the prior generation's passion for the family business. In fact, a recent study demonstrated that only 13% of potential successors in the younger generation shared the owner's passion for the family business.[26] A similar study of family firms in New Zealand noted that 51% of the younger generation were not as interested in the business as the older generation.[27] As a result, business families are best to resist the temptation to paint everyone (i.e., successor generations) with the same brush. Instead, they are wise to pay attention to the individual needs and desires of family members, to encourage and celebrate their individual passions and work to accommodate their individuality.

FINDING YOUR NATURAL BENT

How do we discover our passion? Dr. Norman Wright, a prolific author and family relationship expert, says that parents need to discover their children's "natural bent" and then encourage them to pursue it. When I first read this, our children were young and they all seemed pretty similar to me. So I was puzzled as I tried to think about their "natural bents" and had to admit that I had absolutely no clue!

> *Rather than conform our children to fit into a family business that we have created, we should help them to discover their God-given talents, abilities and passions.*

But it all came together one Christmas afternoon when our four-year-old son, Jon, disappeared for a time. We searched the house and called out his name, but there was no response. Finally, we found him sitting cross-legged behind a closed door in his

---

26. Mark Fischetti, *The MassMutual Family Entrepreneurship Study: What Every Entrepreneur Wants to Know About Being in Business with a Family Member* (Philadelphia: Family Business Publishing Company, 2010), 8.

27. Kosmos Smyrnios and Lucio Dana, *The MGI New Zealand Family and Private Business Survey* (New Zealand: MGI, 2009), 3.

bedroom, clearly oblivious to our calls. He was staring, almost trance-like, at the brand new Fisher Price stereo he had received for Christmas. He was totally captivated by the music, and that day I realized that I had uncovered his natural bent—he loved music and was destined to do something in his life that was connected to it. True to this expectation, Jon started composing music in high school and recorded his first CD (largely comprised of original songs) while at university. He had discovered his passion.

GETTING ON A PONY I DIDN'T WANT TO RIDE

When my dad first proposed that my siblings and I purchase Dominion Construction, I was hesitant. I knew deep inside that I had no passion for the construction business, but at that time I didn't know how to articulate these feelings. So, instead, I responded with the following two concerns:

- I was concerned about the culture of the company. Over the years, the employees had become very dependent on the company in a way that I regarded as unhealthy. They seemed to have what I would describe as an entitlement mentality, expecting our family and the company to look after them. This needed to change, and it would be a challenge.
- I was initially reluctant to buy the business because I was more interested in real estate development than I was in construction.

Yet, as my brother-in-law pointed out, I could more easily pursue my real estate goals by using the platform of Dominion than by renting an office on my own and starting to look for deals. With Dominion, I had the support of a talent pool of 150 professionals, offices in five cities, established relationships for banking and bonding, and proven expertise in design, construction and finance.

In spite of my misgivings, I decided to participate in the purchase of the company and immediately realized that my first task was to learn the construction business. After all, if I was going to be the company president within a few years, I needed to prepare for these responsibilities. As a result, my desire to become a real estate developer was quickly, but temporarily, put on hold.

I dedicated myself to the task and was honoured to be chosen by the board to serve as company president just two years later. But this brought with it an even greater responsibility to focus on what was best for the company (construction), rather than what was best for me (real estate development). So, I put my desires on hold again, and for the next five years I focused on leading a construction company.

Once I saddled up to ride this pony, I wasn't about to dismount until I learned how to ride her! Yet, much to my surprise, these "riding lessons" swiftly gobbled up 10 years of my life. During that time, we made great progress as a company, but I became more and more distant from my real career interests and my passion for real estate development.

GETTING OFF THE PONY

I have previously explained how my brother-in-law, Phil, offered to buy my interest in the business. Under the terms of our shareholders' agreement, I had 60 days to accept his offer or to counter it by offering to buy his shares, at a price at least 5% higher than what he had offered.

During those 60 days, I was scheduled to go on a retreat with my two closest friends, Carson Pue and Bob Kuhn.[28] I recall telling them that I felt pulled in opposite directions. One direction would pull me towards our construction business and allow me to feel like I was being faithful to my heritage and the legacy of Dad and Granddad. The other direction constantly pulled at me to pursue my own interests and to be true to my own passion. I remember thinking that if I bought Dominion, it would mean borrowing money, going in debt and taking on the responsibility of becoming the sole owner of the business. This not only sounded risky, it was also downright scary. If I sold my shares in Dominion, I would be starting my life and my career all over again, at the age of 43. It would be like letting go of a flying trapeze without a safety net.

As we discussed this, Carson said, "As your friends, we will be with you and support you, regardless of what decision you make." I knew his words were genuine, and it helped to know that I would have his and Bob's support, no matter what. In addition, my wife, Alison, also said she would support me regardless of what direction I chose to take. However, I still lingered with my decision, not wanting to move forward on my own. At this point, Bob helped to nudge me towards a decision by asking several penetrating questions.

"If someone walked down Burrard Street, downtown Vancouver, and offered to sell you a construction company, would you buy it?"

I replied with a firm "No."

"Why not?" he persisted.

"Because I decided back in grade 10 that I didn't want to be in construction."

"Then why are you looking at buying Dominion?" he replied.

[28.] This life-changing event is discussed more fully in chapter 18 on life calling. You can read more about my relationship with Carson and Bob in my award-winning book *The Company You Keep*. To order a copy, go to www.nxtstp.net.

"Because it's not just a construction company, it is my heritage and my legacy." Indeed, it had also become my identity.

Bob then stunned me by saying, "David, I'm a lawyer, and a construction company is just a legal construct, nothing more!"

His jarring remarks made me sit up and take notice. Something shifted for me, and I remember thinking, if I did buy a construction company, would I hire "me" to run it?

As I contemplated this question, I mused about what it takes to be a successful leader. This took me back to my encounter with Tom Landry several years earlier. I remembered that he had been successful, in large measure, because he *loved* football. In contrast, I didn't even *like* construction. So how could I ever expect to be successful as the leader of a construction company?

That's when I blurted out the words that eventually changed my life: "You know, if I did buy a construction company, I wouldn't hire me to run it."

Even as I uttered those words, I realized that a decision had been made. How could I buy the business and run the company if I knew, in my heart of hearts, that I didn't believe I was a good candidate to run the company? I resolved then and there, with the support of my two closest friends, to sell the business.

OWNERSHIP AND MANAGEMENT ARE DIFFERENT

I don't regret the decision to sell Dominion, but, as I look back, I now realize that I made this decision based on a very common misunderstanding. Like so many in family businesses, I had assumed that if you own a company, you have to run it. I had observed my dad and granddad as "owners/managers" and that was all I knew about leadership in a family enterprise.

However, with hindsight and the benefit of study and reflection regarding family business, I've come to realize that second and third generation (or any successive generation) owners should be very open to hiring others to run their family firms. Too often, family business successors don't even think about that option, even though their commitment to preserving the family legacy may be better served by being dedicated owners, rather than ill-equipped managers.

PASSION TRUMPS TRADITION

Unfortunately, not all families realize that finding one's passion is as important as keeping in touch with family traditions. This is not to say that family firms or family traditions are not important. They are very important, particularly if there is a tradition of working in a certain industry. However, I believe that passion is even more important and, when it is ignored, families sometimes unwittingly force their children to live lives of quiet desperation.

One of my family business clients confided in me that he had enjoyed working in his family business for over two decades. However, as his role changed, he felt as if he was dying a death of a thousand cuts. For ten years, he endured the pain, partly because he wanted to be loyal to the family, but mostly because he didn't realize he had a choice. His wife told me that he had become depressed and sometimes seemed suicidal. Isn't it tragic that a successful business, carefully preserved for the benefit of the next generation, could become the very thing that destroys that generation? Thankfully, in his case, we were able to engage in a process to liberate this fine family business successor, and he is now pursuing his true passion through serving others and building schools for the less fortunate in other countries. He has discovered his passion and his life now counts for more than just preserving a family tradition.

I believe that without abandoning the role of being wise stewards of the businesses that have been created by prior generations, all persons associated with a family business should be encouraged to discover their calling and to not spend their lives slavishly seeking to simply preserve a business they have inherited.

HELPING OFFSPRING TO DISCOVER THEIR PASSION

A balanced approach to succession involves giving the next generation confidence, exposing them to the business when they are young, and then freeing them to choose a career that brings out their passion.

1. GIVE YOUR CHILDREN CONFIDENCE

One of the most important gifts that parents can give to their children is self-confidence. I was fortunate to have a dad who did this for me, and I strongly encourage parents to tell—and show—their kids continually that they believe in them. This will help the children to have the courage and confidence to develop their own interests and passions.

2. INVITE KIDS TO WORK FOR THE FAMILY FIRM IN THE SUMMER

A summer job in the family business can be a great opportunity for teenagers to develop both a solid work ethic and an orientation to the family company. It is a great way for kids to become acquainted with the business and have an opportunity to earn some of their university expenses. At the same time, they can explore, in a non-threatening environment, whether or not they have a passion for the family business.

3. FREE SUCCESSORS TO FOLLOW THEIR PASSIONS

Offspring of successful business leaders are at risk of being stifled in their personal and career growth because they are usually expected to follow in their parents' footsteps by working in the family enterprise. They may feel obliged to work for their mom or dad, even though the career path has no correlation with their skills or interests. Instead, successors should be encouraged to discover and follow their own passions, wherever that leads them. For some, like my dad, this pursuit will lead to working in the family firm.

For others, it may mean they do not. This is probably as it should be. If they are not "hard-wired" with an interest in the family business, why would we want to force them to work there? One of the greatest gifts we can give to a young person is the freedom to discover their unique gifts and abilities. If they do this and end up working in the family business, it will not be out of obligation. Sometimes, their passion may lead the company to expand or morph into new areas. This can result in a double win, where the needs of both the business and the successors are met.

CONCLUSION

After I left Dominion, it was very hard for me to adjust to a life outside the family business. Even now, a dozen years later, it remains difficult to comprehend the fact that our family is no longer associated with the leadership of either Bentall Real Estate Services or Dominion Construction. But leav-

> *A family business deserves owners who want to be owners, not owners who are forced to be.*
> *Aronoff and Ward (2002)*

ing the family business was absolutely the best decision for me, both personally and professionally. It has freed me to discover my own path in life and to pursue what I am passionate about.[29] My experience has shown me that it is far more important to follow one's personal passion than to be a slave to a family legacy that doesn't capture that passion.

[29.] See chapter 18 for more on what this has meant for me personally.

PART II

LESSONS
FROM THE
Bentall
FAMILY

CHAPTER 9
LEARNING FROM OUR MISTAKES

The Bentall Family has a proud heritage. Both Granddad and Dad achieved many things that are worth emulating. However, our family also made many mistakes, especially when it comes to the inter-relationship of family and business. In this chapter, I would like to explain ten of the most serious mistakes we made and then offer suggestions that will help other business families avoid committing these same mistakes.

1. IMPATIENCE AND PRESUMPTION

I had been encouraged by my dad to aspire to be president. In and of itself, that wasn't a bad thing, but it served to fuel a strong presumption that one day the top job would be mine, and I incorrectly assumed that I would succeed my uncle as president when he retired.

> *Successors need to cultivate patience. If they prove themselves worthy, their chance to lead will come.*

In retrospect, I can see how these factors contributed to my impatience and kept me from submitting to organizational authority. It is obvious that I would have benefited from some guidance and patience regarding my lofty expectations. Our family should have known that there was another option—a non-family president, perhaps serving for ten years in between my uncle and me. A far more balanced approach for raising the next generation of potential leaders is to:

• Encourage children to aspire to senior roles.

• Encourage them to be patient.

• Don't allow them to presume that any job is a guarantee based on family ties alone.

Other would-be successors would be wise to recognize the importance of developing and exercising patience. If they prove themselves worthy, their chance to lead may come.

> *Successors must learn to submit to organizational authority, because a good leader must first learn to be a good follower.*

2. CRITICAL SPIRIT AND INSUBORDINATION

Uncle Bob invited me to consider joining the family firm and, initially, was very supportive. Unfortunately, once I joined the company, I often disagreed with his business strategy (and almost everything else). Instead of respecting his experience and his senior position in the company, I was openly critical of him (both to his face and behind his back). I now realize that my critical spirit and insubordination combined to give my uncle ample justification to eventually want to remove me from the company.

Successors have only three honourable responses when they don't agree with the direction of the company or its senior leadership:

• Respectfully offer their dissenting opinion to those in authority.

• Accept the decisions of those in authority after having offered their views.

• Follow their leadership and keep quiet about their concerns.

If a successor can't manage to utilize the above approaches, then he or she would be wise to seek work elsewhere.

3. FOCUS ON HARD ISSUES

Harvard professor "By" Barnes has said that business families are often guilty of letting the hard drive out the soft. That is, they typically let hard issues (sales, profit, taxes, etc.) receive priority over soft issues (relationships, family harmony and communications). At The Bentall Group, we trusted our

> *Anticipate conflict and plan in advance how you will resolve disagreements. When the house is on fire, it is too late to shop for a fire extinguisher!*

professional advisors to guide us in matters not related to the core business (such as taxes, accounting and estate planning). In fact, we had the best technical advice money could buy to sort out the hard issues, but we didn't pay any attention to all the soft (relational) issues that needed urgent consideration.

> *Meet regularly as a family to provide an opportunity to talk about feelings and relationships, before they become unmanageable.*

Uncle Bob was frustrated being forced to be subordinate to my dad for over 20 years. Uncle Howard sometimes felt out of the loop because he didn't work in the business on a daily basis. Sadly, my dad was unaware of how much his brothers were struggling and how deeply rooted these feelings were. In fact, he was naive to the fact that he contributed greatly to their angst. If the brothers had met regularly as co-owners, or even as brothers, to air their differences, they could potentially have resolved these concerns before they became unmanageable. Had they realized the need to invest in family communications and long-term family harmony, they might have been able to avoid the further deterioration in relationships that ensued.

4. NO CONFLICT RESOLUTION STRATEGY

Our legal advisors never addressed the fact that the company's shareholders' agreement lacked a conflict resolution mechanism. Consequently, when my father and his brothers found themselves in a major argument after 40 years of co-ownership, they found that their shareholders' agreement was of no help. The documents were actually silent regarding how to resolve an impasse. No one was alert to this potential problem, and so when relationships collapsed, there were no mechanisms in place for dealing with the situation.

To avoid this kind of ending, families in business are wise to acknowledge that conflict is normal and to plan in advance what they will do when it occurs. In addition, if things become untenable, they should have a clear, mutually agreed upon strategy for ending their co-ownership. Obviously, these mechanisms should be in place before disagreements arise. Moreover, if a family can't agree on how to end a partnership prior to beginning it, then they probably shouldn't go into business together. (See part IV for several creative conflict-resolving strategies that other families have utilized.)

> *Transfer voting shares to the next generation in increments to facilitate sharing power between the generations for an interim period.*

5. VOTING CONTROL LOST THROUGH TAX PLANNING

Our tax advisors were excellent, but my dad did not foresee the inadvertent loss of voting control that would come as a result of some share transfers that he was advised to make for tax planning purposes. Specifically, my dad was encouraged to sell some of his shares to his two brothers, so they would each have 25.01% of the company and enjoy better tax treatment (prior to the sale of shares, each of my dad's brothers had approximately 24% of the company). Happily wanting to help his brothers, Dad sold an extra 1% of the company to each of them so that they could enjoy a better tax position. Together they now had over 50% of the shares, and years later this put Dad at a disadvantage when they disagreed regarding future plans.

One of my clients (who prefers to remain anonymous) has an enlightened view on the transfer of voting control. His threefold strategy could be of value for many business families. He recommends:

- Transferring management control to the next generation only after sufficient funds for a secure and stress-free retirement have been withdrawn from the company by the elder generation.
- Training the next generation as owners by transferring some voting shares (but not control) to them and sharing power with them for an extended period of time (five to ten years).
- Only transferring the remaining voting shares (and control) to members of the next generation when they have responsibly accomplished the first two initiatives.

6. NO SHARED VISION

Even though my dad and Uncle Bob worked together for almost four decades, they had never developed an agreed-upon vision or long-term strategy for the company. Rather than helping to bridge this gap between the brothers, members of our senior management team chose sides and thereby contributed further to the disintegration of unity.

By writing a corporate strategy, shareholders can crystallize an agreement on future direction. In addition to unifying the shareholders, this process typically has the following added benefits:

> *Create a shared vision as shareholders, so that all stakeholders will understand the corporate direction.*

- Management develops consensus and unity of purpose.
- Capital reinvestment is encouraged to keep the company strong and growing.
- Successors will be able to understand the corporate direction and may more readily assess what career opportunities may exist for them within the company.

7. NO CEO SELECTION PROCESS

Although there were many other problems and disagreements regarding the future of our family business, the spark that started the fire that eventually de-stroyed our family was the lack of a defined process for selecting the future CEO of the business. A member of the Bentall family had always served as president, and as my dad and uncle approached their retirement, all of our employees were wondering who would be the future leader. I had been work-

> *A CEO selection task force is the wisest and most effective way to select a strong leader for the family business.*

ing in the company for almost ten years and was obviously interested in the job as one of only four corporate vice-presidents—it seemed to me that I was at least a legitimate candidate. Admittedly, the other three corporate VPs were older and had more experience, but they were not family members.

It's astonishing to me, as I look back over this situation, that we had never developed a process for selecting the next CEO. In the absence of a defined pro-cess, the other VPs began jockeying for position, even as my dad was assuming that I was the only logical choice. Rather than leave the CEO selection process to chance or let it become a political battlefield, like we did, wise families in busi-ness proactively establish a transparent, objective process years in advance.

8. CONFLICTING ASSUMPTIONS

Although choosing the next leader for our company was a topic on many people's minds, the job description for this role and the criteria for selection were never agreed to. We were not alone in failing to document the skills required for the next CEO. In a recent survey, "34% of family firms noted that they did not even have written job descriptions for senior management."[30]

In the absence of defined criteria and an objective process for selection, no one even knew what The Bentall Group was looking for in a CEO. In fact, it is interesting to compare the following assumptions that were made:

- Jim, our VP of finance, assumed that a "numbers guy was key to our future."
- Dick, our VP of construction, knew that the top guy had always been a "construction guy."
- Wally, our VP of properties, pointed out that our wealth "was essentially in properties."

[30.] Kosmos Smyrnios and Lucio Dana, *MGI New Zealand Family & Private Business Survey* (New Zealand: MGI, 2007), 7.

- As VP of real estate development, I figured I had the "inside track."

When I served as the chair of the nominating committee at St. George's School in Vancouver, we were given responsibility to search for and select a new head of school. The first step we took was to clarify the qualifications we were looking for in the recruiting process. In an effort to develop a broad consensus regarding this essential information, we met with all staff and held a series of town hall meetings with parents. A consensus readily emerged from this process.

Family companies can expect to enjoy similar results if they seek input regarding the qualities needed in the future CEO from the following stakeholders: senior management and staff, all shareholders, the board of directors, and the family council.

> *Agree on the skills and experience that will be needed for the company's future leader.*

9. UNMET EXPECTATIONS

Although I was barely past my 30th birthday, I began to solidify an expectation that I would be the next president. This was not just an idle presumption, but one that was based on the following rationale:

- I was the only executive who had worked in every geographic region in which we operated.
- My career development had focused on real estate development, and our future profitability was linked to our ability to identify new real estate development opportunities. None of the other corporate VPs had any experience in real estate development.
- I had formal training in real estate with a degree in urban land economics.
- I had completed a two-year apprenticeship at the largest real estate development company in North America.
- My dad had repeatedly told me that if it wasn't for me he would sell the company and that he kept the company because he hoped that I would lead it one day. Since I was the young age of 10, my dad had been grooming me to be president.

Consequently, as the date of my uncle's presumed retirement approached, I became more outspoken about how I envisioned the future of the company. Unfortunately, it was tempting for everyone in the company to think that they knew what would be best, and in the midst of the debate it became virtually impossible for family members and members of the senior executive team to be objective.

The situation eventually deteriorated into a political and emotional dogfight, with everyone seeking to determine who had the power to overrule those with contrary opinions. Two camps clearly became obvious—employees were either loyal to Dad (Clark) or to Bob. I was caught in the crossfire.

Wise business families avoid polarization on the process of CEO selection by developing family employment policies that include clear criteria for how family members may become legitimate candidates for all senior management positions.

10. HIDDEN AGENDAS

Clarify expectations regarding the CEO selection process by addressing the topic in a family employment policy.

In hindsight, it is easy to see that we had wrongly assumed that one of our senior executives was trustworthy and capable of being independent and objective in negotiations. In our naivety, we never considered that he might have his own agenda. That's why it is absolutely essential that families choose their professional facilitators carefully when faced with sensitive family discussions. In short, facilitators should meet the following criteria:

- Objective
- Independent
- Experienced
- Knowledgeable

Traditionally, for the majority of family companies, their most trusted advisor has been the company's accountant. More recently, family business owners indicate that their spouse has replaced their accountant as their most trusted advisor.[31] Unfortunately, most accountants and most spouses are not trained facilitators. Moreover, there is significant potential for conflicts of interest with both these groups. Therefore, to select an appropriate facilitator, families need to resist the temptation to simply ask for help from whoever is "close at hand."

In order to avoid any conflict of interest, the following individuals should all be disqualified from serving as an independent facilitator:

- Staff or employees
- Senior management
- Corporate lawyer
- Company accountant
- Spouses

[31.] "American Family Business Survey" (Kennesaw: Mass Mutual, 2007), 5.

Choose a facilitator who has no conflicts of interest.

CONCLUSION

Looking back, we did so many things wrong, how could we have expected to have anything other than a disaster? We never invested time to learn how to integrate family and business and instead managed the succession process "by the seat of our pants." Fortunately, there are many books, articles, courses and research that can help to guide families to better outcomes than we experienced. The complete dissolution of our family business could have been avoided if we had had the wisdom to apply some simple yet profound strategies proactively to address succession, both in management and ownership. It is my fervent hope that others will learn from our mistakes and choose more wisely than we did.

CHAPTER 10

NEW PARADIGMS AND THE QUEST FOR MASTERY

Chet Raley is regarded by many as the best water ski coach in the world. This is the main reason why, over the past decade, I've made 40 trips to Florida to practice my slalom skiing under his tutelage. Professionally, he has a background that includes a degree in psychology and experience as a counsellor and teacher. He's also a former college wrestler with a black belt in karate. His father, who coached Chet for over three decades, is an aeronautical engineer. By working together for decades, they have endeavoured to understand the science of the sport water skiing. Chet's primary style of coaching is to train for mastery. He accomplishes this by being a magical combination of encourager, perfectionist, mind reader, storyteller and mad scientist!

When I first meet Chet, I had already been water-skiing competitively for half a dozen years. Each year, I had placed in the top ten (in my age group) at Canada's National Water Ski Championships. But, wanting to perform better, I turned to Chet for help.

A water ski slalom course consists of six buoys, anchored in the water. Success is measured by how many buoys one can navigate successfully without falling. If a skier successfully goes around all six buoys, the rope is shortened to make it more difficult for the next run. In fact, the rope is shortened after each successful pass until competitors ultimately fall or fail to get around a buoy.

The rope starts at a length of 75 feet and is first shortened by 15 feet (called "15 off"). The next step is to remove a cumulative total of 22 feet ("22 off"), then "28 off," and so on. The shortest the rope will go is "43 off."

When I first went down to Florida to ski with Chet, I had skied the course at "35 off" over 200 times in practice and 20 times in tournaments. My next goal was to learn to ski "38 off," but much to my dismay, my entire first week of training was spent skiing at "28 off." I reminded Chet that I hadn't come all the way across the continent to "play around at easy line lengths." After all, I could accomplish that at home and save a lot of money, too.

THE QUEST FOR MASTERY

That's when Chet explained to me the art of mastery. As he explained, if I couldn't ski with correct technique at the longer line lengths, then I wouldn't be able to do so at the shorter line lengths. Therefore, if I hoped to one day ski at "38 off," I first needed to learn to ski properly at easier line lengths. He noted that once I had "mastered" each line length, he would shorten the rope.

As this began to sink in, I realized what this meant: I would need to start all over again and learn to do things right, at each line length. This was a very discouraging realization. I was hoping for a quick fix, but instead I was introduced to a quest for mastery.

Looking back, it took me almost 10 years training with Chet to learn how to regularly complete the course at "38 off." However because of Chet's amazing coaching, many hours spent seeking mastery, and the wonderful support of family and friends, I've learned to ski well enough to achieve virtually all of my water skiing goals. By adopting Chet's approach, I was fortunate to win a gold medal in 2009, at each of the Provincial, Western and Canadian National Water Ski Championships. As an added bonus, that season I also established a new Canadian national record in my age group (52-60) with a score of 3.5 at "39 off." This past year, I was thrilled to win again and become the Canadian National Champion for 2011.

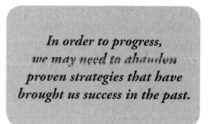

In order to progress, we may need to abandon proven strategies that have brought us success in the past.

Now I can see clearly that if I had continued on the same training path (skiing the same way I had always skied), I would never have learned to ski at "38 off." It just wasn't possible using the techniques that had been successful in the past. My old habits of "trying hard" and "working at it" simply weren't sufficient to allow me to achieve my goals. Instead, I needed to abandon what had given me success in previous years and learn to do things right. In other words, I needed a paradigm shift.

MASTERY IN FAMILY BUSINESS

Similarly, families who want successfully to navigate the tumultuous waters of business succession will typically need to abandon some of the old habits or techniques that have served them successfully in the past. This is not easy to admit. Just as it was difficult for me to "unlearn" the water skiing techniques that had served me well for almost four decades, it will be challenging for business families to abandon past patterns, especially if they have enjoyed substantial success.

A paradigm shift is essential for most families who want to successfully integrate family and business. It will require rethinking how to do almost everything. Most people don't want to do this, and that's why so many family businesses struggle to maintain both financial and relational success. However, the good news is that the principles needed are not that difficult, nor painful. They simply take time, dedication, and a willingness to let go of old thinking and old patterns of behaviour.

In this chapter, I would like to explore the "old" and ineffective paradigms of thinking that are so common in family business today and explain some new paradigms that should be considered by all those who are eager to pass their legacy to the next generation.

The following chart contrasts the "old" paradigms that in the long term may cause harm to family companies, with the "new" paradigms that our family was able to successfully apply when we were given a second chance at getting succession right (when we acquired Dominion).

Figure 3. Mastery in Contrast to Traditional Thinking

Old Pardigm (Traditional thinking)	New Pardigm (Mastering new approaches)
Treat all family members the same	Accommodate individual interests and preferences
Harmonize objectives	Accept differing objectives
Keep family and business separate	Proactively work towards the integration of family and business
Plow all profits back into the company for growth	Remove money from the business to fund retirement
Pay dividends when there is profit	Establish dividend policies

Old Pardigm (Traditional thinking) cont.	New Pardigm (Mastering new approaches) cont.
Don't talk about the "elephant in the room"	Talk about issues and concerns, so they can be addressed and resolved
Avoid conflict	Anticipate conflict and "proactively manage it"

My dad and his brothers were caught in the traditional paradigms common to family business. If my sisters and I were going to be successful as co-owners, we were going to need to embrace new ideas and master new skills. The following are some of the key things we did to create a more successful family business dynamic.

1. ACCOMMODATE INDIVIDUAL PREFERENCES

As I was growing up, my dad had attempted to "homogenize" his children so as to treat us all the same. This was well intentioned, since it was based on the idea that he wanted to be fair. However, by being a slave to equality (and defining it as treating everyone the same), Dad was missing the opportunity to allow for individual differences.

It was not inappropriate to expect my sisters and me to have equal ownership and votes and to all serve on our company board. However, because of the different objectives each of us voiced, we decided to structure our business interests to accommodate these personal preferences. Specific-

If families are slaves to equality, they can miss opportunities to allow for important individual differences.

ally, Helen was able to sell some of her shares in the company, and as a result, she was able to pay for a renovation of her home. This resulted in her becoming a 20% owner of Dominion, while Mary and I each became 40% owners. Nevertheless, we wanted Helen to have an equal vote in shareholder matters, and so our shareholders' agreement provided for her to have the same votes as Mary and me.

2. ACCEPT DIFFERING OBJECTIVES

My siblings and I each had radically different objectives when we were looking at the potential acquisition of Dominion. Yet, rather than trying to force everyone to have common objectives, we supported one another in achieving a host of differing goals. By articulating our own hopes and dreams, we were able to work towards a collaborative arrangement that satisfied everyone's needs.

As we did, other families in business will have members with differing objectives. Some may want active involvement in the business on a day-to-day basis. Some may want to be more passive investors, while others may want a governing role. All of these different preferences can be accommodated if a family will take the time to discuss everyone's goals and then develop a plan that addresses the individual aspirations of various family members.

In our situation, we made room for different types of owners, as represented in the following chart:

Figure 4. Different Types of Owners for Dominion Construction

Investing Owner	-Desires a long-term financial return -No involvement in governance or management	MARY GEORGE (my sister)
Governing Owner	-Active role on the board of directors -No involvement in management	HELEN BURNHAM (my sister)
Managing Owner	-Active role in management	DAVID BENTALL

As our experience vividly illustrates, it is possible for family members to act collaboratively, even if they have radically different objectives.

3. WORK AT THE INTEGRATION OF FAMILY AND BUSINESS

For much of the 20th century, academics and business owners alike argued that family and business should be kept separate. In fact, even the idea of studying family interactions in the context of a business school was frowned upon; those who wanted to study family dynamics were directed towards studies in psychology or sociology.

However, over the past 15-20 years, a solid base of research related to family business has been developed. No longer do we always have to guess at what works when it comes to integrating family and business. Rather, we can study what research has revealed and learn from families and advisors who have pioneered a fresh understanding of best practices. Since approximately 85% of all companies worldwide may be classified as family businesses, it is important that families learn how to integrate family and business. The time for crossing our fingers and hoping that it will all work out is long gone.

One way that our family worked at this integration was to include family members at the boardroom table as illustrated below:

- When Dad retired after 50 years of employment with our company, he initially served as our board chair. Later, we welcomed him at our board meetings as an honorary chairman and he continued to take part in board discussions, even as his health and memory deteriorated. In fact, he continued attending meetings until just before he died at age 84.

- My sister Helen was warmly included at board meetings in spite of the fact that she had no formal training or business education. It was a delight to have her involved, and over time she learned a lot and made important contributions, particularly related to our human resource planning and compensation policies.

- Many families shun the in-laws, believing that they will only make things more complicated. We bucked this trend by inviting our brother-in-law, Phil George, to join our board as our sister Mary's representative. Not only was he an intelligent, constructive member of the board, but he also brought significant insight and experience to our fledgling real estate development activities.

4. REMOVE SUBSTANTIAL FUNDS FROM THE COMPANY FOR RETIREMENT

Granddad had built the company by annually reinvesting virtually all earnings back into the business. My dad followed his example and advised me, while I was growing up, that this should be my approach. Many families' fortunes have been built by this simple formula, and it is hard to argue against the wisdom of this approach. However, as retirement age arrives, a different strategy may be needed to accommodate the needs of multiple generations. For example, to ensure Mom and Dad were looked after in their golden years, my siblings and I provided a formal funding arrangement to ensure that they were guaranteed an after-tax income that was sufficient for their living expenses (as well as travel and medical needs). Once this was in place, Dad not only felt secure financially, but he also became more comfortable about surrendering management control to our generation.

I have spoken of this principle many times because it is critical, and yet often ignored. How can the next generation expect to be given management authority and responsibility if the prior generation's retirement is at risk and dependent upon the decisions their inheritors will make?

This is why it is unrealistic and perhaps even unfair to ask an entrepreneur to surrender management control of a company unless he or she has been able to withdraw sufficient resources from the business to enable them to provide financially for their future. Naive to this reality, successors typically want the opportunity to exercise substantial (or complete) management control over the family business long before the elder generation's needs have even been discussed.

To avoid this problem, families should develop a plan to enable the elder generation to fund their lifestyle and retirement needs, separate and apart from the family business.

Thomas Deans, in his somewhat controversial book *Every Family Business*, addresses this problem by recommending that would-be inheritors buy the family business from their elders.[32] This approach provides the elder generation with the opportunity to liquidate their investment in the family firm and to provide for their retirement. Although I'm not generally supportive of an outright sale of the business between generations, I would suggest that it is essential for any succession plan to have as one of its first priorities the financial well-being of the elder generation.

In other words, if the next generation expects the elder generation to take their hands off the steering wheel and let them "steer the ship," then the successors ought to develop a plan to provide financially for their elders (as depicted in the following diagram). Ideally, this should be done through investments that are safely outside the company. If this is done, the retirement funding will not be subject to risk related to any management decisions made by the next generation.

Figure 5. Transfer of Authority Linked to Retirement Funding

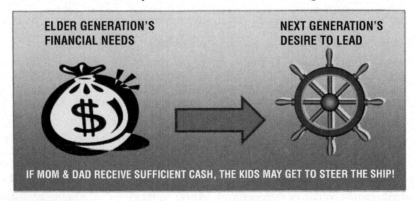

ELDER GENERATION'S FINANCIAL NEEDS

NEXT GENERATION'S DESIRE TO LEAD

IF MOM & DAD RECEIVE SUFFICIENT CASH, THE KIDS MAY GET TO STEER THE SHIP!

[32.] Thomas Deans, *Every Family Business* (Orangeville: Détente Financial Press, 2008).

5. ESTABLISH DIVIDEND POLICIES

Because the root of most family businesses can be traced back to an entrepreneur, corporate earnings are often viewed as something due to the owner/founder. Therefore, dividends are seldom discussed or planned for (except for tax and accounting purposes). Unfortunately, long after many companies have grown past the owner/founder stage, the idea of paying regular planned dividends to shareholders remains anathema.

As a result of not having an established formal dividend policy, two extremes often occur. One, the vast majority of earnings may be paid out to shareholders. As a consequence, shareholders are at risk of starving the company for needed reinvestment capital and potentially impairing its long-term prospects for survival. Or, two, reaching the opposite extreme, family companies may pay too little by way of dividends. This can occur because *In an American family business survey nearly two out of three (64%) of family firms reported that they don't have a formal dividend policy.*[33]
the company needs cash or because the elder generation wants to avoid spoiling the next generation. Regardless of whether the company pays out too much or too little in dividends, a pattern of regular dividends is often never established.

In our situation, Mary, Helen and I discussed dividend policy explicitly, even before we acquired the business. We decided to place a moratorium on dividends for five years to ensure adequate capital for growth. Even more importantly, we wanted to pay off the loans incurred when acquiring the business. Once these obligations had been met and we had eliminated the debts we had with my brother and The Bentall Group, we commenced a modest dividend payment program. The actual amount paid out was determined by our board, after they had reviewed the capital requirements of the firm.

Unfortunately, all too often dividends are a taboo subject in a family firm, because no one wants to fuel expectations that may not be met if the company doesn't perform. Moreover, inheritors are reluctant to raise the topic out of the fear that they may appear greedy. Although there are many excuses for avoiding the topic, wise families have the courage to discuss the dividend policy openly.

[33.] Laird Norton Tyee, *Laird Norton Tyee Family Business Survey: Family to Family* (Seattle: 2007), 19.

6. TALK ABOUT ISSUES AND CONCERNS

Like most people, I grew up in a household where my parents would avoid all unpleasantness and controversy if they could. However, after witnessing the blow-up between our dad and his brothers, we decided that it was better to address problems when they were small, rather than waiting until they escalated or became unmanageable. My sister Helen was the first to suggest that we all meet with a family counsellor to "clear the air" and talk about any

> *My parents met several times with the four of us siblings, together with a family counsellor, just to "clear the air."*

issues or concerns we had. It was a challenging meeting, especially for Mom and Dad, who were very uncomfortable with the idea of talking about our problems with a paid professional in the room. However, after a slow start we had several useful sessions together. Because of this experience, it later became far more natural to raise problems and talk them through.

As an example, one of my sisters and I had a difference of opinion regarding some of our promotional materials. I was eager to inform our customer base that the Bentall family was still the owner of Dominion. I wanted to explain that they could still expect the same quality and integrity that had been synonymous with our family for over seven decades. To this end, I wanted to have a glossy photo of my sisters and me on the front cover of our new corporate brochure. This was a challenge for my sister Mary, because she was reluctant to be publicly associated with the company and didn't want her picture to appear anywhere. This caused some tension and a disagreement between us. I asked if we could talk it through.

Quite simply, Mary wanted her ownership to remain a private matter. Yet there were business ramifications to her decision. I thought her decision might make it more difficult for us to retain the confidence of those customers who were concerned about the company having recently been sold. By listening to each other and developing a shared understanding of the two divergent views, we were able to reach a mutual accommodation. In the end, I abandoned my preference for a prominent photo on the front cover of the brochure and Mary surrendered her absolute ban on pictures of the shareholders. As a compromise, we agreed to have a small photo of all company owners, together with the board, on the back of the new brochure. In the grand scheme of things, I suppose it wasn't a big deal. However, it was significant that we were able to talk it through respectfully. This was a new approach for us, and we were learning to collaborate.

7. ANTICIPATE CONFLICT

Every family in business has the potential for serious conflict, and it is extremely important to have a conflict resolution mechanism in place to deal with disputes before they arise. As noted earlier, Dad and his brothers had no such mechanism in their shareholders' agreement. Therefore, when they found themselves at odds with each other, they had no way to sort out their disagreements. Now that I work as an advisor to families, I recommend that before becoming joint owners of any asset (even a summer cottage) families should decide how they wish to end their partnership in the future. If they can't reach agreement on how to dissolve their co-ownership arrangements before they start, then I recommend they not become partners.

CONCLUSION

As both a youngster and as an adult, I have spent over four decades waterskiing and I am very thankful to have had some success over that period. However, along the way I had reached a level of performance where I was stuck. For several years I remained on a plateau, unable to progress. No matter what I did, I couldn't seem to improve. In order to break free, I submitted to the tutelage of an expert coach. He showed me that I needed to abandon my old paradigms and develop completely different skills. This was not only physically challenging, but emotionally as well. It meant leaving behind many of the habits that I was comfortable and familiar with and that had been the foundation for my success to that point.

Similarly, families in business who want to successfully navigate the transition from one generation to the next will usually need to adopt fundamentally new strategies. Rather than clinging to traditional thinking, they will need to embrace new paradigms and master new skills. To do this, they may need to find a family business expert who will be able to mentor them (like I did for my skiing). It may take courage and dedication to abandon familiar and successful strategies, but having a coach or facilitator to assist can accelerate the learning process. Ultimately, those families who are willing to open their minds to new horizons and approaches will discover that they can develop new and different skills that will enable them to scale new heights. By doing so, both the family and the business are more likely to survive and prosper.

CHAPTER 11

WORKING OUTSIDE THE FAMILY FIRM

In the summer of 1938, Dad had graduated from UBC and immediately joined our family firm. Forty years later, when I graduated from the same school, he naturally expected me to do what he did. In fact, he couldn't imagine me doing anything other than work for our family enterprise.

My father is not alone. The vast majority of family business owners eagerly anticipate the prospect of their children working in their companies. They dream of the day when their offspring will be able to extend, and hopefully amplify, their business success. For some, it is virtually treasonous to suggest that their kids do anything other than work for the family firm.

COMPELLING ATTRACTIONS

There are many persuasive arguments utilized to induce graduates to join the family firm straight out of college or high school. Some of the most common are:

- We need your help to address challenges in the business.
- We will pay you more and give you more authority than anyone else.
- You will be able to progress faster in your career by working with us.
- There is so much to learn; even if you work here for your whole life you will never learn everything there is to know.
- Our business is unique, and what you might learn elsewhere won't apply.
- We can't retire unless you learn the business and take over responsibility for running it.

When young adults graduate from school, they typically lack confidence and are uncertain regarding how to start their careers. It can be very intimidating to face highly educated, aggressive competition when entering the marketplace, looking for full-time employment. Without any work experience,

> *All too often, successors are pressured into joining the family firm, either by guilt or because they don't know where to get another job.*

it can be very challenging to land your first job. As a result, the prospect of a secure position, an immediate paycheque and the support of family can all work together to make the family firm look enormously attractive. On top of all this, most families also add a touch of guilt with the standard line "Aren't you grateful for what we've done for you?" Sound familiar?

OPPORTUNITIES TO LEARN

Initially, I was very thankful I chose to join our family firm right out of school. I was promptly given opportunities to lead. I enjoyed challenging and stimulating management initiatives that included HR planning, organizational design, production scheduling and marketing. I had a great mentor in Paul Schoeber, the GM of BC Millwork Products. He was an encourager and a great role model, and he gave me plenty of opportunity to learn and grow.

Soon I was invited to work at the head office alongside Uncle Bob, who was then president and CEO of The Bentall Group. I was thrilled to spearhead a corporate rebranding initiative and facilitate strategic planning for all seven of our strategic business units. Then, within a year, my wife and I moved to Calgary, where I was asked to take on leasing, development and marketing responsibilities within our Alberta division.

No one could argue that I was not given a great start in my career. During my initial four years with the company, I had significant exposure to virtually all facets of the business. It was a great time of growth and development for me as a young executive. Looking back, I am also happy to say that I made a positive contribution in each of my roles.

SEEDS OF DISCONTENT

Unfortunately, over time I became increasingly dissatisfied with the direction the company was going. Although I lacked the experience to make such judgments, I had concluded that the company was too risk-averse and that we were missing too many opportunities through a lack of aggressiveness. To further

131

exacerbate the problem, I was having difficulty accepting my uncle's leadership. I tried to articulate my concerns, both to him and to other members of the executive. However, I was too immature and impatient in my approach. It is no wonder that I was unsuccessful in having my voice heard. It wasn't long before I decided that it would be best if I could quietly withdraw rather than cause a major upset. I reasoned that I needed to get out of Dodge, before someone got shot.

APPLYING ELSEWHERE

I decided that if I wanted to excel in my career, I should endeavour to learn from the best, so I began my search for a job elsewhere by making a list of the largest real estate companies in Canada. I think all future leaders of family businesses should have similar aspirations for excellence. In business today, competition is fierce, and it is essential for would-be successors to seek the best mentoring and career development opportunities they can find.

Without too much difficulty I was able to get job interviews at three of the most prominent real estate development companies in Canada (Trizec, Campeau and Bramalea). However, nothing materialized from these meetings. I then met with Dr. Michael Goldberg, who was dean of the business school at my alma mater. He offered to connect me with Cadillac Fairview (at that time, it was the biggest publicly held real estate company in North America). Dr. Goldberg knew the company's president, Bernie Chert, who had also graduated from the same university as I had.

GETTING MY DAD'S SUPPORT

Even though my dad was not supportive of this initiative, I kept him informed about my progress. Every month, he would routinely fly to Toronto for board meetings, and I suggested to him that on his next trip perhaps he could meet with Bernie. Reluctantly, Dad agreed to do so. As a proud father and a gifted salesman, I think that once Dad was in Bernie's office, he couldn't resist advocating for me. Consequently, when Dad phoned me after the

It's not that difficult to get a job outside the family firm, especially with the support and connections of the elder generation.

meeting, he announced, "I think I've found you a job!"

Before a formal job offer was made, I flew to Edmonton to meet with Jim Bullock, president of the Shopping Centre Group for Cadillac Fairview. He made it clear from the start that he expected me to "really work" and that this would not be just a 9 to 5 job. Sadly, most family business inheritors don't understand what it means to really work. They may *think* they understand and they may even try hard. However, unless they have worked for an intelligent, demanding, non-family senior executive, they may never understand what it is like to live and work in the real world. Jim wanted me to know that he expected me to overcome this stereotype.

WHAT I LEARNED

For two years, I lived in Toronto and worked at Cadillac Fairview. They were some of the happiest days of my entire career. I enjoyed the people I worked with, the projects I worked on, and the tremendous opportunities I was given. There are four significant lessons that I learned, as a young executive, that were extremely memorable:

1. DECISION-MAKING

Jim Bullock bluntly told me that I was expected to make decisions, explaining that if his executive team expected him to make all the decisions, "nothing would ever get done." Jim explained that I would likely make some mistakes; "But," he said, "that's OK, as long as you don't make the same mistake twice." (This was in sharp contrast to my experience at our family firm, where I had never been expected to make any decisions and where executives, including me, lived in fear of making mistakes.) I was thrilled with the trust that Jim placed in my abilities, especially in comparison with the lack of authority and responsibility that I was given at our company.

2. MANAGING RISK

One of the key reasons that I left our company was to check out a theory I had been privately nursing for years. My hypothesis was that our firm was missing many business opportunities because we were too risk-averse. Much to my surprise, my experience working in Toronto proved my theory wrong. Instead, I learned that our family could afford to be even more risk-averse, because I realized that there is a big difference between risk and aggressiveness. Under Jim Bullock's mentoring, I discovered that through a wise combination of prudent risk management and aggressiveness, many real estate development deals can be done without taking on undue risk. (He was a master dealmaker and managed risk very astutely.)

3. REALIZING I DIDN'T NEED TO KNOW EVERYTHING

One afternoon while I was working in Toronto, a soil engineer made an important presentation regarding a new project I was working on. It was a complicated situation, and a lot of money was resting on his opinion. Much to my astonishment, in front of a dozen senior executives one of our senior vice-presidents admitted he didn't understand the report and asked the engineer to explain it all again. I was amazed! Prior to that day, I had suffered under the mistaken assumption that, as Charles Bentall's grandson and Clark Bentall's son, I could never admit that there was anything I didn't understand. This experience helped me to realize how vitally important it is for anyone to ask questions when they don't understand critical concepts or issues. It also showed me that there's no shame in not understanding something, especially if you're responsible for the project. That day I was freed from the need to pretend I knew it all.

4. ADMITTING THAT I MIGHT BE WRONG

After my two years at Cadillac Fairview, I wrote a letter to Uncle Bob, asking if there might be an opportunity for me to rejoin the family firm. To buttress my application, I obtained a letter of reference from Mr. George Lawtey, who had been my immediate supervisor during my time in Toronto. It was very complimentary, prompting my father to say that it was the most amazing letter of reference he had ever seen. However, George included the observation that "David suffers from a need to always be right." It would take many years and many painful experiences for the truth of this statement to sink in. However, George was the one who first helped me to see that this was an area where I needed to grow.

> *Working outside the family firm is like a "rite of passage," demonstrating to all stakeholders that the successors are capable and competent.*

I BECOME A MAN

As my time working in Ontario drew to a close, our family took a vacation in Florida. As Dad and I walked together one night, he put his hand on my shoulder and confessed, "David, you know I was dead set against you ever working outside the company. You were dead right, I was dead wrong. It was the best thing you ever did." With those words, I became a man. In some cultures in a bygone era, when a man reached adulthood his father would give him a hunting knife to symbolize that he was no longer a child. But for me it was when my dad admitted that he could be wrong and that I could be right. In his eyes, I was no longer his little boy. In his mind, I had now become a man.

By this time, I had already completed a five-year business degree, been married for four years, become a father twice, and worked as an executive in the family firm for four years. However, it was not until I had worked outside the family company that my dad saw me and accepted me as an adult and someone capable of standing on his own two feet. Sadly, the vast majority of business successors never have the courage to fly on their own and, as a result, never receive the acceptance or affirmation that I enjoyed on that memorable night. As a general rule, it is not possible to earn the confidence and respect of the elder generation without working outside the family firm, at least for a few years. There are rare exceptions to this rule, but they are just those…exceptions.

BENEFITS OF WORKING OUTSIDE THE FAMILY FIRM

Many important benefits can be realized by providing offspring an opportunity to work outside the family business. The following outlines four of the main advantages:

1. KNOWLEDGE AND EXPERIENCE

If a family business successor works in another company, he or she can gain specific industry knowledge and general management experience that can be brought back to the family firm. As I mentioned earlier, the projects I worked on in Toronto taught me to be more aggressive, while still managing risk. These experiences had a direct impact on successfully launching some new real estate projects when I returned to The Bentall Group. By way of contrast, it can be very difficult to generate new ideas if a person only experiences "the same way we have always done it" at the family firm.

2. ACCEPTANCE BY CO-WORKERS

Rather than being seen as someone simply riding on Daddy's coattails, family business successors can demonstrate their competence to their co-workers and peers by proving themselves elsewhere. When I returned to our family firm, I worked with many executives who had more years of experiences than I did. However, the majority of them were able to accept me as "part of the team" because of the relevant experience and success I had enjoyed in a non-family work environment. The fact that I had worked in a highly respected company gave me a measure of credibility that I could not have established on my own.

3. ACCEPTANCE BY FAMILY

My siblings are 10, 12 and 15 years older than I am. As a result, I've always been perceived as their "little brother." This was evident when I worked on a project with my brother after my return to Vancouver. It was very difficult for him to accept me in a leadership position, simply because I was so much younger than he was. Similarly, when I later assumed the role of president at Dominion, my sisters had some challenges accepting me as "the guy in charge." Thankfully, all of my siblings were eventually able to accept me in these roles. However, I imagine it would have been virtually impossible for us to work together had I not been able to demonstrate competence through my work experience and record of accomplishments at Cadillac Fairview.

4. ACCEPTANCE OF SELF

Growing up in the shadow of a successful father can cause family business successors to suffer from an acute sense of inadequacy. I was no exception. This was further complicated by the tension that existed between Uncle Bob and me and the resultant criticism that flowed between us. To say that my self-esteem was fragile would be an understatement. Consequently, two years of working outside our family firm, where I was appreciated for who I was and for what I could accomplish, was a godsend. Many times, I was able to reflect on this experience in order to bolster my confidence.

After working elsewhere, successors will be viewed differently by the rest of the family, by other employees and, most importantly, by themselves.

It is tragic that we sentence the vast majority of family business successors to a life where they are robbed of the opportunity to genuinely and objectively prove themselves. There is nothing that can take the place of being able to look in the mirror each morning and know that you were able to "make it" in the real world. Working outside the family firm provides this vitally important opportunity.

REDUCING TENSION

The fact that I had obtained relevant work experience elsewhere assisted members of our family to see me differently. They realized that I had developed relevant knowledge and competencies that could not only aid in my career development but also make me an asset to our business. These factors helped my siblings accept me in my role. However, for the vast majority of family firms,

136

family member employment is, unfortunately, a significant issue. Wise families minimize these problems by establishing employment policies that require relevant outside work experience. As my situation illustrates, relevant outside work experience can mitigate these kinds of challenges.

NEGOTIATING RE-ENTRY TO THE FAMILY FIRM

Paul Desmarais Jr. is the chairman of Power Corporation, a very substantial family-controlled Canadian corporation that owns many well-known enterprises, including The Investors Group and Great West Life. Paul earned the respect of his peers by gaining considerable executive experience working in both London and New York before joining his family firm. He demonstrated wisdom in his career planning and has encouraged his offspring to follow his example. In fact, he once told me that he and his brother hoped that their children would become such a success elsewhere that one day he would "beg them to return" to the family firm.

Charles Flavelle, the owner and president of Purdy's Chocolates in Canada, didn't actually "beg" his daughter Karen to rejoin the family firm. However, after 12 years of working outside the family firm, she was able to join her family's company on her own terms because of her success working elsewhere. She was also able to avoid feeling as if the family enterprise was her only option. In fact, she was quite content to continue her professional career in Toronto, until her dad made her an offer that was attractive enough to encourage her to move to Vancouver. (See Part III for a more detailed description of her experience.) Enabling successors to create a foundation for their career by working outside the family enterprise is a philosophy that virtually all experts in the field endorse. To be precise, most family business advisors strongly recommend that successors get a minimum of three to five years of work experience outside the family business.[34]

Unfortunately, it is all too common for family firms to have no specified prerequisites for offspring wanting to work in the family enterprise. Those who do require relevant external job experience are generally very lenient, with over 50% of firms (in a recent family business study) only requiring a nominal experience of one or two years.[35] The same study revealed that over one-third of family employment policies now require at least three to five years outside experience prior to joining the family firm, and this is a positive trend.

[34] Craig Aronoff and John Ward, *Another Kind of Hero: Preparing Successors for Leadership* (Marietta: Family Enterprise Publishers, 1992), 10.
[35] Kosmos Smyrnios and Lucio Dana, *MGI New Zealand Family & Private Business Survey* (New Zealand: MGI, 2007), 17.

The following table summarizes the results of the study:

Figure 6. Family Employment Policies

REQUIRED MINIMUM OUTSIDE WORK EXPERIENCE	PERCENTAGE OF FAMILY FIRMS SURVEYED
1 year	31%
1-2 years	28%
3-5 years	36%
More than 5 years	4%

WHY LEAVE THE FAMILY BUSINESS?

This past year, in my MBA class, I taught a student from Spain who was feeling pressure to return home after graduation to work with his father in the family company. Together we generated the following list of reasons why he should consider not returning to the family firm without first working outside the company:

1. If he can achieve success in a role outside the family firm, he will be able to demonstrate to his family that he is a capable executive and thereby earn their respect.
2. If he decides to return to the family firm in the future after enjoying success elsewhere, non-family employees will be able to see him as competent and not just as "Daddy's boy."
3. When he looks in the mirror after proving himself in another firm, he will know in his heart of hearts that he is competent. This will increase his self-confidence and reduce his self-doubt.
4. If he returns to the family firm, he will know that he is employable elsewhere and will not feel "stuck" in the family company (or family) because he will know that he could leave at any time and be employable.
5. When he completes his MBA, it will be the ideal time to look for outside work. If he rejoins the family firm and later wants to venture outside, it may be much more difficult to get a job because potential employers will see him either as a castoff from his family firm or someone who will likely leave to rejoin the family business.
6. If he decides to return to the family firm in the future, he may do so on

his own terms and should be able to negotiate an appropriate role and suitable compensation.

7. In a new work environment, away from family influences, he may be freer to discover his unique talents and skills.

8. Working in circumstances where his parents are not "superintending" his progress would likely be a healthy step towards his individualization as an adult.

> *Would-be successors should pursue their careers independent of the family firm. Their goal should be to achieve such success that the family will "beg" them to return.*

9. If in the future he decides to rejoin the family firm, he will able to bring back skills and experience obtained elsewhere, and he can contribute these to the family company.

10. If he decides ultimately not to return to the family firm, he will know:
    a) The family will survive without him.
    b) The company will be able to function without his input.
    c) He may have found his passion and may be living his own dream (rather than living someone else's dream).

11. If he decides to return, and does so for the right reasons, he will likely be more committed to the family firm and will be able to genuinely and passionately contribute to its success. He will discover that it is possible to love his family and not work in the same business. (On the other hand, if his family says he must demonstrate love by working in the business, he will be able to explain that they are demanding an inappropriate form of love.)

12. His relationship with his father may be much better if they can avoid the tension and conflict that has come from trying to work together in the past.

CONCLUSION

Personally, I have thought a lot about the importance of working outside the family firm, because it had such a positive and profound impact on my own career. I developed more skills and experience, and my self-confidence was significantly impacted as a result of my two years working at Cadillac Fairview. Since commencing my work as a family business advisor over a dozen years ago, I have encountered many families where, like me, successors have worked outside the family firm for a substantial period of time. Without exception, their experience has contributed to a healthier environment in both the family and the business. On the other hand, whenever I have seen real challenges in a family business, it could almost always be traced to a situation where successors had no experience working outside the family firm. I recognize that it can be unpopular to propose that a successor get a job outside the family firm for five to ten years. However, this strategy usually gives families in business the best chance to succeed, both financially and relationally. A family employment policy or family culture that requires significant outside work experience is one of the most important ways a family can increase the odds for their long-term success.

> *With outside experience, successors will not feel "stuck" in the family firm. If they know they are employable elsewhere, they will feel confident enough to leave if appropriate.*

CHAPTER 12

NEW PERSPECTIVES

The vast majority of assumptions that people make about family businesses are false. I recognize that this is a bold statement. However, I am invariably confronted by inaccurate beliefs whenever I mention that I consult and teach in the area of family business. Many commonly held misperceptions are so widely accepted that they have taken on almost a mythical proportion. The following are some of the most ubiquitous and mistaken beliefs.

COMMON MISPERCEPTIONS ABOUT FAMILY BUSINESSES
1. They are small- or medium-sized enterprises.
2. The first generation will start it, the second will build it and the third will destroy it.
3. They are less efficient and pay an economic penalty for being family-owned or managed.
4. They are destined to fail because of family strife or sibling rivalry.
5. They should learn how to do things properly by copying businesses that are not family controlled.
6. There is tension between the priorities of the business and the family. To resolve this tension, it is important to put the business first.
7. Succession is a taboo subject. If discussed, it will inevitably lead to the disintegration of family relationships.
8. The key priority of the succession process is assessing which family member has the potential to be the next leader of the business.

9. Succession should not be talked about too early, as it will create expectations that may never be able to be satisfied.

In contrast to how things are commonly seen, I would like to offer a more accurate perspective for all nine of these "myths."

FAMILY BUSINESSES ARE OFTEN SUBSTANTIAL IN SIZE

Many well-known, family-controlled companies are world leaders in their industries: Michelin Tire, Hallmark Cards, Estée Lauder, L.L. Bean, Wal-Mart and Cargill Grain are all family companies that have annual sales or total assets measured in the billions of dollars. Wal-Mart Inc., the largest family firm in the United States, had 2.1 million employees and annual revenues of over $400 billion in 2009.[36]

In addition, consider the following statistics:[37]

- 90% of all US firms are family owned or controlled.
- 33% of the companies in the Fortune 500 are family businesses.
- ½ of the US GDP is attributed to family businesses.
- ½ of total US wages are paid by family businesses.

Furthermore, it is estimated that "a wealth transfer of at least $41 trillion will take place in the United States by the year 2052."[38] Much of this wealth in held in family controlled corporations.

Because of these facts, we ought to adjust our thinking about family businesses and acknowledge that they are much more than just Mom and Pop operations. Rather, family businesses are often substantial, and together they provide the economic engine of the global economy.

FAMILY BUSINESSES ARE LONGER LASTING

> "Family firms generally perform better and last longer."
> John Davis

The idea that family companies are large and potentially long lasting goes against the conventional wisdom that assumes a family will go from "shirtsleeves to shirtsleeves in three generations." In other words, it is commonly assumed that the third generation

---

[36.] "Wal-Mart 2009 Annual Report" (Bentonville: Wal-Mart Stores, Inc., 2009).

[37.] Nancy Bowman-Upton, "Transferring Management in the Family-Owned Business" (1991), http://archive.sba.gov/idc/groups/public/documents/sba_homepage/serv_sbp_exit.pdf.

[38.] John T. Havens and Paul G. Schervish, "Why the $41 Trillion Wealth Transfer Estimate Is Still Valid," *The Journal of Gift Planning* 7 (2001), 11-15, 47-50.

will fail to carry the family business forward. In fact, there is an expression for this presumed failure in many cultures, such as "clogs to clogs" in Holland and "rice paddy to rice paddy" in China. However, the truth is that family firms generally "perform better and last longer."[39] In truth, a family firm will, on average, last twice as long as a non-family firm. As an example, a contemporary study found that the average lifespan of a company is 12 years, whereas the average life span of a family company is 24 years.[40]

To illustrate how resilient family firms can be, the following are the five longest lasting family businesses in America:[41]

1. **Zildjian Co.** is the world-renowned manufacturer of Zildjian cymbals. The company traces its origin back to 1623. Originally established in Turkey, the company now employs members of the 15th generation of the Zildjian family.
2. **Tuttle Farms** is a 240-acre farm now in its 12th generation under the Tuttle family. It grows vegetables and strawberries and operates a retail shop on site. It was founded by the Tuttle family in 1635.
3. **Shirley Plantation** is Virginia's oldest plantation, settled in 1613. It was purchased and has been managed by the Hill/Carter family since 1638.
4. **Barker Farm** is a family farm now run by the 11th generation of Barkers, founded in 1642.
5. **The Seaside Inn and Cottages** is the oldest inn in America, founded by the Mason family in 1667.

> *The average lifespan of a family company is 24 years, whereas the average lifespan of other companies is only 12 years.*

Around the world, there are many companies that are much older than those in North America. In fact, *Time Magazine* reports, "Kongo Gumi Co. is run by Masakazu Kongo, 55, the 40th Kongo to lead the 1,410-year-old company, believed to be the world's oldest family enterprise."[42]

[39.] John Davis, "Family Enterprises: Beyond the Three Circles," at Family Firm Institute Annual Conference (Boston: Harvard Business School, 2011).
[40.] "Family Business Facts, Figures and Fun," Conway Centre for Family Business. http://www.familybusinesscenter.com.
[41.] "Monthly Message June 2008," Conway Centre for Family Business, accessed March 12, 2012, http://www.familybusinesscenter.com/public/files/newsletters/2008-06.pdf.
[42.] Hanna Kite, "Meet the World's Oldest Family Firm," *Time Magazine* (April 14, 2004), http://www.time.com/time/magazine/article/0,9171,993900,00.html.

FAMILY BUSINESSES PRODUCE BETTER RETURNS FOR THEIR INVESTORS

As professionals and academics around the world study family companies, they are discovering and spreading the word that family business is good business. Most strikingly, the current research shows that family firms typically outperform non-family firms in terms of economic return. In other words, family business is a better economic model. If you need convincing, have a look at the following statistics.

FAMILY CONTROLLED FIRMS COMPARED TO NON-FAMILY CONTROLLED FIRMS

Figure 7. Family Firms Outperform Non-Family Firms in the USA

Annual/Average	Family Firm	Non-Family Firms
Revenue growth	23.4%	10.8%
Income growth	21.1%	12.6%
Total shareholder return	15.6%	11.2%

Source: Comparison of average annual results for all firms in the S & P 500 from 1992-2002.[43]

Figure 8. Family Firms Outperform Non-Family Firms in France

Annual/Average	Family Firms	Non-Family Firms
Return on Equity	25.2%	15.8%
Return on Capital	18.5%	12.6%

Source: Comparison study of 47 matched pairs by size and industry from the largest 1,000 industrial French companies (1982-1992).[44]

[43.] Danny Miller and Isabelle LeBreton-Miller, *Managing for the Long Run, Lessons in Competitive Advantage from Great Family Businesses* (Boston: Harvard Business School Press, 2005), 15.
[44.] Ibid.

GOOD GOVERNANCE IS THE KEY TO LONG-TERM FAMILY BUSINESS STABILITY

Poor relationships between siblings (sibling rivalry) is commonly assumed to be the reason why a family business has failed or been torn apart. It is true that siblings are sometimes jealous of one another, and their relational challenges can boil over into the family business, with negative effects. However, to blame sibling rivalry for the deterioration of a family business is usually far too simplistic. In many

Blaming sibling rivalry for all the challenges of a family business is too simplistic.

circumstances, the real culprit has been the lack of good governance processes and structures. Although this may be overlooked by some, as a company and a family grow, so do their needs for proper governance. With this comes an ever-increasing requirement for the investment of time and energy, and so governance often suffers from direct competition with the urgent demands of the business.

As discussed throughout this book, if families choose to invest the time to create an effective family council and a well-functioning board of directors (with independent members), they will create governance mechanisms that can provide opportunity and support for siblings to work through their relational challenges productively.

FAMILY BUSINESS IS GOOD BUSINESS

The family owners of S.C. Johnson, one of the world's most respected corporations, are so convinced that family business is good business, that their firm's official slogan simply reads, "S.C. Johnson…a family company." They take pride in the fact that they are a family-owned firm, and like many other business families they have a dedication and commitment to excellence.

Some people assume that if family businesses perform well, then it is in spite of being family-owned, not because of being family-owned. Authors and researchers Danny and Isabelle Miller have thoughtfully examined why it is that family businesses are so effective. They offer four compelling explanations as to why family-controlled companies tend to out-perform their non-family counterparts:[45]

1. **They make a priority of *continuity*.** That is, they invest for the long run and are not driven by quarterly earnings. One obvious reason is that family businesses are investing for their children and grandchildren.

[45.] Ibid.

2. **They are people who take *command*.** They take action and tend to be more decisive. This is, in part, because management and ownership are more closely aligned, if not one and the same. Therefore, family firms can often respond more quickly to opportunities in the marketplace.

3. **They are builders of *community*.** Their culture is more inclusive. By extending their family circle to include employees, family business owners are usually able to develop a cohesive, loyal culture.

4. **They build better *connections*.** Given that the tenure of a public company CEO is often less than five years and family business leaders are often in their role for decades, family companies have an edge in competing for the loyalty and support of key customers and suppliers. Not only are these relationships longer lasting, they tend to be more of the win-win variety.

FAMILY SHOULD BE THE PRIORITY OVER BUSINESS

Whenever families are involved in a business together, there is a natural built-in tension between family and business. Inevitably, there will be times when what appears to be best for the business and what appears to be best for the family may be in conflict. For example, the business may require capital for expansion at a time when the family wants dividends to fund their lifestyle needs. Similarly, the business and family may have different priorities if a member of the successor generation is not doing a good job at work. While it might appear to be best for the business to simply fire him or her, this may cause considerable upset within the family.

> *Family businesses are a better economic model.*

In dealing with tensions between family and business, many family business leaders assume that the business should come first. If it doesn't, so the logic goes, it will create an unhealthy situation where the family's needs and wants will eventually be permitted to ruin the business. This risk is obviously real, and family members should not be permitted to put the business in jeopardy simply to serve their own self-interest. However, there is more to the picture than this.

If a family determines that business is their first priority, then it is virtually inevitable that the family business will one day be sold. This is because unless the family remains a priority, there will be no reason to train members of the next generation to lead, nor will there be any reason to transition ownership to them. In addition, if business comes first, it may be too easy for a member of the family to be "sacrificed on the altar of the business" by being either fired too readily or marginalized because they don't fit the current needs of the business. Another reason for placing the priority on the family is that a strong family can provide a strong foundation upon which to build a strong business. However, the reverse is not true. A company is not equipped to create or develop a strong family. In fact, the currency of success in these two spheres is radically different. In business, success is measured by profits earned; whereas in a family, the yardstick is love. Both profits and love are essential, but love is more important.

As we all know, left to themselves all things tend to deteriorate or degenerate. Family relationships are the same. Unless families invest in building healthy relationships and good communications, poor relationships and bad communications will naturally result. Unfortunately, often family members working in a business are either too busy or are unaware of the need to invest in building stronger relationships.

It is helpful to think about a family business as an organization with two bottom lines: a financial one and a relational one. Both deserve attention. Leaders ought to therefore work at keeping communication lines open between family members (i.e., creating and preserving loving relationships). In parallel with this, they should manage the business professionally and with excellence (without letting it be overrun by family preference or incompetence).

Wise families recognize that family is more important than any business, and so they put family first. However, in managing the delicate balance between the two systems, they put family ahead of business, without permitting either to dominate. Family business executive Ron Mannix summarizes it well when he states, "You run the business as if it were a family and you run the family like a business"; he also states, "if it is done well, it is always family first, business second."[46]

SUCCESSION DOES NOT NEED TO BE A TABOO SUBJECT

In his classic article "The Succession Conspiracy," Ivan Lansberg writes that it seems as though there is a conspiracy to avoid the topic of succession in family business.[47] He notes that the elder generation doesn't want to talk about succession because they don't want to confront their own mortality, while the next generation doesn't want to raise the subject for fear of being presumptuous.

[46.] Rick Pilger, "Ron Mannix: Decidedly Different," *New Trail* (Edmonton: Alberta Business Family Institute), http://www.uofaweb.ualberta.ca/newtrail/nav03.cfm?nav03=420 14&nav02=41993&nav01=41992.

[47.] Ivan Lansberg, "The Succession Conspiracy," *Family Business Review* 1 (1998), 119-143.

At the same time, members of the management team don't bring up the topic because they are comfortable with the status quo and don't want to rock the boat.

Consequently, the vast majority of family firms drift aimlessly through time, ignoring the fact that they have a date with destiny, when the elder generation will no longer be around. Sadly, they are like a naive boatload of tourists enjoying the beautiful scenery as their boat is being swept down river towards the Niagara Falls.

Today, there are many good books and educational seminars that can help families to address the topic of succession. Unfortunately, too few families in business are willing or interested in learning about it. There are a host of reasons for this neglect, but the following is a representative list:

- If the family members are getting along well, they assume they don't need help.
- If the family members are not getting along, they don't want to talk about it.
- Some people assume that if the "technical planning" is done, there is nothing more to do (i.e., if an estate freeze, family trust or current will are in place, then everything is looked after).
- The business has enough *current* challenges without talking about the future.
- It is presumed that business and family should be kept separate, and so there is no need to talk about their integration.

In spite of these challenges, it has been my experience that when families pluck up the courage to thoughtfully discuss the subject of succession, the perceived problems almost immediately shrink in size. Often, just getting the issues out in the open can make them seem smaller and much more manageable.

If your primary goal is the long-term survival of the business, you must make sure that healthy family relationships are your first priority.

I am not suggesting that the succession process is easy. However, in our family's experience, matters became much worse simply because we were afraid to talk about them. If our family had had the courage to talk openly and consistently about succession, we might have been able to develop more effective solutions.

START BY ASKING THE KIDS IF THEY WANT TO BE PARTNERS

Families in business ought to be proactive in addressing the matter of succession, rather than just letting time, circumstances or a potential crisis dictate when the discussion occurs. But, where should a family start? It all depends on whom you ask:

- A lawyer may suggest starting with a will or an estate freeze.
- An accountant may recommend a family trust or tax minimization plan.
- A financial planner might recommend some retirement planning.
- An estate planner would likely propose some life insurance.
- A corporate strategist may start with a strategic plan.
- A psychologist might ask the elder generation what their desires are.
- An HR professional would probably start by identifying potential successors.

All of these are legitimate places to begin. However, I have come to believe that it is best to start the succession process by asking the next generation to articulate their hopes and dreams for the future. Specifically, do they want to own the business, and do they want to be partners with their siblings? If they confirm they are indeed interested in owning the family enterprise, then considering how this could be accomplished becomes the first priority to be addressed. If they are not interested, then a plan to transfer ownership to them would be redundant.

> *Ask your children if they want to be partners with each other. This will help kick-start the succession planning process.*

Typically, the next generation is the last to be consulted regarding succession. Parents and their advisors often make the assumption that successive generations will want to own and/or manage what may be passed down to them. In addition, owners will rarely ask successors if they want to be in a business with their siblings; nor will they ask if they are interested in learning to become knowledgeable owners.

One of my colleagues, a trust and estate planning expert, confided in me that she was tired of following her clients' instructions and "forcing succession plans down kids' throats." During her long career, she had virtually never been in a situation where the elder generation was willing to explore what the next generation really wanted. It was just assumed that "Father knows best!"

I once asked a good friend if he had ever sat down with his two children to ask if they wanted to be partners. He assured me that he had, and he explained that the kids were happy with the idea. But when I asked if he had ever offered the kids an alternative, the answer was quite different. I asked what he would think about each having their own half of his estate, independent of the other. He emphatically replied, "I don't want that. Besides, it would never work, because we can't divide up the business."

As this situation illustrates, unless the option of being independent is genuinely considered, successors are not really being given a choice. This friend I am speaking of is a wise, loving father and a capable, successful businessman. However, he also represents the vast majority of business owners who are not prepared to discuss options with their offspring.

When planning for the future, there is an extremely important question that should be asked of all families with multiple children: Do the siblings (or cousins) want to be partners or co-owners with one another? The fact that they have the same parents doesn't necessarily mean they are be well suited to being business partners. While we can't choose our family, we should be able to choose our business partners. In essence, there should be no involuntary shareholders. In other words, no one should be required to own shares of a company with their siblings (or anyone else). The succession planning process, when wisely initiated, should begin by asking offspring if they want to be partners with each other. The answer to this question is foundational to everything that follows.

START THINKING ABOUT SUCCESSION WHEN YOUR KIDS START ELEMENTARY SCHOOL

There is no easy time to begin discussing potentially becoming owners of a business. Consequently, the conversation seldom occurs. Too often it is simply assumed that the next generation would want to own the business one day. After all, who wouldn't want the opportunity to benefit from the financial success of your parents' family business? Certainly those who have toiled night and day for years are unlikely to understand why anyone might not want to inherit the family business.

Consider the following reasons given for deferring discussions of succession with your children:

- When the kids are just toddlers, they won't sit still to talk about anything.
- When the kids are preteens, they are too young to understand.
- When the kids are teens, they are too self-absorbed and immature.
- When the kids are in their 20s, they are focused on starting their own careers.

- When the kids are in their 30s, they are busy starting their own families.
- When the kids are in their 40s, their career and education decisions have mostly been made.
- When the kids are in their 50s, they are nearing the zenith of their careers, and it's probably too late.
- When the kids are in their 60s, they are planning their own retirement and it's certainly too late.

As this list clearly illuminates, there is no obvious time to begin discussing succession with the next generation. Nonetheless, it could be argued that it is ideal to start the process when offspring are in their preteens. At this stage, parents can begin to orient their family to the business through age-appropriate activities. Then, when kids are in their teens, their education regarding the business may include summer employment. By their 20s, with a foundation of awareness already established, more detailed discussions can occur. By the time they are in their 30s, potential inheritors can be well prepared to begin discussing the pros and cons of potentially becoming business partners. Each of these steps may seem a bit too early for some. However, as noted above, if the discussion is deferred until kids are in their 40s and 50s, there is a possibility that it may indeed be too late.

CONCLUSION

When our kids were young, it was my privilege to help with the coaching duties for my daughter Christy's soccer team. In order to qualify for this role, I was required to take some training in coaching theory. In one course I was taught that "the foundation of all coaching is the power of observation." This sweeping statement was reinforced by the notion that until you can see what is being done correctly and what is being done incorrectly, how can you assist anyone to improve? With this in mind, it is no wonder that coaches for professional football teams (and a myriad of other sports) spend countless hours dissecting game films. They want to see clearly what is happening on the field or court, so that they can coach wisely.

Being able to see clearly is a prerequisite for many things. A family business is no different. In order to wisely manage, lead and plan for a family business, many of us need to see more clearly. Often that means putting on a different set of glasses. In this chapter, I have outlined nine common misperceptions related to families in business and offered a new way of looking at each. It is my hope that by seeing more accurately the realities of family business, business families can make wiser choices in the future.

CHAPTER 13

SEPARATING MANAGEMENT FROM OWNERSHIP

SUCCESSION IS NOT A TECHNICAL MATTER; IT IS A RELATIONAL ONE

Instinctively, most family business owners will call their accountant or their lawyer when they want to discuss succession. Obviously there are technical matters to be considered, including legal, accounting, tax, financial, insurance, estate and testamentary issues. However, a well-developed succession plan will be designed to serve the best interests of a family and their business. Unfortunately, all too often technical solutions will be allowed to overshadow discussions between family members regarding their needs and desires for the future.

To avoid this happening, families in business are wise to recognize that succession planning is not a technical matter but a relational one. Rather than having technicians driving the process, family dreams and family discussions should lead the way. To accomplish this, it is best to talk about the future, together as a group. Usually the support of a trained facilitator will aid the process.

SEPARATE MANAGEMENT FROM OWNERSHIP

The first step to discussing succession intelligently requires family business owners and their families to separate the discussions of management succession and ownership succession. Far too often, the lines between management and ownership succession are badly blurred. I know I often merged the two in my own thinking, partly because my grandfather and my father before me had both been owner-managers. Consequently it never occurred to me that the ownership succession and management succession were two very separate topics, each deserving proper attention.

Some family business owners may realize it is important to differentiate between ownership and management. However, they may conclude that only those who are involved in management should be permitted to be owners. In some cases this may be an appropriate solution. However, in most situations there is no legitimate reason to require offspring to be managers in order to own shares. Although I am not a manager at a public corporation like Coca-Cola or Apple, this doesn't disqualify me from the opportunity to own shares in either company. Similarly, why should anyone be required to be a manager in a family business in order to own shares?

> *The first step to intelligently discussing ownership succession is to separate it from the discussion of management succession.*

Some will argue, quite rightly, that company management contributes to the creation of shareholder value, and so managers should have the opportunity to own shares. Obviously this is a persuasive argument, and it is one of the reasons why many public companies grant stock options for their senior executives. Frankly, it is hard to argue against the importance, suitability and numerous benefits of having members of the management team own shares, and in most cases, it can be particularly helpful in creating alignment between the goals of ownership and management.

However, in the majority of corporations, the bulk of the equity invested in the business does not come from management. Rather, management is typically entrusted with funds invested by owners and is expected to wisely manage these resources. When siblings or cousins are co-owners in a business, it is not uncommon for a few members of the family to manage on behalf of the rest of their generation. In these situations, it would be severely limiting and potentially short-sighted to say that only those who work in the company should be permitted to own shares. Without devaluing the importance of management, it is obviously not a necessity for anyone to be part of the management group in order to be a good shareholder, and vice versa.

WHAT ARE THE RESPONSIBILITIES OF SHAREHOLDERS?

The job description of an owner includes the responsibility to "establish the values, vision and goals that will guide the business."[48] These are topics that family members, young and old, well-educated or not, can all understand. When my sisters and I acquired Dominion Construction, it wasn't difficult for us to discuss and agree upon the values, vision and goals for our new company. To some, discussing these matters may initially appear to be superfluous or even irrelevant. However, it was precisely the absence of alignment on these basic topics that ultimately led to the falling out between my dad and his brothers. Both shareholders in a family business and inheritors in a family business owe it to themselves to spend the time to discuss and reach agreement on these topics. Ultimately, they provide the foundation for all other decisions. (Refer to chapter 6 for more detail regarding how my sisters and I dealt with these important elements.)

WHAT DOES IT TAKE TO BE A COMPETENT SHAREHOLDER?

When addressing my MBA class at UBC, Sacha McLean, now vice chairman and CEO of his family's helicopter business, Blackcomb Aviation, insightfully noted that "there ought to be a minimum qualification in order to become a shareholder in a family business."[49] This is such simple common sense—so why do family business owners seldom think about this? Perhaps it is because few recognize that becoming a competent owner is a skill that can be developed over time. We tend to see ownership as a privilege, not a responsibility. Just like the owner of a new Jaguar or Mercedes, an individual ought to learn about what they own so they can become responsible for maintaining its value.

Similarly, it would be nonsensical and foolish for my wife, Alison, and me to buy a car for one of our kids and then give it to them without at least requiring them to have a driver's license or without explaining to them the importance of regularly changing the oil. Being able to drive is an appropriate minimum standard for owning a car, and if a car owner doesn't change the oil, their investment will not be worth much in the long run.

> *"There ought to be a minimum qualification to become a shareholder of a family business."*
> Sacha McLean

[48.] Craig E. Aronoff and John L. Ward, *Family Business Ownership: How to Be An Effective Shareholder* (Marietta: Family Enterprise Publishers 2002), 27.
[49.] Sacha McLean, 2011 interview with David Bentall.

I know of one father who would not allow his three teenage girls to drive the family car until they had each put on a pair of overalls and demonstrated to him that they could change a flat tire. Similarly, offspring of a family business owner should be required to meet a "minimum standard" before they receive any shares of the company. If we were to clarify expectations and codify this, we might require at least the following prerequisites:

- An ability to read financial statements (or a willingness to learn how to read them).
- A dedication to invest in ongoing education related to the company and its industry.
- A commitment to attend quarterly meetings of the board and/or shareholders.

Obviously, each family is free to choose their own standard, but learning the basics about the business and knowing how to read the company's financial statements would be a good place to start. After all, accounting is the language of business, and it is the primary tool for monitoring the ongoing success of a business. Financial statements are also the means by which the shareholders, board and management communicate. A person doesn't need to be a CA or have a business degree to be able to read financial statements. There are workshops and courses available that can assist Inheritors to acquire this basic knowledge. Sadly, this minimum expectation is often never articulated.

LEARNING ABOUT WHAT YOU OWN

One of my clients owns several apartment buildings. He and his wife have four children, who are in their 20s and just getting started in their careers. In the future, it is anticipated that they will own a portfolio of real estate assets. It is very unlikely any of them will work for the company.

To date, because of other career and personal priorities, they haven't shown much interest in learning about the business. Like many business owners, my client has had difficulty explaining to them that ownership involves more than just receiving dividends or collecting the rent.

Over the past few years, one of their 40-year-old apartment buildings experienced numerous broken water pipes and substantial water damage. The cost of patching and repairing the copper pipes was considerable. The plumbers and other tradesmen had to work overtime to provide tenants with water on an urgent basis. These costs were paid for by the owners and were not recoverable from their renters. His children, as future owners, would obviously rather avoid similar costs in the future.

One option to avoid these ongoing maintenance costs would be to set aside sufficient capital to replace all the pipes in the building. Unfortunately, this would wipe out virtually all earnings from the building for an extended period. On the other hand, if the pipes are not replaced soon, some tenants may vacate the building for fear of damage to their personal property, and this would also result in income being lost to the family.

My client suggested it would be a good idea to assign his offspring the responsibility to determine whether or not to replace the pipes. They could be asked to research the situation and bring forward a formal recommendation to the company's board of directors.

Interestingly, my client also explained to me that replacing the pipes would not only mitigate the risk of future leaks but also create the capacity to add dishwashers to the building. If these appliances were added to each apartment, the market rents that could be charged would increase substantially. It might even be possible for the owners to not only afford the new plumbing but also improve their bottom-line profits.

The following are just some of the questions the future shareholders could obtain answers to through this one simple exercise:

- What kind of water does Vancouver have, and how does it impact piping over an extended period of time?
- What has been the cost to repair the pipes each year?
- What would it cost to replace all the copper pipes?
- What rents could be charged if there were dishwashers in every suite?
- What are other competing buildings doing? Do they have dishwashers?
- What will be the value of the building in the future if they add dishwashers? What if they don't?
- What would a bank require before they would be willing to provide a loan for the repairs?

There are many ways to train the next generation of shareholders. However, one of the best ways is to get them involved in researching the pros and cons of decisions the company is facing. Additionally, if the situation has financial implications for the inheritors they will be more motivated to learn and more likely to remember what they discover.

PARENTS HAVE MORE INFLUENCE THAN THEY REALIZE

In preparing heirs to be inheritors in a business, the elder generation may have much more power and influence than they perceive, especially in relation to encouraging or even requiring their offspring to learn about the responsibilities of ownership. For example, it would have been entirely reasonable for the recently noted client to say, "I am prepared to share a percentage of the company's annual net earnings with you, starting within the next year or two. However, prior to doing so, I would request that you prepare to become knowledgeable and collaborative owners. If you want to participate in the earnings, then there are a few things that I need you to do in order to demonstrate that you are becoming capable and deserving of being co-owners:

1. Work together as a team to develop a well-researched recommendation regarding what should be done about the copper pipes.
2. Once approved, implement the plan on behalf of the family."

By completing these two relatively simple tasks, the next generation would not only have the potential to learn about the business but also have an opportunity to work together and learn about one another as potential co-owners. In addition to an assignment like this, potential inheritors might be asked to complete a workshop on financial management or attend an introductory course on property management (or other relevant industry courses).

LESSONS FOR ALL FUTURE OWNERS

At first blush, learning everything there is to know about a business seems like a daunting task. However, the following steps provide a logical method by which young owners can learn about their family's business:

1. Understand what it is (visit your business).
2. Understand how it performs (review the financials).
3. Understand what others are doing (research the market).
4. Listen to others (get expert advice).
5. Keep on top of things (have regular meetings).
6. Listen to those who are wise (recruit a board).
7. Choose strong management (hire a CEO).
8. Think ahead (participate in the development of the strategic plan).
9. Compare alternatives (perform or review analyses).
10. Have the courage to act (be entrepreneurial).

If this seems too complicated, one of my colleagues has simplified the mentorship process for new shareholders by stating that future owners simply need to read, read and read! They can start by reading the company's financials and all other information they can obtain about the company, its markets and its competition. In addition, they can read about the economy, marketing, leadership and governance.

In previous generations, there wasn't much information available to read about family businesses. Now there is a wealth of expert resources, quality research, and helpful books that relate to family business. For those who are just getting started, one of the most accessible and comprehensive places to start is with the *Family Business Leadership Series* published by Family Enterprise Publishers.[50] This excellent encyclopedic resource provides pithy commentary on virtually every topic related to family business, including compensation, succession, governance and how to manage conflict.

BECOMING WORTHY OF WHAT YOU OWN

Company founders have often worked tirelessly to create a business out of nothing. It is only after they have sacrificed for years, worked long hours and survived numerous setbacks that they have finally arrived at their "mountaintop" of success. From the top of the hill, the view is amazing. The air is clear, and opportunities on the horizon seem limitless.

In most cases, their kids have little or no understanding of how hard it was to climb to these heights. In effect, they have been coddled in a backpack while Mom and Dad did the hard work of climbing! Yet most loving parents don't want to throw their kids down the hill and ask them to start climbing the hill of financial success on their own. They may want them to earn a university degree or earn their place in the business by starting at the bottom, but parents typically want their kids to have more than they had.

As my father did for my siblings and me, most parents are inclined to gift their kids the shares of the business when they die. If this is the plan, it can be said that the inheritors will have done nothing to earn those shares. This can result in a sense of guilt, a lack of commitment or even a lack of appreciation for what they have received. To counteract the potential for these feelings, wise families outline expectations and responsibilities that the next generation can take on in order to feel like they have done something to earn their shares.

---

50. http://www.efamilybusiness.com/index.cfm.

For one of my clients who has two university-aged daughters, we created an initial four-year shareholders' training program. The following is a comprehensive list of the items we have asked the girls to do as they begin their journey towards becoming knowledgeable and capable owners:

1. Complete a weekend workshop regarding accounting and financial management.
2. Read Stephen Covey's book *7 Habits of Highly Effective People*.[51]
3. Visit the company's operations to meet the people and learn what they do.
4. Attend an industry seminar to learn about the business.
5. Subscribe to a national business news service and read it every day.
6. Complete a workshop on family business with the rest of the family.
7. Read John Ward's book *Creating Effective Boards for Private Enterprises*.[52]
8. Travel with their family to another country for a weekend to build a house for a poor family. (This will help them to develop gratitude and experience working together as a team.)
9. Attend the Chester Karrass Negotiating Seminar.[53]
10. Read *Getting to Yes: Negotiating Agreement Without Giving In* by Roger Fisher, William L. Ury and Bruce Patton.[54]
11. Join Toastmasters and participate actively for two years.
12. Join the board of the United Way or Rotary Club to give back to the community and to develop leadership skills.

Notice that none of the foregoing requires working for the company. In addition, to orient them to the business, these girls have been offered summer work experience within the family firm. Additionally, during the balance of the year, each is expected to read monthly reports related to a specific element of the company operations. All this may sound like too much to do, yet their inheritance will be substantial, and so this actually seems like a small price to pay.

> *The elder generation should help inheritors to develop a multi-year shareholder-training program. Successors can then feel more worthy of what they will own.*

[51.] Stephen Covey, *7 Habits of Highly Effective People* (New York: Free Press, 2004).

[52.] John L. Ward, *Creating Effective Boards for Private Enterprises* (San Francisco: Jossey-Bass Inc, 1991).

[53.] Information about this seminar is available at http://www.karrass.com.

[54.] Roger Fisher, William L. Ury and Bruce Patton. *Getting to Yes: Negotiating Agreement Without Giving In* (New York: Penguin Group, 2011).

Actually, it's hard to judge what is right for each family, but the key is to be pro-active and to develop a curriculum that will help prepare inheritors to become knowledgeable and informed owners.

CONCLUSION

When I decided to sell my interest in our family company, Dominion Construction, I did so because I didn't have a passion for the job and therefore did not feel well suited to be its president. However, in hindsight, I now realize I was confusing ownership and management. Obviously, the "job" of an owner and the "role" of a company president are very different. If I had been more conscious of the potential to separate ownership from management in a family firm, I might have made a different choice. I might have been happy to remain as an owner while choosing not to be a manager.

As family business owners transition from one generation to the next, it becomes more important to differentiate between the roles of management and ownership and to specifically emphasize the preparation of future shareholders. With appropriate preparation and training, family members can become knowledgeable and competent shareholders of a company. They can actually become the "best" kind of shareholders, because as family members they will typically have a sense of heritage and an emotional commitment to the enterprise. This is not easily replicated by those for whom a business is simply a financial investment.

Becoming a competent manager of a family owned business may be a challenging prospect beyond the reach of some family inheritors. However, becoming a "knowledgeable and competent owner" is a worthy ambition for successors, and one that should be realistically attainable by most. The first step is to differentiate between ownership and management, and then to develop a plan for becoming a wise owner.

CHAPTER 14

FAMILY BUSINESS BOARDS

INTRODUCTION

"Every family corporation has a board of directors, because boards are required by law. But the fact that every family corporation has a board doesn't mean that these boards direct anything. Most family business boards are lucky if they meet, much less direct."[55]

Our family company, The Bentall Group, had a board, at least on paper. But it never formally met. In order to comply with legislative requirements, the directors would annually execute paperwork, indicating either that they had met, or that they were waiving their right to meet. They would also sign documents approving the financial statements. But that was about it. The company had nothing you could call governance. Like most family-owned companies that I have encountered, management was responsible to run the company, but they were not accountable to anyone; nor did they have the guidance or support that a board would have been able to provide.

THE BENTALL GROUP STRUGGLES TO CREATE A BOARD

I recall my dad educating me regarding our board by explaining, "When Uncle Bob and I meet, we are effectively like the board of directors, because we have majority ownership of the company." Sadly, this statement also belied the

---

[55.] Danco, Leon and Donald J. Jonovic, *Outside Directors in the Family Owned Business: Why, When, Who and How* (Cleveland: University Press, Center for Family Business, 1981), 17.

fact that there were two other significant owners of the company who were also directors. I know Dad didn't mean to belittle them; he simply reasoned that Howard, his elder brother and a pastor, was not active in the business and trusted the others to make the right decisions. Similarly, Frank Worster, vice-president of finance, who had been given shares by our family, was expected to trust the others with major decisions, in part because he had a smaller stake in the company.

In hindsight, it is easy to imagine how Dad's perspective—that he and Bob had the only voices that mattered—created a situation where the others resented him. Had the four owners met as a board, just quarterly, to discuss the future direction of the company, it could have made a remarkable difference. Through such meetings, Uncle Howard would have had the opportunity to be included and educated on the business, rather than feeling "left out" all the time. Even more importantly, Uncle Bob would have had a legitimate forum to discuss his strategic priorities with my dad, and the potential would have existed for them to find mutually agreeable solutions for the future.

Ironically, for many years Uncle Bob wanted to create an effective board for The Bentall Group. He also wanted to include three outside independent members. In reading about the importance of professionalizing a family firm, he had learned that a formal board of directors could be of significant value, particularly in dealing with succession. But Dad was definitely not keen on the idea. This was quite surprising, since he personally sat on many prestigious and effective boards. In fact, at one point in time his directorships included the TD Bank, BC Forest Products, Finning Tractor, Scott Paper, Cominco and Expo '86. When he turned 70, he had to retire from all of these, but International Forest Products then invited him to join their board.

When I asked him why he didn't want a board, he mentioned two key objections. First, he said, "Our business is unique, and outside directors wouldn't understand what it is we do." Second, he said he wanted to avoid anyone knowing the details of our business. This is probably why he argued, "We can have a board when everything is running the way we want it to." It is amazing to me that a man whose advice and expertise was so highly sought after by other companies could not imagine how his own company could have benefited from the same kind of input that he was paid to offer others.

After many years of debate, my dad finally agreed, and Bob recruited three outsiders to join the board. The new directors met just a handful of times before Bob decided to terminate the experiment. This was unfortunate in the extreme, because they likely would have been able to effectively mediate some of the challenges our family was about to face. We will never know what might have happened, but I am convinced that my dad and his brothers could have found better solutions to their inter-family struggles if they had availed themselves of the benefit of wise, independent counsel. Instead, shortly after the board was disbanded, Bob met with the other shareholders (not including my dad) and charted a new course for the future of the company (and one that Dad did not agree with).

Astonishingly, it is estimated that less than 1% of family companies have the wisdom or foresight necessary to constitute an effective board. In fact, "Based on [his] observations [of] over two decades with many tens of thousands of businesses…family business expert Leon Danco discovered that 'less than one family-owned, privately held company out of 200 has…created and used a working board consisting of a majority of contributory outside directors.'"[56]

CREATING AN EFFECTIVE BOARD AT DOMINION

Having seen The Bentall Group fall apart, in part because it had not had an effective board, when my sisters and I acquired Dominion in 1988 we decided we would do things differently. When drafting our shareholders' agreement, Helen, Mary and I, as the new shareholders, decided that each one of us would be able to appoint a director to the board, even though our shareholdings were unequal (20%, 40% and 40% respectively). As mentioned earlier, Dad was our initial chair, and Dick Meyers was our vice chair. Together with the three shareholders' representatives, we had a board of five.

Although this arrangement may seem extraordinarily simple, it was profound, and we enjoyed many benefits as a result. The most readily apparent advantages were the following:

- As shareholders, we had a forum where we could discuss and debate and then develop a unified direction for the business.
- As owners of the company, we had a vehicle through which we could officially communicate our priorities and goals, including our financial expectations.
- As owners, we were effectively precluded from providing ad hoc direction to employees (which is commonplace in many family companies).
- We were able to clearly articulate the difference between the board and management (unlike the previous generation's arrangement, where the line between the role of board and management was very fuzzy).

---

[56] Danco, Leon and Donald J. Jonovic, *Outside Directors in the Family Owned Business: Why, When, Who and How* (Cleveland: University Press, Center for Family Business, 1981), 24.

Our board was charged with the following responsibilities:
- Approving the company's strategic plan
- Approving our annual plans and budgets
- Approving all major capital expenditures and any new real estate investments
- Approving all construction contracts above a specified dollar amount
- Approving all compensation, including bonuses and profit sharing arrangements
- Selecting and appraising the CEO of the company

SUCCESSION NEEDED AT THE BOARD LEVEL

A few years after we formed the board, my dad became afflicted with Alzheimer's disease and his health began to deteriorate. We knew changes had to be made on the day that he arrived at a board meeting in a haze of confusion and tried to get our meeting started. Dad walked into the offices, looked right at Dick Meyers and addressed him as Phil. He then explained that he had just gotten off the phone with Mary (meaning Helen), who had called to explain she would be late. He then looked at Phil and me, addressing us as Chuck and Dick, and asked if we could start the meeting anyway. Recognizing what he meant, I was able to translate, and we were able to move ahead. Although we all chuckled uncomfortably, it was now tragically apparent that something wasn't right with Dad's brain functioning. We realized that unfortunately changes to the board would have to be made.

Dad's situation now precluded him serving effectively as chairman, so we elevated him to the position of honorary chair (this meant he could attend any or all meetings but was no longer responsible to chair the meetings and no longer held an official vote). Dick was appointed chair in our dad's place, but he was also now 65 and moving towards retirement. Although he continued to make a strong contribution at the board level, we didn't know how long he would continue to do so. As a result of Dad and Dick's changing statuses, we determined that we would be wise to strengthen the board by electing two independent, non-family board members. This had been contemplated in our shareholders' agreement, with the only requirement being that any additional board appointments would require the unanimous agreement of all three shareholders.

ATTRACTING INDEPENDENT BOARD MEMBERS

As we considered potential board members, we reflected on our strategic plan and identified two important priorities. The first was that we planned to expand geographically into California. Second, we planned to develop more small shopping centres for resale (essentially functioning as a "merchant developer"). As we considered these two priorities, we noted that they coincided with two significant experience gaps. Namely, we didn't know anyone in California and we had no one in the organization with shopping centre expertise. Consequently, we decided to recruit board members who could help fill these "knowledge gaps."

We began by approaching Geoff Moore, a shopping centre expert from Toronto (founder of Geoffrey Moore & Associates), and Gordie Mackenzie, a seasoned real estate executive who had originally worked with Vancouver-based Daon Developments and who was now residing in California. When we initially asked them to join our board, they declined, and each one offered very similar objections. Each stated the following:

1. They didn't know much about our industry.
2. They didn't want to get embroiled in a family business squabble.
3. They lived in other cities and didn't want to travel to Vancouver for board meetings.
4. They didn't have the time.

However, when I explained to Geoff that we wanted his help with shopping centre developments, his attitude changed almost instantly. Explaining that this was his primary business passion, he readily agreed to join the board. Similarly, Gordie's attitude changed very quickly once we explained that we wanted him to help us build a network in Southern California. Both men agreed to serve as directors because we had shown them that we valued their specific identifiable skills and knowledge. Once they understood this, they were both more than happy to help us.

Several years later, I attended a seminar on board recruiting and learned the wisdom of recruiting to fill specific needs. Marjorie Engle, an expert in board recruiting for private companies, spoke at the event and explained that "every director should be a strategy."[57] In other words, each potential director should be invited to join the board because they have the potential to offer specific skills and experience that the enterprise needs. Just as we had done in recruiting Geoff and Gordie, she recommended that board candidates be recruited specifically to help fill strategic gaps.

Now that I have been working as an advisor to other families in business for the past ten years, I have been able to consistently utilize Marjorie Engle's strategy

---

[57.] Marjorie Engle, Governance Workshop (UBC, 2006). Marjorie is vice president of Allen, Gibbs & Houlik, L.C.

in helping recruit board members for numerous family firms. It has yielded sensational results. (See part IV for a more complete outline of the recruiting process.) Marjorie argues that this approach results in several important benefits:

1. Board members know why they are on the board and what they are expected to contribute.
2. Management can readily see how each board member can add value. This enhances the board's credibility and usefulness.
3. Board members will know when their job is done and when it is appropriate for them to withdraw from the board.

In addition to the three benefits mentioned above, recruiting in a sharply focused fashion helps to ensure that the best board candidates are much more likely to agree to serve. (In other words, they are more likely to say yes when asked to join a board.)

WHY COMPANIES RESIST CREATING A BOARD

Years ago, Dad said he didn't want to have a board because he wanted to preserve our family's privacy. Beneath that statement, I think the real reason he resisted was that he didn't want anyone to discover that we weren't actually as large or as financially successful as some perhaps thought. In addition, having sat on many boards, he probably didn't want to face the scrutiny and accountability that he recognized would come with a proper board. These are understandable reactions. However, having talked to many others about the topic, the most common excuses given to me by family business owners for not creating a board are as follows:

- We have been successful without one.
- They would just add bureaucracy and slow down our decision-making.
- We don't know where to find good board members.
- It would be a waste of time.
- We can't afford it.
- No one who is any good would agree to serve on our board.
- Our business is unique, and an outsider would never be able to understand or add value.

According to a study of family firms in New Zealand, the top two reasons for not having non-family directors on the board are that "family members have all the skills required" (23.4%) and the family has a "desire to retain privacy" (17%).[58]

[58.] Kosmos Smyrnios and Lucio Dana, *New Zealand Family & Private Business Survey* (New Zealand: 2007), 3, 13.

Others may resist having a board because they say their company is too small. However, size of the business is much less important when compared to preparation. I know of a family firm with thirty employees with three independent directors on their board. They could do it because shareholders and management were unified about what they wanted to achieve and were willing to invite accountability from supportive independent directors.[59] "Shareholders who can articulate a unified message to new independent directors is a huge indicator of readiness."[60]

MATCH THE EXPERTISE TO THE NEED

Over the past couple of years, I have had the privilege of spearheading the board recruiting efforts for numerous family enterprises. Virtually all of these companies have initially resisted the idea, citing some of the listed objections. However, in every case, once we decided to proceed, we have been able to successfully assemble a suitable and potent brain trust in relatively short order. Focusing on specific knowledge and experience in our recruiting has accelerated the process as well as the effectiveness of each board we have recruited.

To illustrate how we have articulated the precise skill sets we have targeted, the following is a list of some of the different board member profiles we have gone after:
- Experience in transitioning from an entrepreneurial to professionally managed firm
- Proven success in developing marketing and sales initiatives
- Successful experience with family business succession
- Ability to mentor the next generation regarding finance and accounting
- Expertise in industrial real estate property acquisitions
- Asset allocation and investment portfolio management experience
- Ability to drive operational excellence and growth
- Credibility to assist the elder generation transition from an operational to a strategic role
- Experience in developing a domestic retail marketing initiative

DON'T START WITH NAMES

When a company or an individual begins a board search, it is almost instinctive to begin listing names of potential candidates. I know this was in-

---

59. Stephen McClure, 2012 interview with David Bentall. Stephen McClure is the principal of The Family Business Consulting Group.
60. Christopher Eckrich and Stephen McClure, "Toward Greater Objectivity on Your Board," *The Family Business Advisor* 9 (Marietta: Family Enterprise Publishers, 2002).

> *When recruiting a board, don't start with names, and don't recruit your friends, family or advisors.*

itially my natural impulse when recruiting our board at Dominion. Naturally, the first places people typically look are to friends, family, existing advisors and senior management. Unfortunately, these are usually four of the worst places to look.

We should discount each of these for the following reasons:

- Friends: You already have the advice of your friends; you don't need to put them on the board to get their feedback. Moreover, friends will find it hard to offer objective advice for fear of negatively impacting your relationship.
- Family: Family members may be capable and interested. However, managing the interface between family and business is one of the key roles of a board for a family firm, and family members are not well suited to do this objectively. (For exceptions to this rule, see comments following regarding family members on the board.)
- Advisors: The expertise and opinions of your professional advisors (such as your lawyer and accountant) are already available to you. Why pay them a second time for their input? More importantly, advisors who have a financial relationship with your company will be very reluctant to speak their minds on delicate issues for fear of damaging their pre-existing business relationship. In short, they will invariably have a conflict of interest.
- Senior Management: Your company's senior executives may be invited to attend board meetings, and may even do so on a regular basis. (It is not unusual for a report from the CFO or VP of finance to be a feature on the board's standing agenda.) However, board members should ideally be those who have a broader perspective than that of most senior managers. Moreover, two of the roles of the board are to assist the CEO in assessing the performance of, and compensation for, his team. For these reasons, senior management should generally not be invited to serve as board members.

If a company wants to create a truly strategic board, it is essential to start not with names but with clear criteria, as explained previously.

FAMILY MEMBERS ON THE BOARD

Unless they have begun to think about governance strategically, family firms tend to predominantly have family members serving on their board. In fact, a recent study revealed that 54% of family firms surveyed indicated that their board consisted of family members only.[61] In contrast, many experts suggest that the ideal family business board is one constituted entirely of independent board members. This approach virtually ensures that all board members are chosen for their expertise rather than based on familial relationships. It is difficult to argue with this approach.

However, as a practical matter, it has been my experience that this "ideal" is often too radical for many families. Instead, I have seen good success with what I describe as a "mixed board," where their family ownership is represented on the board, balanced with strong, independent advisors. This type of board can be particularly appropriate for a sibling partnership that may want to accommodate non-management owners. Family

> *Business owners must seek the help of a risk-taking peer, someone who is not beholden to them in any way other than through a moral sense of commitment to what the owners are trying to do with the business.*
> **Leon Danco**

board members can then include those who want to learn to be good owners, as well as those who may be eager to keep a watchful eye on a sibling who is running the business. In effect, a "mixed board" can introduce appropriate accountability, help to keep peace in the family and simultaneously increase the business knowledge and understanding of business inheritors.

THEY WILL BE EXCITED TO HELP

The first time that I had the privilege of helping recruit board members involved interviews with six candidates for three board positions. The family CEO and his three sons all participated in the interviews. When we had finished the interview process, all four of the family members looked at me in astonishment, saying, "Where did you find these guys?" They gushed with incredulity, thinking that it was all too good to be true. But it wasn't—all six candidates were willing to serve if selected. Everyone was happy then, and even more so today as the business has prospered with the input of the new board.

HOW DO YOU FIND THESE PEOPLE?

If done properly, recruiting for a board can be a wonderful experience. In fact, it is one of the most gratifying things I have done in my professional career. The methodology I now use involves a series of nearly 20 steps. The most significant steps are as follows:

---

[61]. Laird Norton Tyee, *Laird Norton Tyee Family Business Survey* (Seattle: 2007), 17.

1. Develop a strategic plan and obtain management and shareholder approval.
2. Identify knowledge gaps in the strategic plan that can be filled by board members.
3. Create a prospectus summarizing the strategy and the knowledge gaps.
4. Identify "centres of influence" who know the company.
5. Share the prospectus with them and ask them to help generate a list of potential candidates.
6. Keep searching until a healthy list of well-qualified prospects is identified.
7. Review all candidates in light of the strategic plan and knowledge gaps.
8. Interview at least two candidates for each board position.
9. Make it a goal to find a good "fit" for both the company and the potential candidates.

HOW MANY BOARD MEMBERS DO YOU NEED?

If a company recruits only one independent board member, this person is placed in a difficult situation. If the board member agrees with what is being proposed, then the recommendation will go forward. If he or she objects, the opposite will likely happen. Consequently, instead of functioning like a member of the board, a sole independent director is forced to act like a single arbiter or a second CEO. Obviously, this is an unhealthy situation.

Two independent board members are better than one, but with two independents, the situation can boil down to one being in favour, with the other opposed. Again, this is not the best arrangement. Simply in terms of numbers, three independent directors are exponentially better than one or two. With three, there can be healthy debate, and no one board member feels all alone or in the spotlight. More than three may be appropriate, depending on the size of the company, but it is best to have at least three independents, whenever possible.

HOW MUCH DOES IT COST?

Board members should be paid, but frankly, they are almost always worth far more than their compensation. After all, how do you estimate the value of decades of experience, available on a moment's notice? In some ways, a board member's fees are often little more than an honorarium. Board members who are well chosen and who do their homework typically deserve every penny they receive.

In Canada, a recent study showed that directors' fees for public companies varied widely, with annual retainers ranging from a low of $7,800 to a high of $390,000 per year.[62] Obviously, the size of the company, the nature of the business, and the amount of time expected from a director all influence these figures. With such a wide variance in figures, it would be unwise to generalize regarding what a director in a private family company might expect to be paid. Nonetheless, as a point of reference, some family companies might find it helpful to know the figures for Canadian public companies with sales of less than $500 million per year. In 2010, these firms paid an average retainer of approximately $40,000 per year.[63] For these same firms, the average meeting fees paid to directors were $1,500 per year.[64]

Instead of comparing with public corporations, and as a rule of thumb, some find it helpful to "use the salary of a company's CEO as the basis of comparison (excluding the CEO's bonuses and dividends and perks)."[65] If the CEO is paid $250,000 per year for 250 days' work, they are essentially receiving payment of $1,000 per day. If this is the case, it may be appropriate to consider paying board members on the basis of $1,000 per day. One of my clients, with a CEO salary in this range, estimated that their advisory board members would be required to devote approximately twelve days per year to their duties, including attending meetings, preparing for meetings, and keeping current on industry trends and information related to the company. To compensate them, it was agreed to pay an annual retainer of $8,000 per year plus $1,000 per quarterly meeting. In total, this amounted to $12,000 plus any disbursements. This was deemed an appropriate gesture of appreciation for the time commitment that these advisors were making. With the cost of three independent advisory board members totalling $36,000 per year, the shareholders realized that this expense was much less than hiring an experienced executive assistant.

Regardless of what a company decides to pay their board members, when compared to the cost of consulting advice or additional

> *As a general rule it may be appropriate to pay board members approximately the same daily rate as the CEO.*

[62.] Korn/Ferry International, "Corporate Governance and Director Compensation in Canada: A Review of 2011" (2011), 56.

[63.] Ibid., 54.

[64.] Ibid., 56.

[65.] James E. Barrett, "A Formula For Paying Your Outside Directors," *The Family Business Compensation Handbook*, ed. Barbara Spector (Philadelphia: The Family Business Magazine, 2001).

executive talent, a functioning board is probably the most cost-effective source of advice an enterprise can ever obtain.

Some family firms fear that creating a formal board may be overkill for a smaller private family firm. In some cases, this may be true. If a company is very small, it may want to start with a board of advisors, who may agree to serve for a nominal fee. Or perhaps the company may offer some of its products or services to advisors in lieu of cash. However, one way or another, willing advisors can usually be found, and appropriate compensation is not usually a problem.

Typically, when creating a board a family firm will want to pay both an annual retainer and a meeting fee. The former may be regarded as the cost to "buy ongoing advice," while the latter "encourages and rewards meeting attendance." As a general rule, it is customary to also provide dinner the day before board meetings and lunch on the day of meetings. These "social occasions" make the experience more personal and also encourage directors to connect with members of the family and senior management.

WHAT ABOUT LEGAL LIABILITY?

Some terrific board candidates are unwilling to serve on a family business board for fear of the legal liability. In some cases, this may be overcome through the purchase of directors' and officers' insurance or through the provision of formal indemnity agreements. However, in some circumstances neither of these mechanisms are suitable or affordable. Sometimes, the family shareholders may not be ready for the perceived "major step" of creating a formal, legal board. In each of these situations, an advisory board is a worthwhile option to consider. Regardless of why this option is chosen, an advisory board can provide many of the benefits of a true board. Even without having legal authority, a well-chosen group of advisors can provide expertise and advice, hold management accountable, and bring independent, objective judgment to the table.

BENEFITS OF A BOARD

The benefits of a strong board are numerous and include the following:
- Keeping the business focused on the future
- Ensuring that family issues do not dominate the business agenda for the company
- Assisting the CEO with the succession process
- Mentoring and keeping the CEO accountable

- Reviewing and approving executive compensation
- Providing expertise and advice in areas where the company may be lacking
- Asking penetrating questions that help to keep management sharp

HELPING FAMILIES STAY OUT OF TROUBLE

A board can also help business families avoid some of their most common challenges. Specifically, a strong board can be very helpful by assisting with the following areas.

- Emotional, subjective decision-making can be replaced with rational, objective decision-making.
- Family quarrels can be replaced with family communication and harmony.
- Insecurity in a crisis can be replaced with stability and confidence.
- A lack of a mechanism for intergenerational transition can be replaced with structure and guidance for succession.
- Difficulties related to family personnel decisions can be replaced with supportive, objective input for family employees.
- A lack of accountability for family members working in the business can be replaced with a heightened sense of responsibility.
- A lack of focus can be replaced with a strong emphasis on clear business priorities.

BOARDS SHOULD FOCUS ON POLICY

World-renowned board expert John Carver emphasizes that boards should not be focused on the day-to-day affairs of the business. Instead, he emphasizes the importance of boards actively serving as policy makers for the enterprise and says that a board's primary role is to determine the results toward which the organization should be striving. He calls this focusing on ends rather than means. "Ends" have to do with organizational mission and are outwardly directed, rather than inwardly focused. Therefore, a board that is doing its job properly should be thinking about its mission and its "ends." A board can do this by constantly seeking to answer the question "How will the world be different as a result of our being in business?"[66]

[66.] John Carver, *Boards that Make a Difference: A New Design for Leadership in Nonprofit and Public Organizations* (San Francisco: Jossey-Bass, 2006), 58.

HELPING WITH THE SUCCESSION PROCESS

A well-constituted board can be especially useful for a family business when they are trying to navigate the turbulent waters of succession. Selecting the next leader within a family firm can often create a challenge for a family firm and there are sometimes difficult questions to answer, including whether the next generation is ready to assume leadership, or which sibling would be the best CEO. A formal board, with non-family membership, can create an environment where these topics can be discussed in a professional manner and where healthy decision-making processes may be cultivated. Rather than a family being left alone to wrestle with these kinds of potentially contentious decisions, a well-chosen board can be an invaluable resource. Sometimes the independent members of the board may be asked to serve as a CEO selection task force, and they can bring both objectivity and professionalism to the process.

> *Well-chosen directors can help bridge the gap between generations by providing mentoring and a sounding board.*

RESPECT, TRUST AND CANDOUR

In his article "What Makes Great Boards Great," Jeffrey A. Sonnenfeld writes, "Great boards are less a function of good structure and more a function of chemistry."[67] In explaining how to create optimum relationships, the author also notes,

> They seem to get into a virtuous cycle in which one good quality builds on another. Team members develop mutual respect; because they respect one another, they develop trust; because they trust one another, they share difficult information; because they all have the same reasonably complete information, they can challenge one another's conclusions coherently; because a spirited give-and-take becomes the norm, they learn to adjust their own interpretations in response to intelligent questions.

This is a description of the kind of mature, constructive board discourse where the best ideas win, not the person who holds the most votes or the most shares. It is also a world where the elder generation is respected for their wisdom and experience, and the younger generation gets a fair hearing for their new ideas. It is the kind of environment that all family companies would benefit from creating.

[67.] Jeffrey A. Sonnenfeld, "What Makes Great Boards Great," *Harvard Business Review* 80 (2002), 106.

ADVICE

If a family business elects to form a board, it is critical to take the advice of the board seriously. Otherwise, the family is wasting everyone's time, and is also likely to lose its board. This occurred a few years ago to a very creative entrepreneur who had recruited a three-person advisory board. He had already successfully established a leading edge product for the recording industry. His revolutionary invention was of such high quality that it had gained worldwide acclaim and was being used by such music legends as George Harrison and Elton John. However, to augment his management experience, he recruited three independents, including myself, to support him.

When we asked him what he wanted from us, he explained he wanted us to function "essentially, and in most respects, as if we were a true legal board," without the legal liability. We agreed, and were given nominal stock options as a means of ensuring that we were aligned with his interests.

After just three meetings, we fired ourselves, because we were not being effective. Our friend genuinely wanted our input, but, as the sole owner and founder of the company, he just couldn't bring himself to respond to our advice. It was a disappointing experience for everyone, but not a unique one. Like this entrepreneur, it can be difficult for business owners to share power and decision-making with a board, even if it might be in their best interest.

DECIDING BY CONSENSUS

Recently, I was speaking with Jason McLean. He is a lawyer by training and was recently appointed CEO of his family's business, The McLean Group of Companies. He explained that the board of The McLean Group has only four people on it, all of whom are family members. Over the years, they have been encouraged to develop a larger board, and they are now planning to do so. However, what intrigued me was the fact that their board had an even number of members. This troubled me, as I could foresee the potential for deadlocks to materialize.

When I raised this concern, he explained that whenever they can't agree, they "sleep on it" and try for consensus again the next day. This seemed like wishful thinking to me. However, Jason reassured me that it had worked well for them for over a decade already. He then pointed out that their father, David McLean, had enjoyed a similar experience with CN Rail, where he has been chair for almost 20 years. Cited for numerous governance excellence awards, CN is one of the most successful privatizations in Canadian history, and the company boasted revenue of \$8.3 billion in 2010.[68] David explained to me that for over 18 years he has consistently encouraged the board to operate by consensus. He maintains that "the discipline of seeking consensus leads to better decisions and a more unified approach to governance."[69]

This echoes my own experience as president of Dominion Construction. Although we were a much smaller company, we worked by consensus, not only at our board, but also at the shareholder level and within our management committee. We had three shareholders, five members of the board and twelve on the management committee. It was most difficult with the largest of these groups, but we made it work. We were also successful in growing the company significantly during a decade when our leadership was known for collaboration and consensus.

Some people think this approach is not realistic. However, according to independent research, "A group can reach consensus decision-making 75% of the time if they build the process step by step."[70] I strongly advocate this approach for business families, because consensus decision-making ensures that no one is left behind. It also can help to build unity and mutual respect. Without a commitment to consensus decision-making, there is a risk that some shareholders in a family business will dominate and others will be marginalized. This can lead to divisiveness and a political environment, especially when inheritors are endeavouring to establish a fledgling sibling partnership.

In contrast, consensus decision-making tends to lead to better decisions, while at the same time forging unity within the group. In other words, "the goal of a consensus-building process is not only to resolve a specific issue, but also to enrich communication and understanding, so that future problems can be resolved more effectively and alienation is diminished."[71]

I will admit that consensus decision-making takes time and dedication, and it is considered by some to be impractical. In fact, when recruited for a family board a few years ago, all the external candidates were surprised that this was my client's ap-

---

[68.] "The Journey Continues 2010 Annual Report CN" (Montreal: Canadian National Railway Company, 2011), 2.

[69.] David McLean, 2012 interview with David Bentall. David is board chair of The McLean Group and board chair of CN Rail.

[70.] David Straus, *How To Make Collaboration Work* (San Francisco: Berret-Koehler Publishers, Inc., 2002).

[71.] Ellen Frankenberg, "If Your Family Business Has Grown Your Decision-Making Style Needs to Grow Too," *Frankenberg Group* (2012), http://www.frankenberggroup.com/published-articles/47-if-your-family-business-has-grown-your-decision-making-style-needs-to-grow-too.html.

proach. The potential board members maintained that consensus was a nice idea, but they all thought that this would eventually bog things down or curtail growth. They initially felt my client needed to be more realistic. However, in time they came to see that this philosophy was central to the unity the family enjoyed.

Business leaders who are sceptical of this approach may find it helpful to consider the record of accomplishment and astonishing commercial success that has been experienced by many world-renowned Japanese corporations. Their business executives typically consult more extensively and utilize a more consensus-oriented approach to decision-making. The success of this collaborative style of leadership has been remarkable and has often been noted as more effective. Adopting this approach may take quite an adjustment, especially on the part of an entrepreneurial founder. This is because decisions by consensus require a high degree of unity and mutual trust. However, one of the benefits of this approach is that it helps to maintain unity and mutual trust, which are both essential elements for the long-term health of a family firm.

WE ALL NEED MENTORS

One of my mentors is Peter Legge, the publisher of *BC Business Magazine* and one of the most sought after public speakers in Canada. He is famous for saying, "Ten years from now, you will be the same person as you are today except for the people you meet, the places you go and the books you read."[72] Others talk about the amazing influence others have on us by stating that most of us are "the average of our five closest friends." There is no denying it; the people we spend time with have an inestimable influence on us, for better or worse. Realizing this, why

> *"Ten years from now, you will be the same person as you are today except for the people you meet, the places you go and the books you read."*
> *Peter Legge*

would any leader not want to surround himself or herself with high quality board members who could help mentor and guide? It may take some effort to recruit and orient them, but the benefits can be enormous.

CONCLUSION

Creating a board is one of the most important things a family business will ever do. In fact, I have come to believe that if you only do one thing to help

---

[72.] Peter Legge, 2012 interview with David Bentall. Peter is co-founder and CEO of Canada Wide Media Group Limited.

ensure a smooth transition from one generation to the next in a family business, you should create a board of directors with outside independent members.

CHAPTER 15

MONEY, KIDS AND PARENTING

On his 40th birthday, Zig Ziglar, the world-renowned speaker and writer, received a happy birthday call from his sister. Much to his surprise, she seemed a little over eager to find out what their parents had given him for this birthday. When he told her that it was an all-expenses-paid week away on a cruise ship, she was ecstatic!

Puzzled by her reaction, he asked her why she was so thrilled. After all, he reminded her, "It's my birthday, not yours!" She then explained that she was excited because their mom and dad always treated them the same, and so she now knew with certainty that she would also be going on a cruise for her 40th!

As he reflected on this, Zig observed that parents should be so consistent in how they treat their kids so that their offspring will know, with confidence, that they will all be treated fairly in the future.[73]

EQUAL TREATMENT SHOULD BE THE BENCHMARK

When advising my business family clients, I emphasize the importance of making it a habit to treat all offspring equally. When a family matriarch once protested against my advice, saying it was her money and she could do what she wanted to with it, I agreed. Parents can choose to favour one child over another. But, as I pointed out to her, parents also have to be ready to deal with the consequences of their actions. One of the best ways to ensure that children become

---

[73] Zig Ziglar, *Raising Positive Children in a Negative World* (Nashville: Thomas Nelson, 1985).

bitter and resentful towards one another is to treat them unequally. It is also a surefire way to undermine children's respect for their parents.

When Mom and Dad don't treat their offspring equally, it can lead to jealousy, bitterness and relational breakdown among the kids. Without thinking about the origin of these feelings, parents often mislabel these problems as sibling rivalry, even though they may have had a hand in creating these problems for their kids. Undetected, these feelings may lurk underground for years before erupting explosively, often after Mom and Dad have passed away.

INEQUALITY BETWEEN BROTHERS

Perhaps my dad could have used some advice in this area. He was always giving generously to us children, but we sometimes felt he wasn't as fair as he might have been. For example, when Dad wanted to reward my brother, Chuck, for completing his university education, he presented him with a brand new car. Chuck had studied long and hard for seven years to complete both a bachelor of arts and a bachelor of architecture. His perseverance was rewarded with a metallic blue, convertible Austin Healey 3000, complete with chrome spoke wheels. It was a beautiful and fabulous gift, and I believe that Chuck was appropriately appreciative of Dad's generosity.

However, when I was in grade 10, Dad decided that I could make use of a car. My cousin was selling his mint condition Fiat Spider convertible—just two years old and equipped with a throaty "Stebro" muffler and mag wheels. Like my brother, I was genuinely appreciative of Dad's generosity, but, as a 17-year-old, it never occurred to me that I was getting my first car nine years earlier than when my older brother got his first set of wheels.

I never heard Chuck complain about this situation, but I believe that this stark contrast in treatment must have contributed to his feeling that Dad may have loved me more. When talking to Chuck about this recently, he said these decisions made him feel that I was spoiled and made it hard for him to want to spend time with me. Understandably, it also made it hard for him to enjoy time with our dad, as he was often reminded of how he had been treated unequally. Happily, on my 50th birthday Chuck took me out for lunch to my favourite restaurant and gave me a beautiful pen to mark the occasion. We've sort of "started over," but it is too bad we lost so many years, in part because of Dad's naivety.

FAIR DOESN'T ALWAYS MEAN EQUAL

I personally believe that endeavouring to treat all of our children equally is a critical starting point. However, in his best-selling book *Joy at Work*, Ray Bakke offers an important, sharply contrasting opinion. Highlighting the difference between fairness and equality, he states that fairness means treating everyone *differently*.[74] I understand what he means, because I have seen many situations where fairness is not equality. Unfortunately, I have heard many parents say "fair doesn't mean equal" simply as a way of justifying how they have chosen to treat their offspring. These words can be used as a smokescreen to divert attention away from inequities or as an excuse for not doing the hard work of treating children fairly.

Permit me to share a simple example that demonstrates that fairness and equality are not always the same thing. A family I was working with had a business on an island and planned to have annual shareholders' meetings there. One of the five shareholders lived onsite; one lived about an hour's drive away. Two others lived five hours away and could access the island by ferry. The fifth shareholder was a teacher who lived in the Middle East. We discussed providing cost reimbursements for everyone to attend the meeting. Estimated costs for the group members were $0, $40, $200 and $5,000 respectively. Clearly, paying everyone an equal amount of $1,000 would not be fair. It would be a windfall for several and a hardship for the sibling who had the farthest to travel. On the other hand, it would be fair to pay each person's out of pocket expenses to attend the meeting, but this would certainly not be equal.

DIVIDENDS AND EQUALITY

As my siblings and I transitioned into adult life, there were times when we each wanted more money than we had earned (typically for a major repair or large purchase). In these situations, Dad permitted us to take advances from the company instead of borrowing from a bank or using a credit card. Shortly after Alison and I were married, we borrowed $10,000 to help with the purchase of a second car. Each month, we tried to save a little bit to enable us to pay off this loan as soon as we could.

Much to our surprise, at the end of the year Dad paid off this debt for us, explaining that the Canadian Revenue Agency (CRA, Canada's federal tax authority) did not look favourably on shareholders who had debts that remained

---

[74.] Dennis W. Bakke, *Joy at Work: A Revolutionary Approach to Fun on the Job* (Seattle: PVG, 2005), 29.

outstanding over the year-end. Not only that, but Dad advised that he did this every year for all four children, based on the following rationale:

1. He needed to do this to avoid problems with the CRA.
2. It was equal treatment for all his children.
3. It was fair because "whoever needs the most, gets the most."

I told my dad that I had a problem with this arrangement. I explained that if there was to be money available for us each year, then I would like to know in advance so I could plan and budget accordingly. In time, this resulted in Dad providing an annual budgeted dividend, so all four of us could know what we could expect. It wasn't a huge amount, but at least we all felt it was fair.

DISCUSS MONEY AS A FAMILY

My eldest sister, Helen, was married when she was only 19 and before her 30th birthday had given birth to seven children. After her first marriage of 20 years fell apart, she found herself unemployed, without child support and providing for a household full of teenagers. I recall sitting in the den at my Mom and Dad's home when Helen dropped by and, during the conversation, asked if Dad could potentially provide her with some financial assistance. My dad loved his daughter and recognized that she needed his help if she was going to make it through. At the same time, he realized that if he gave her more money, this would create some inequities with the rest of his children.

Dad really wanted to help Helen, but he wanted to do so without creating hard feelings among the rest of his family. Rather than attempting to balance these two competing interests, he deferred to us, saying, "You kids work it out." Consequently, the four of us siblings were given the responsibility of determining how to divide up the annual dividends that were available for distribution. Dad explained that we were at liberty to give some money to Helen, loan her the money on conditions we found acceptable, or advise her that she would simply have to make it on her own.

I was ecstatic that Dad was willing to trust us with this decision and saw it as a vote of confidence in the next generation. I also felt that it was something of the beginning of the succession process (since I hoped that one day we would also have responsibility for the family foundation and the family business). However, when I talked to my siblings, both Chuck and Mary felt there had been some unfairness regarding how Dad had handled things in the past, and they wanted to deal with this first.

Frankly, I wasn't aware that there were any inequities that needed to be addressed. In time I came to realize that there were. Consequently, the four of us agreed to a financial review of the previous five years to determine what had actually occurred. Much to my surprise, the analysis showed that in spite of Dad's honest efforts to treat us fairly, there had been significant inequalities. Even more surprisingly, I discovered that I had been one of the ones who had received substantially more than the others. I realized that any fair-minded person would probably agree that there should be some retroactive adjustments.

RIGHTING THE WRONGS

After six or eight meetings, and quite a delay, we were able to determine a financial solution that we thought was fair to everyone. For this, we had the help of a neutral third party who met privately with each of us and who carefully listened to what we each wanted and needed in a settlement. Our facilitator then wrote out a draft proposal for all of us to review. After a few revisions, we were all able to sign a deal to provide retroactive equality.

In essence, we all agreed to help each other out. Our agreement could be summarized as follows:

1. We helped Chuck by providing him funds to pay for his planned home renovations.
2. We helped Helen by forgiving her for having received more than others had in the past. (But she didn't get the additional funds she had been hoping for.)
3. We helped Mary by permitting her to have ownership of half of a summer cottage, deemed to be worth approximately the amount owing to her.
4. We helped me by allowing me to pay back the extra funds I had received in the past.

After this was all agreed to, I went to the bank, took out a mortgage on our home, and paid my siblings an amount sufficient to provide redress for Dad's excess generosity to me. Understandably, I wasn't excited about the deal, but I did this willingly, in recognition of the fact that I had been given more than my siblings, and with a view to improving relationships in the family.

Years later, I had the opportunity to counsel another family whose circumstances were similar. In this other family, there were

> *Wise families have the courage to examine how much money has been given to each sibling in the past and then agree on how to correct any inequities.*

five children, and the eldest had received substantially more than his younger siblings. Voluntarily, he offered to pay the extra into a fund that would be divided amongst the other family members to achieve equality. I will never forget his words at the end of our meeting as he thanked his siblings for giving him the opportunity to pay the money back. He stated, "Knowing that I had received more than the rest of you has been bothering me for a long time. Thank you for allowing me to clear my conscience and for the opportunity to build relationships with each of you [his siblings] without this money in the way!"

TREATING OUR KIDS FAIRLY

Having experienced genuine challenges in working things out with my siblings, I was determined to make sure Alison and I didn't create the same kind of inequities with our kids. I wanted to make sure that how we dispensed money would not drive a wedge between any of our children. Consequently, we have worked diligently to treat our children equally in regards to love and money. However, as I mentioned previously, equal is not always fair, and this was certainly the case when it came to their sporting activities.

When our daughter Christy started to play soccer, we happily bought her new cleats and shin pads. When she started playing goalkeeper, we had no problem with paying for her first pair of goalie gloves. But as she entered her teens, I remember being shocked that her new goalie gloves cost over $100 per pair. All of my concern over these expenses vanished when our son Jon started playing hockey. Skates, padded shorts, shoulder pads and other related expenses were a lot more expensive than Christy's gloves. Now we were also buying a $300 aluminum, supposedly unbreakable hockey stick and an extra one—just in case it did break! We had promised to pay for our kids' sports equipment, not to give them each an equal amount of money. Happily, this didn't seem to cause any problem for either Christy or Jon.

When our youngest child, Stephanie, took up horseback riding, even hockey started to look cheap. She started riding at age three, and she won her first competition when she was just four years old. Over time, lessons became more frequent; then came the purchase of her first horse, and then her second. One new saddle added up to all we had spent over the years on hockey and soccer combined. Certainly, this wasn't equal.

> *It may be uncomfortable, but families can learn to talk about money in such a way that misunderstandings can be avoided and corrected.*

We began to wonder if paying for all our kids' sports equipment was still a good idea. One day, I asked my wife, Alison, if it would still be fair to pay for Stephanie's riding if it became an enormous annual expense. She agreed that if the costs became extreme, this would no longer be fair. The next year, riding related expenses skyrocketed. In addition to the normal expenses for horse shows, lessons and tack, we also had to pay for major surgery and related veterinary bills. After talking it through, we agreed that in the future any costs over $1,000 per month should be Stephanie's responsibility.

In essence, we were putting a cap on how much we were prepared to pay for our daughter's riding in any given year. We proposed this at a family meeting with all the kids, and everyone agreed that this made sense. Stephanie continued to ride for several more years, and her "extra expenses" were deducted from other funds she might otherwise have received.

DETERMINING AN APPROPRIATE ALLOWANCE

For several years, Alison and I struggled to decide what to pay our kids as an allowance. I argued strenuously that we needed to teach them that money should be earned and reasoned that giving the kids money doesn't emphasize the need to work for it. After several years of debate, I stumbled upon a very helpful book entitled *Raising Money-Smart Kids* by Ron and Judy Blue. They settled the matter for us by explaining that one of the first things we need to teach children is that "money is a scarce resource."[75] They explained that in order to assist young people in understanding this, the best thing we can do as parents is to give our kids an allowance so they can learn to manage money. They suggest that it is best to do this with relatively modest amounts of money. Kids can learn by trial and error.

It was hard for me to admit that Alison had been right all along, but it was fantastic to get some objective advice to help us resolve the impasse. Subsequently we followed the Blues' advice and provided our kids with a monthly allowance. We did this during the balance of their time living at home. This change relieved a lot of tension around the house and transferred responsibility for some of the money decisions to our children.

When the kids were young, we started their financial education with the aid of three glass jars. The first one was labelled "savings," the second "giving" and the third "spending." To help the kids learn to think in these terms, we had them

---

[75.] Ron Blue and Judy Blue, *Raising Money-Smart Kids: How to Teach Your Children the Secrets of Earning, Saving, Investing and Spending Wisely* (Nashville: T. Nelson Publishers, 1992).

put 10% of their allowance in each of the first two jars, and then gave them freedom to do what they wanted with the rest.

TRANSFER FINANCIAL RESPONSIBILITY

However, our big breakthrough came years later, when we transferred to our teenagers the funds budgeted for their clothes. Because they were all in independent schools, we offered to pay for all their required clothing items, including school uniforms, school shoes, overcoats, gym strip, running shoes, socks and underwear. When I reviewed this list, I thought that the kids would not really need much more money for other things. Alison pointed out that they would need casual clothes for the weekends, as well as for special occasions. We settled on a relatively generous allowance ($1,000 per year, in 1990). Because we had been liberal in this discretionary clothing allowance, we were able to remain firm that there were no exceptions, regardless of whether or not they ran out of money.

I recall the first time I went shopping for running shoes with our daughter Jenny after we had introduced this new regime. She wanted a pair of the latest style in sneakers. She found exactly what she was looking for—at a cost of $129. After tax, this purchase would use up almost 15% of her clothing budget for the year. Without hesitation, Jenny put the shoes back on the shelf and walked out of the store. I was relieved, but astonished. No arguments; no pleading for more money; just recognition that this was more of "her money" than she wanted to spend.

When teenagers are given an appropriate allowance for purchasing their own clothes, a major source of intergenerational stress can be eliminated.

Within 15 minutes, Jenny found exactly the same shoes for considerably less dollars. Obviously, she was learning to manage money. At the same time, I was coming to realize how much better it was for our relationship. We had now eliminated almost all the arguing over money simply by giving the kids some freedom and by transferring some financial responsibility to them.

BALANCE LOVE AND CONSEQUENCES

Like most teenagers, Jonathan found it hard to wait for some of the things he wanted to buy. When he was in high school, we encouraged him to earn some extra money so he could save up for his first car and the stereo he wanted to install in it. In his graduation year, he scraped together enough cash to acquire a

30-year-old Cougar from one of our closest friends. However, our son couldn't imagine driving it without music, so he borrowed money from one of his schoolmates to buy a cassette deck. He borrowed more money for new speakers and a few other items he wanted. He was in car heaven, at least for a while.

But Jon soon found it hard to afford gas for the car, let alone pay back the debts he had incurred. To make matters worse, we had paid for the first three months car insurance as our way of partnering with him in achieving this important goal. Now, he needed to find a way to pay not only for the insurance but his other debts as well. As we reviewed his circumstances, we realized that, in essence, our son had become insolvent.

I realized that Jon needed a fresh start, yet he also needed to learn how important it is to not be careless with debt. I prayed for wisdom. Then it struck me. I could help Jon by taking responsibility for all his debts and wipe the slate clean, so he could start over. This would be showing him love, support and grace. After talking it all through, I offered to repay all of Jon's debts, in exchange for title to his car (which was worth much less than he owed). Jon reluctantly agreed to my proposal and we put the car up for sale.

It was a painful lesson, but Jon has since told me that through this experience he learned how important it is to never borrow money, unless it is to acquire an appreciating asset, such as a home.

PROVIDE A GOOD START IN LIFE

Dave Phillips, an internationally recognized speaker and sought after resource for executives and their families, has spoken widely about the essentials that are necessary to give our kids a good start in life. Based on his extensive experience, he recommends that we:

1. Provide our children with opportunities to help others who have much less than we do. Usually this is best done by travelling to a poorer country where they can develop a deeper sense of gratitude. These kinds of trips can also help our young people to realize that what they have is not a birthright but rather a wonderful gift not to be taken for granted. Our family has now made six trips to Mexico to help out with missions and building projects. I can't think of anything more important that we have ever done to help our children understand how fortunate they really are.

2. Encourage our kids to develop a moral and spiritual foundation for their lives. One of the best ways to do this is through involvement in a summer camping program. Our children developed independence, responsibility

and leadership skills at a wonderful youth camp over several summers. Beyond that, they also developed great lifelong friendships and came to a meaningful understanding of how God can make a difference in a person's life.

In addition to these two suggestions from Dave, we decided that it would also be important to help our kids to get a good start in life by assisting them to get a good education. Because I was not raised in a private school environment, I had a negative perception of "all boys" or "all girls" schools. However, a lot has changed since I was in school, and I think our four children benefited substantially from the private school educations they received at St George's and Crofton House schools in Vancouver. These schools provided a well-rounded education that included artistic, musical and athletic opportunities beyond what the public system was able to offer. Alison and I believe we made a good investment in providing this academic "head start" for our kids. Parents who have sufficient resources and want to give some of it to their kids could start the process by investing some of the money in a good education for their offspring.

CLARIFY FINANCIAL EXPECTATIONS AS KIDS BECOME ADULTS

In their excellent book *The Financially Intelligent Parent*, John and Eileen Gallo recommend that parents write a letter to their children, outlining what to expect as they mature and become adults.[76] For some, it may be appropriate to commemorate their high school graduation or an 18th birthday. The date itself is not critical; the critical point is the act of taking the time to celebrate and mark your child's transition into adulthood. With our four children, we spelled out clearly what we were willing to pay for and what they were responsible to earn.

Many parents want to avoid their children having to suffer. But they ought to avoid the temptation to overindulge them.

We agreed to help them with the costs of their university education, but we had clear expectations regarding what they would be responsible to earn along the way. We also agreed to assist them with their first car and a down payment for their first home, again on very specific terms.

---

[76] John and Eileen Gallo, *The Financially Intelligent Parent: 8 Steps to Raising Successful, Generous, Responsible Children* (New York: New American Library/Penguin Group, 2005).

188

RESIST THE TEMPTATION TO GIVE YOUR KIDS TOO MUCH TOO SOON

Dr. Lee Hausner is author of the book *Children of Paradise*, and she is well known for her work with the Hollywood set in California.[77] While many of her ultra-wealthy clients have wrestled with lazy and unmotivated kids, Dr. Hausner's advice has remained unequivocal. She says that the only way to help your kids become independent is to cease treating them as dependents. One of her recommendations is that parents require their adult children to get a job and pay rent. She also says that kids should be warned that if they don't earn their keep, Mom and Dad may physically remove their belongings from the house. Young people will get the message that you mean business when they are staring at the blank walls in an apartment that you have found for them, even if you have moved them in and paid the first couple of months' rent. They will soon realize that the ball is now squarely in their court.

Unfortunately, many family trusts provide for regular payments to beneficiaries beginning when they turn 21. While payments at this stage may be appropriate to fund education or to help with the down payment on a first home, there are real dangers in regularly paying out large sums of money to young adults. The potential for this kind of largess to undermine creativity, initiative and self-responsibility is enormous. Even worse, ready access to cash can sometimes contribute to drug and alcohol abuse. To avoid these problems, Dr. Hausner counsels affluent parents to avoid the regular or significant distribution of funds to their children at "any time during the early career building years."[78] Just like a butterfly who must struggle to get out of its cocoon to develop its wings, our children should be permitted the opportunity to struggle, especially if we want them to learn how to fly.

DELAYED GRATIFICATION AND WORK FOR WHAT YOU WANT

A young man I know once begged his parents to buy him a car while he was still in high school. His mother wisely explained that she and her husband did not want to rob him of the satisfaction that they anticipated he would experience when he had saved up

Children should not be given any substantial wealth until they are through their prime career building years.

[77.] Lee Hausner, *Children of Paradise, Successful Parenting for Prosperous Families* (Irvine: Plaza Press, 2005).

[78.] Ibid., 234.

the money required to buy his first car. Undeterred, the son continued to press his case. "Why can't you just help me, Mom?" he pleaded. She responded, "Because we love you too much to make things too easy for you." The young man, realizing he had lost his case, sadly concluded the exchange by saying, "Couldn't you just love me a little less?" This young man was disappointed, but I believe that his parents got it right. Many parents don't love their kids enough and give in too easily to their children's requests.

CONCLUSION

Many parents I know confuse the following:
• Love and Generosity
• Love and Giving
• Love and Helping

Wise parents see the differences between these attributes and learn how to love their children without being too generous, without giving them too much, and without helping them when it would be unwise to do so. Those who have accumulated or inherited wealth need to resist the temptation to salve their guilty consciences by simply giving their kids material possessions.

They don't need more money or more stuff. They need more of their parents' time and more of their love. In addition, they need their parents to display more wisdom by being scrupulously fair in how they disperse money among siblings. Finally, they need parents who will be more thoughtful in modelling for them how to be wise stewards of their resources. Parents can be wise in what they do with their money, and it can be a great blessing to their children. If they are unwise, their money can end up being a curse. If I was to have a slogan for wise parenting, it might be something like this:

Don't Give Them Money and Don't Give Them Things;
Instead...
Give Them Roots and Give Them Wings!

CHAPTER 16

GOVERNANCE AND FAMILY MEETINGS

Families in business can learn a lot from our fair-feathered friends, the geese. Although they have long been considered a nuisance in our public parks, these birds display the kinds of skills and behaviours that would benefit any family or family business. They co-operate, encourage one another and act in harmony to support their leader. Any businessperson would be thrilled to have employees who behave this way.

Geese are well known for flying in a V formation as they head south for the winter. As each bird flaps its wings, this formation creates uplift for the bird immediately following and, through this action, the whole flock gains over 70% greater flying range than if each bird flew on its own.

Whenever a goose falls out of formation, it feels the drag and resistance of trying to go it alone and quickly gets back into formation to take advantage of the lifting power of the bird immediately in front. When the lead goose gets tired, he rotates back in the formation and another goose flies the point. The geese honk from behind to encourage those up front to keep up their speed, and when a goose is injured and falls to the ground, two others drop out of formation to support it. They stay with the struggling bird until it regains enough strength to rejoin the group or dies.

Like a flock of geese, families function better when they encourage one another and take turns doing the hard jobs. They can get where they are going much more quickly and easily if they stay in formation with those who are headed in the same direction and if they travel on the thrust of one another.

Unfortunately, it seems like geese have more loyalty to their own kind than many people do in family businesses. All too many family members are discarded by the side of the road, while the rest carry on without them. Obviously, families in business don't need to fly in a V formation. However, in order to provide mutual support and to create synergy, like geese do, wise families are purposeful about their direction and their relationships. One of the most powerful things a family can do is to have regular family meetings. These discussions are a form of governance for a family in business and are typically the best way for a family to begin exploring how they would like to govern their shared interests. This chapter will consider when and why to conduct family meetings and how they can help to create and maintain family unity. In addition, because the concept of governance is easily misunderstood within the context of a family business, we will first define governance and explore what constitutes good governance.

FACTS AND DISAGREEMENTS

A friend of mine recently retired from a long and successful career as a litigation lawyer. When I asked him what he had learned from a lifetime spent "arguing" on behalf of his clients, he responded with the revealing words "When all the facts are known, virtually all disputes disappear."

This observation suggests that a lack of communication is typically the root of all disagreements. If this is true in the courtroom, it is also true in family relations. If family members don't stay in regular communication with their loved ones, they will inevitably suffer the consequences. On the other hand, if they invest time in developing good communications within the family this will provide a foundation upon which to build good governance for their family enterprise.

WHAT IS GOVERNANCE ANYWAY?

Since the Enron scandal, the word "governance" has been bandied about in business circles. Shareholders, academics and politicians are now all seeking the holy grail of good governance. Yet many people wrongly consider governance only in terms of public corporations and rules relating to their boards of directors. What does this word "governance" actually mean? And how does governance apply to families in business? According to *The Random House College Dictionary*, governance is

> *Governance is composed of two essential elements: COMMUNICATION and DECISION-MAKING.*

192

"a method or system of government or management." This is a good, concise definition. However, it is not prescriptive. To help my clients and students understand governance, I have found it helpful to think of governance as a combination of communication and decision-making. In other words, the two essential elements of any governance system are communication and decision-making.

COMMUNICATION

Let's look first at how communication is essential to governance. I have worked with many families who are trying to manage or govern the intergenerational succession process. Typically, they have not had much prior communication about what their succession plan might be (if it even exists). The elder generation will usually not know how to bring up sensitive topics, like who will own the family cottage or how their estate will be distributed when they die. Similarly, the next generation will have difficulty trying to get Mom and Dad to address these topics. Everyone is afraid the discussions might cause an argument.

Not surprisingly, in the vast majority of families there are simply no regular opportunities for dialogue or a time when it is safe to raise these kinds of topics. Usually no one has thought about this as being a communication problem. Instead, succession-planning problems are often simplistically blamed on either sibling rivalry or a founder who won't let go of the reins. These are genuine issues to be mindful of, but they are not usually the root problem. All too often, the root problem is simply a lack of good communication.

For example, I know of a business family that recently experienced a breakdown between two siblings. At first blush it appeared that one was just jealous of the other having a new home. However, upon closer inspection, a lack of communication was causing some of their troubles. In this particular situation, Mom and Dad loaned funds to one of their children to enable him to purchase a new house. This loan is an interest-bearing debt, and the young couple are expected to pay it back. In addition, it is secured against their future inheritance, and as a result they may receive less from their parents' estate in the future. However, because the details of the loan arrangements were not communicated to the rest of the family, there has been speculation about what the arrangements actually are. Some of the siblings have assumed that a special gift has been given to one child that was not available to others in the family. Had there been simple, transparent communication regarding all this, at a family meeting, it would have prevented this needless hurt and misunderstanding.

DECISION-MAKING

When raising a family, Mom and Dad are typically in charge of all decisions, large and small. Similarly, when building a business, Mom or Dad (if an entrepreneurial leader) is usually responsible for most decisions. However, over time, as children become adults and as a business matures, there are many decisions in the home and company that could benefit from the input of others. For example, the next generation may have a much better idea regarding how a family business could introduce new technology or take advantage of social media channels when marketing its products. More importantly, if the next generation is expected to shoulder the responsibility to make all the decisions one day, their elders would be wise to include them in decision-making discussions. This will provide an opportunity for the parents to mentor their kids in regard to making good decisions.

WHAT IS EFFECTIVE GOVERNANCE?

Every family in business has established patterns of communication (whether good or bad) and decision-making norms (which may also be good or bad). How then can a family determine what good governance is? In other words, how does a family in business know if its communication and decision-making are appropriate or effective? A family may be judged to have effective governance if they have systems and processes that make revolution unnecessary.

> *Effective governance includes SYSTEMS AND PROCESSES THAT MAKE REVOLUTION UNNECESSARY.*

In other words, effective governance involves the development of appropriate communication channels and decision-making bodies that make it possible for everyone's voice to be heard in an appropriate way. When these kinds of structures and governing mechanisms exist, individuals are able to deal with their issues and concerns in a respectful and appropriate fashion. Consequently, individuals don't need to wait until they are frustrated to the boiling point; nor do they need to lash out in destructive ways. Reflect on the tragedy associated with any of history's violent political revolutions. There is little doubt that those who revolted were clamouring for a voice (communication) and a change in power (decision-making). The Russian and French Revolutions certainly were occasioned by those who desired to be heard, and they wanted to change how decisions were made. The same thing can happen in a family business, when one group of owners or other stakeholders loses confidence in those who hold the power. Sadly, this is what happened with my two uncles, who were co-owners of The Bentall Group yet felt their voices were not being heard. Consequently, they determined that a change was warranted.

START WITH THE FAMILY

When thinking about how to create appropriate governance for any family in business, the question often arises as to where to begin. Good governance for a family enterprise should begin with the family. This is because without unity in the family, unity within the family business will be at risk. Moreover, a cohesive family can provide a foundation upon which a business may be built, but a business cannot provide the foundation for building a cohesive family. In other words, a business may be capable of many things, but it can't build a strong family. Not only is this not its role, it is just not equipped to do so. A business is designed for satisfying customers, making things and earning a profit, not building family relationships. Philippe de Gaspé Beaubien summarizes it best when he states, "A strong family can build a strong business; but a strong business cannot build a strong family."[79]

FAMILY MEETINGS

Open lines of communication are essential for a family who wants to establish an enduring family business. The simplest and most important starting place is with a commitment to holding regular family meetings. These gatherings should be held at least twice annually, and they are usually invaluable in helping the family learn how to communicate and make decisions together. Experts jokingly say that a family needs to meet more often than annually, because if they just meet once a year, it is not really a family meeting; it is just a reunion.

The following are three of the primary purposes for holding family meetings:
• Developing and educating the family (building knowledge)
• Making rules and decisions that impact the family (developing unity)
• Resolving and avoiding conflict (providing an escape valve for problems)

Starting when the children are very young, family meetings can address topics like bedtime, allowances and rules related to homework. When the children are older, family holidays and charitable giving are good topics to discuss.

[79.] Kim Green, "A Family Affair: Making Sense of Change," *New Trail* (Edmonton: Alberta Business Family Institute), http://www.uofaweb.ualberta.ca/newtrail/nav03.cfm?nav03=42014&nav02=41993&nav01=41992.

Ultimately, meetings can graduate over time to include family employment policies, investment strategies and succession planning. By having regular meetings, families can pro-actively build unity and learn to solve problems.

We started having family meetings with our children when they were ages two, four and six years old (see chapter 17 for more details). Some people think that our experience is extreme, but family business expert Nan-b De Gaspé Beaubien, who started holding regular family meetings with her husband and their three children when they were in their teens, claims that "if we had it to do over again, we would have started having family meetings much sooner."[80]

A good friend of mine is a senior executive with an international real estate brokerage firm. He told me that he and his wife held weekly family meetings with their three boys as they were growing up. In hindsight, he realized that this simple routine provided an escape valve for issues and concerns to be discussed before they became unmanageable. This dad told me that on one occasion he had to make amends to one of his young lads because the gardening duties hadn't been apportioned out fairly. Their family meeting gave his young son a time and place to respectfully raise his concerns, and Dad's mistake was corrected.

Getting the family together to talk regularly may not seem revolutionary, but it is one of the most important ways to build long-term harmony and to avoid relational breakdowns, especially for business-owning families.

RETAIN A FACILITATOR

Just getting everybody together won't guarantee success. Well-established communication patterns, where Mom and Dad may be tempted to dominate, don't evaporate simply by getting everyone in the same room. Similarly, strained relationships between siblings or any other familial dysfunction can't be ironed out without some work. One of the most effective ways to change the family dynamics is through the introduction of a professional facilitator. An independent voice can help and encourage family members to be on their best behaviour. They can also help break old patterns of dominance by some parents and help to establish a more egalitarian, harmonious environment for everyone.

Occasionally, in circumstances where there is profound family dysfunction, a family may be unable to unlock emotional or relational challenges that may have existed for decades. Meeting together can even exacerbate the situation or prolong the agony. In these situations, a psychologist or counsellor may be required

---

[80]. Nan-B De Gaspé Beaubien, Governance Seminar, 2008. Nan-B is co-chair of the Business Families Foundation, Montreal.

to help break old habits or to dislodge a relational logjam. I have had the privilege of partnering with a psychologist in working with some of my family clients, and together we have been able to help resolve some complicated and enduring challenges. If the root problem is not relational but rather business related, an individual with specific industry knowledge may be needed to help the family address some specific business concerns.

DON'T WAIT FOR A CRISIS

Unfortunately, many families wait until a crisis before starting to get the family together to talk. By then, it may be too late. In our nuclear family, our first formal family meeting wasn't held until after the situation between my dad and his brothers had already erupted. By then it was too late for us to do anything meaningful to help the situation.

Some people claim it is too hard to get everyone together or that people will just argue. If that's the case, then it is very likely that there will be bigger problems down the road. Rather than waiting until problems are unmanageable, wise families make it a habit to meet frequently and proactively. When families in business invest the time required to hold regular family meetings they are able to share their dreams, learn to make decisions together, plan for the future and have a forum to discuss concerns.

G3 FAMILY MEETINGS

Alison and I started having annual family meetings with our kids to discuss our charitable giving, household chores and family vacations. Over time, we added conversations about allowances, saving for a college education and how to earn money for a first car.

We also borrowed an excellent strategy for including fun from Philippe De Gaspé Beaubien. His family has a rule that requires "one hour of family fun for every 20 minutes of meeting time."[81] Consequently, a few

> *"Our family meetings have one hour of fun for every 20 minutes of meeting time."*
> *Philippe De Gaspé Beaubien*

years ago, we spent a couple of days snowboarding together as a family and held our annual family meeting over pizza après-ski. Holding the meeting at a resort made it more appealing to the kids; combining it with a snowboarding trip made it easier for our teenage children to put the dates on their calendars.

[81.] Philippe De Gaspé Beaubien, 2008, personal communication with David Bentall. Philippe is co-chair of the Business Families Foundation, Montreal.

I admit that getting everyone together over the years hasn't been easy, but I am convinced that it has been worth the effort. Recently, I was delighted to witness our youngest daughter standing in front of a flip chart, leading the annual discussion of our charitable giving. The older kids became more engaged in the process when our eldest received her Jeep TJ upon graduation, and our son, who had recently become engaged, became interested in details of our family's first house purchase assistance plan.

A CODE OF CONDUCT

Whenever I facilitate an initial meeting for a family, our first joint exercise involves creating a code of conduct for the discussions. We begin by asking the family to each describe what kind of behaviour would help to create a safe and productive environment. It is amazing how easily members of the family can articulate what this would look like. The following are some responses that have been proposed by various family clients for their respective codes of conduct:

- Speak your mind, not what you think others want to hear.
- Be attentive to other people's feelings.
- Be collaborative, not competitive.
- Share the air time (no one should be able to hide or dominate).
- Share concerns face to face, not behind each other's backs.
- Seek facts before drawing conclusions.
- Have a clear agenda and stick to it.
- Don't condescend or minimize others.
- No personal attacks.
- Demonstrate mutual respect.
- Don't walk over the end of others' sentences; i.e., no interrupting.
- Look forward not backward; be solution oriented.
- Be honest and forgiving.

Through the process of creating a code of conduct, and with the support of a skilled facilitator, families can learn new behaviours. By starting with small, manageable chunks of time, families can begin to learn new patterns of relating. A facilitator can help support and guide families as they replace old parent-child relationships with adult-adult interactions. Like any new skill, learning to communicate differently takes time, discipline and patience. However, with encouragement and coaching most families can discover how to have healthy and constructive dialogue together.

GETTING STARTED

There is often anxiety or apprehension about getting everyone together for an initial family meeting. This hesitancy can be alleviated and a foundation established for a good first meeting by having a neutral party conduct individual interviews with every member the family before getting the group together. The following are the two questions that I typically ask in such interviews:

1. What are the topics or issues you believe this family should be talking about?

2. What do you think your family should do about these subjects?

Armed with answers to these questions, I'm able to prepare a report of themes. Without attribution, and using non-critical language, I am able to help a family by sensitively putting on the table the topics everyone believes should be addressed. This provides the basis for discussion and problem solving. (A detailed sample agenda for an initial family meeting is included in part IV.)

MEETING FOR FOUR HOURS IS MAGICAL

I have discovered that family meetings tend to function best when they last for at least four hours. Initially, I was hesitant to schedule meetings that were this long, believing that families would not have the patience to sit together for so much time. However, I have come to realize that there is almost something magical about meeting for four hours. It usually takes the first three hours for family members to get comfortable and to begin exploring in a cautious fashion. However, when the fourth hour arrives, families are usually ready to make decisions and to grapple with the difficult topics at hand.

When I first started working as an advisor to families in business, we would typically meet for dinner and then meet in the evening. I did this so as not to interfere with the needs of the family's business. This also made scheduling much easier, because I was happy to accommodate my clients during the evening hours. However, family business advisor Gord Wusyk wisely counselled me to revise this approach, stating that he will not work with a family unless they are prepared to meet during the day.[82] This is because there are numerous negative consequences inherent to evening meetings; these include the following:

> *Family meetings should be held during the day, so everyone can give their best energy to the topics at hand.*

[82.] Gordon Wusyk, 2011 communication with David Bentall. Gordon is founder, president and CEO of Predictable Futures Inc. and author of *Drift, Drown or Decide* (Edmonton: Predictable Futures, 2010).

- Family members are usually too tired to be productive for the whole meeting.
- Evening meetings imply that the really important work happens during the day.
- A subtle message may be communicated that family meetings aren't of high value.
- Evening meetings also interfere with times when families should be eating dinner together, helping children with homework or enjoying some "down-time" at home.

LEARNING OPPORTUNITIES

Family meetings should include some time for learning. Some say that families that play together stay together; others say that families who pray together stay together. I think both are true, but I would add that families that learn together stay together. This is because shared learning helps create common knowledge and this contributes to unity.

The following are a sample of learning opportunities that are appropriate for family meetings:

- Five ways to handle conflict
- Individual and family values inventory
- Characteristics of an effective sibling team
- Ten benefits of an effective board
- The different roles of management, shareholders and the board
- The CEO selection process

At one family meeting I attended, everyone was asked to identify what values had been the most important to them in the past two months. They then compared these values with the values they wanted to have in the future. Not surprisingly, the 85-year-old patriarch noted that the values on both of his lists were the same. In contrast, a 17-year-old member of G3 discovered that, in the future, he wanted all of his values to be different. These were memorable moments for everyone present.

THIS IS NOT A BUSINESS MEETING

Some people resist holding family meetings because they don't want to introduce such formality to their family relationships or because they are afraid the business will dominate their family relationships. However, *a family meeting is not a business meeting*. Business matters can be discussed at a family meeting, but a family meeting exists for the purpose of getting the family together to talk about many subjects and not just business.

Our eldest daughter, Christy, has now attended regular family meetings within our family for over 20 years. A year ago, she remarked that she finally understood that these meetings were for her benefit (and for her siblings'). She finally understood that our purpose was to educate and to enable their input into the decisions we were making as a family. Reflecting on her new understanding, she explained that she had previously thought that I wanted to make a business out of our family. With disarming candour she quipped, "Just like some young girls enjoy playing house, I thought just you wanted to 'play business' with us."

DECIDE BY CONSENSUS

As discussed in chapter 15, I am an advocate of consensus decision-making. I believe it is a very powerful tool for family meetings. Family business expert Peter Leach states it even more strongly. He observes, "The goal for the family's planning process is consensus."[83] I first discovered the potential benefits of consensus decision-making when my sisters and I bought Dominion Construction. At our strategic retreat with our senior executives, each of us was to prioritize the utility of 15 objects that could be used to help us survive if our plane had crashed in the frozen tundra of the North. We then worked in groups and decided by consensus how to rank the same objects. We had some highly intelligent people in our company who argued strenuously for their respective rankings, but consensus decision-making always resulted in a list that was better than the best and the brightest had chosen. This exercise revealed to us all that even those with higher IQs make better decisions if they are willing to submit to a consensus decision-making process that includes the input of others.

It is my experience that consensus decision-making is the best way to create an environment where harmony in the family can be built and maintained. Deciding by consensus not only requires unity but also helps to maintain it. Consensus decision-making requires patience and careful listening, but these inevitably lead to better relations and better decisions.

My experience is not unique. Recently I heard of a highly regarded, internationally recognized family business consultant who, in a moment of exasperation, told his family client that they needed to be

> *Consensus requires unity and maintains unity.*

[83.] Peter Leach. *Family Business: The Essentials* (Great Britain: Profile Books Ltd., 2007), 59.

practical, and because it appeared consensus would not be achieved, they should simply make a decision based on a vote. The family's response was decisive and remarkable. They explained to their advisor that if this was his approach they would need to work with someone else. They explained that if they were going to get along together in the long run they must not allow the divisiveness that comes from voting. Because they are committed to consensus they make decisions in such a way that no one is left behind.

NO RIGHT ANSWERS

For me, being "right" has always been very important. This has caused me all kinds of problems in life, including in my marriage. It has also made it difficult for me to get along with my siblings from time to time. For example, in dealing with a property that the four of us co-own on an island, I recall thinking that my older three siblings were simply not fair if they didn't agree with me. At the time, I thought fairness was something that was objectively determinable (something I could be "right" about). Years later, when studying at the Harvard Business School, I encountered a very memorable case study entitled "Exercises on 'What Is Fair.'"[84] In our class discussion, it was concluded that there were several solutions to a problem, which all could be defended as "mathematically" fair. This interaction with my classmates in Boston radically changed my perspective! It helped me to see that fairness is more of a personal and subjective notion and not an absolute.

With this new understanding, I came to realize how important it is for families to arrive at solutions that they can all endorse. One member of the family may believe they have a fair solution (as I often did). But there may be other solutions that different family members also regard as fair. In these situations, it is critically important for all family members to have an opportunity to be heard and understood. When everyone is listened to respectfully, the family can seek to reach solutions that all parties can live with. In the end, as much as I wish it were not the case, there are no "right" answers, just answers that work for a particular family.

> *It's not about getting the right answer, it's about the discussion.*

DISCUSS SALARIES FOR FAMILY MEMBERS

Compensation can be a volatile subject for families in business, and there can be many different perspectives regarding what is "fair." This can be a difficult

---

[84.] Paul A. Vatter, "Exercises on 'What Is Fair?'" (Boston: Harvard Business School).

matter to resolve, because there are many different scenarios for determining salaries, each of which could be considered fair. For example, the Ferragamo family (manufacturers of Ferragamo shoes, handbags, etc.) sought to avoid controversy over salaries, and so the matriarch of the family decreed that all seven of her children would be paid exactly the same, regardless of their role within the company. This is an egalitarian approach that can, and does, work. Other family companies prefer family employees to be paid a market salary for their job. This approach may help to avoid tension between with the family and other employees, by ensuring that family members are neither given a free ride nor excessively compensated. Both of these compensation philosophies could be considered fair. The point is there isn't simply a "right answer" for most situations within a family business.

In dealing with sensitive issues like compensation, it is important for families to obtain appropriate education and quality information upon which to base their decisions. In addition, they should endeavour to create a healthy environment for discussion if they are to going to be able to reach wise conclusions. As Ruth Steverlynk emphasizes, a family needs to have "a set of principles as to how they will behave when they meet together so they can have healthy honest discussions…but they also need education and information sharing…to make good decisions."[85]

HIGHLIGHTS FROM OUR FAMILY MEETINGS

Two years ago, in one of the most productive meetings our family has held, our middle daughter, Jennifer, led the rest of the family in a goal-setting exercise. She brought an audio recording on goal-setting and provided worksheets to assist all of us in developing goals for the year ahead. In my role as father, I never could have pulled that off! However, she was able to give leadership to her siblings and teach them this life skill. She was effective in this situation in part because she was a peer (not Dad) sharing with her siblings. In addition, her experience with goal-setting as a member of "Generation Y"[86] was rooted in digitally recorded seminars and her work experience at Lululemon. Her background and first-hand knowledge was more compelling for her siblings than any ideas I might have shared as to why goal setting should be important.

Over the past 25 years, our family meetings have involved topics such as charitable giving, family holidays, education planning, investment updates and

---

[85.] Ruth Steverlynk, 2012 interview with David Bentall.

[86.] Generation Y, also known as Millenials, are generally marked by an increased use and familiarity with communications, media and digital technologies.

family fun. More recently, we have been going away overnight to a resort where our family can ski, swim or play tennis. The girls have also enjoyed it when we can include a trip to the spa.

Last year, when our family met in Phoenix as part of a family vacation we devoted one full day to a family retreat. Everyone came prepared to share their life purpose, mission and vision statements with the aid of a PowerPoint presentation. Dave Phillips, who has written a book on the subject, guided us and gave everyone support and feedback on their plans. We all learned a lot from the exercise and got to know each other better. We also took tennis lessons, swam and enjoyed some great meals together. However, the highlight of the weekend for me was Bentall Jeopardy. As a means of exploring numerous important business topics, Jennifer had asked me to give her the 30 key items that I wanted everyone to know. She then created five categories of questions, including finances, vacations, charitable giving, etc. We pitted the boys against the girls, complete with music, timer and buzzer. Through this fun exercise, we were able to communicate important information that needed to be disseminated to the family. I'll never forget our daughter Stephanie saying with a shocked look on her face, "Is this how you tell me we are selling our family boat in 15 years?" Aside from her disappointment, the game was a real success.

INCLUDE SPOUSES IN YOUR MEETINGS

The first formal family meetings our parents ever organized occurred when we were faced with the tragic breakup of our family business. As discussed earlier, this included the momentous decision of whether or not to buy a 75-year-old construction business. You can imagine all the challenges and emotions attached to these discussions.

Some people are surprised that we had our spouses present at these meetings. However, their input was critically important. Firstly, just having them in the room assisted us in being on our best behaviour (because anything we said or did was being observed by our brothers- and sisters-in-law). Secondly, they helped us with some very good suggestions during our problem solving. Thirdly, whatever we decided on would have to eventually be agreed to by our spouses. So, we were best to involve them along the way, rather than trying to "sell them" on our decisions later. Fourthly, and perhaps most importantly, they provided emotional support for each of us as we were dealing with a very challenging circumstance.

For those who may think that spouses should not be included in family meetings, I would propose that they think about the following two statements:

1. Regardless of whether or not they are included in family meetings, spouses will have an influence.
2. Which is better—for spouses to have an informed influence or a uniformed influence?

I have observed over the years that excluding spouses from family discussions often results in misinformation, misunderstandings and a deterioration of relationships. By way of contrast, those families who are inclusive and welcome the input of spouses are able to create and maintain family unity more effectively.

Nonetheless, even as I advocate the involvement of spouses, I also recommend caution. Knowing what to communicate, as well as how and when, is an art that requires both wisdom and sensitivity. For example, a family may want to obtain spouses' input into the selection process for the next CEO, but not in the actual decision. In other words, the family may want input regarding "how to choose," but not "who to choose." Similarly, a family

> *Spouses will have an influence. But it is better for them to have an informed influence.*

may want to explain to spouses why dividends for the coming year will be reduced (how they were determined) and yet they may not want to have spouses involved in setting dividend levels (what they will be). Typically, dividends will be set by the board, and so family members ought to be educated regarding how dividend levels are determined, without assuming responsibility for them. Additionally, when involving spouses, it is important to clarify whether they are being invited to offer their opinion or they are being given a vote. For example, in one family I worked with, there were two daughters who were going to inherit the business equally. The husband of one of the girls also worked for the company. We included him in some of our meetings, but in order to avoid an imbalance of power, he didn't get an official vote when they were making decisions.

FAMILY EMPLOYMENT POLICY

When families meet together, it is important to capture in writing what they agree upon. A written record of their discussions can help to avoid future misunderstandings and to overcome "selective amnesia." For most meetings, a carefully prepared set of minutes will be sufficient. However, over time, as families begin to develop guiding principles for the future, they may wish to establish some written family policies. These are not legal documents but rather "moral agreements," established in the interest of good relations and to help clarify expectations. Families should remember that in many cases, the discussion about a given policy will be more important than the final wording of the policy statement. This is because it is through dialogue that the family develops a shared understanding and shared expectations.

One of the most important topics that should be addressed by way of policy is family employment. This should include specifying what kind of education and experience a family member should have before applying for a job at the family company. A few years ago, the G2 president of a family firm asked for my assistance in developing their family employment policy. She proposed that the following minimum criteria be adopted for any family members who wanted to apply for a manager job at the company:

• A four-year business degree, plus six years relevant experience, or
• An MBA, plus four years appropriate experience, or
• A diploma in business, plus ten years relevant experience.

In order to create a family employment policy, we invited all seven members of G3 (ranging in age from 14-25) to discuss a draft employment policy containing the above provisions. After a rigorous discussion, they unanimously agreed that these criteria were appropriate for anyone aspiring to be president of the company. However, they believed that a lower minimum standard would be appropriate for other management roles. Their recommendation was agreed to by everyone in the family. What was notable about this situation was the dialogue and debate. Through this process, all members of G3 came to understand that they didn't want their family enterprise led by someone who was not well prepared. As a result, they all endorsed a policy that would set a high standard in terms of prerequisites required for the future company president. They did this even though they readily acknowledged that most of them would be unlikely to meet these requirements.

As these cousins discovered, when family members work together to create policies, they realize what is important to them as a family and as individuals. They also have an opportunity to develop communication skills and to learn the art of compromise.

CONCLUSION

Governance is composed of two key activities: communication and decision-making. Effective governance comes from creating structures and processes that make revolution unnecessary. If a family wants to avoid a revolution in their family business, they would be wise to invest the time to have regular family meetings.

It may take several years for a family to develop a strong governance system, but the most important place to start is with governance in the family. This should begin by having regular family gatherings that include fun, education and an orientation to key business topics. By being proactive, unity can be developed and future potential problems can be avoided. As Nan-b De Gaspé Beaubien has often said, "A little time in the planning saves a lot in the fixing."[87]

---

[87] Nan-B De Gaspé Beaubien, 2012 interview with David Bentall.

CHAPTER 17

PHILANTHROPY: WHAT TO DO WITH ALL THE MONEY?

When our kids were young, we always looked forward to decorating the Christmas tree together. It was an event that marked the beginning of the holiday season, and everyone was full of anticipation and excitement. Alison bundled the kids up with woolen caps and mittens, and then we would all pile into the van and head off on our adventure. After carefully selecting the perfect tree, we would stop at McDonalds for an eggnog milkshake. It was a wonderful festive tradition!

When our daughter Christy turned six, we wanted to include her in the process of finalizing year-end charitable donations. The other kids were only two and four years old, but we decided to include everyone. The question was how?

Using Alison's creativity as a former elementary school teacher and my determination to do all this together, we invented a plan. Alison got out a big box of crayons and some construction paper. When we were sprawled on the floor in the living room, we told the kids that this year we wanted everyone to make special decorations for our tree. We explained that every year Mommy and Daddy made donations to selected charities. We told them that we would like them to each create something to put on the tree to remember each special organization. Christy drew a picture of a well to represent the clean water provided by Hope International, Jon cut out a sailboat to remind us of the camp at Keats Island, and Jennifer created a pair of paper eyeglasses to symbolize the work of Operation Eyesight International.

After putting these ornaments on the freshly-cut tree, we wrote a cheque to each organization and let the kids lick the stamps and seal the envelopes. Then we all marched down the block to the mailbox and each of the children had the opportunity to post one of the gifts. This became an annual ritual, as our family commemorated the season of giving by sharing some of our good fortune with others.

LESSONS LEARNED

In time, we started involving the kids in choosing what charities we would support. We started by giving each of them responsibility to allocate $500 or $1,000 among a list of 20 charities. We then held a group discussion to finalize our decisions. Years later, our youngest daughter, Stephanie, led this part of our meeting. It was very satisfying to see our 16-year-old "baby" chairing this part of the get-together and recording our donations on a flip chart.

As a result of these efforts, our kids have not only learned about charitable giving but also about leadership and group decision-making. In addition, they have learned that their voices matter and that they can make a difference in other people's lives.

Generally speaking, family philanthropy is a wonderful arena within which families can develop many skills. Governance and financial literacy are two good examples. In addition, families can learn about group decision-making and how to constructively deal with disagreements.

I can't imagine a safer or more productive way for a family to learn how to collaborate than having them wrestle with whether or not to donate funds to cancer research or to a children's hospital. Through discussions like this, families will develop the capacity to discuss the "undiscussable," and these skills are essential if a family will also be co-owning assets together in the future.

Conversations regarding charitable giving may still be very challenging, but it will be much better for a family to develop these skills through discussions regarding what they will give instead of what they will get. As an added benefit, family members may be able to think more about what they are responsible for rather than what they are entitled to.

Family philanthropy also provides an opportunity to include some members of the family who may otherwise feel left out, perhaps because they are not directly involved in the family business. By being inclusive and sharing leadership responsibilities, charitable giving activities when thoughtfully undertaken can help foster unity and goodwill in the family.

THE RIPPLE EFFECT

Our daughter Christy needed to take out her first mortgage when she purchased her first two-bedroom apartment. She carefully planned her budget to confirm what she could afford. I was thrilled when she volunteered that she could afford to pay the mortgage and still donate $275 a month to charity, including sponsoring a child in Africa. As a young woman earning a modest wage as a fitness trainer, she was joyfully giving away $3,300 per year. This amount, while modest, is over three times the average annual charitable giving per household in America.[88]

A BILLIONAIRE'S EXAMPLE

While I was at university, I met Jimmy Pattison, one of Canada's most celebrated billionaires, while he socialized at a Christmas party in my parents' home. He and my dad nostalgically reminisced about their earlier days, when they didn't have much money. When my dad explained how he had always set aside the first 10% of his earnings to give to the church, Jimmy shared that he had done the same. That evening he also recounted how difficult it had been for him to set aside $12.50 per month for giving when he was only earning $125 per month. However, he said that establishing this pattern early had helped him to maintain the discipline of tithing throughout his whole life.

If you automatically transfer 10% of your income into a separate account each month, charitable giving becomes almost painless.

As a result of overhearing that conversation, I went to the bank and set up a separate account for tithing. From that day on, I have had an automatic transfer made each month from my main bank account into my tithing account. The transfer is equivalent to 10% of my actual or estimated earnings for that period. Perhaps I should have done much more, but at least I have been consistent over the years.

WE ARE ALL RICHER THAN WE THINK

In 2009, an acquaintance shared with me something that radically altered my perspective. Consider the following stunning statistics:

[88.] The average American household contributes approximately $1,000 per year to charity, according to Arthur C. Brooks, "A Nation of Givers," *The American: The Online Magazine of the American Enterprise Institute* (March/April 2008), http://www.american.com/archive/2008/march-april-magazine-contents/a-nation-of-givers/article_print.

- Anyone earning $25,000/year is in the top 10% in the world in annual income.[89]
- An individual with an after-tax income of just $35,000 qualifies in the top 1% in the world.[90]

My friend then explained that he had been a career missionary, working overseas for 20 years before retiring to Vancouver and buying a small home. As a result of inflationary increases in real estate values, he now has $400,000 in equity in his home. He advised that this qualified him for the top 1% in the world in net worth! As astonishing as it sounds, a career missionary, who had never owned or managed a business or bought or sold stocks, and who had never had a high-paying job, is now amongst the world's financial elite.

Given his understanding of the global economic picture and that he is amongst the top 1% in the world in terms of wealth, he told me that it is not logical for him to say that he cannot afford to give to others who are less fortunate. So often, we think we would like to give to help others, if only we had enough for ourselves. If you are reading these pages, I am confident that you are likely in the top 10%, if not in the top 1%, in the world in terms of wealth. If you and I cannot afford to give to others, who can?

If your net worth is $400,000 you are in the top 1% of the world in wealth.

GIVING A LARGER PERCENTAGE

One of my closest friends has a generous heart and has been tithing for years. When he turned 50, he decided to increase this to 11% of his income. By increasing his giving by 1% each year his goal is to be giving away 20% of his income by the time he turns 60.

Inspired by his example, my wife, Alison, and I decided that we would like to gradually increase our giving during our 50s as well. When we asked our financial planner to do some long-term projections to determine the impact of doing this, we were pleasantly surprised. Aided by the tax deductibility of charitable giving in Canada, we were happy to discover that there would be virtually no change to our net worth if we gradually increased our giving by 1% per year over the next decade.

[89] Branko Milanovic, "True World Income Distribution, 1988 and 1993: First Calculations Based on Household Surveys Alone," *Economic Journal* 112 (2002), 30.
[90] Annalyn Censky, "Americans Make Up Half of the World's Richest 1%," *CNN Money* (New York, 2012), http://money.cnn.com/2012/01/04/news/economy/world_richest/index.htm.

Henry Parsons Crowell, the founder of Quaker Oats, did much more than this. Shortly after he started the now famous food company, he prayed and asked God to bless his business. In return, he pledged 90% of what he earned to charity. God must have been listening! Over time, Quaker Oats became an extraordinarily successful enterprise. As a result, Mr. Crowell became a wonderful benefactor who helped many organizations, particularly those in the Chicago area.

I am inspired by him, as I have been by the following individuals I am proud to have known:

- A real estate executive whose goal is to give away $1 million during his lifetime
- An immigrant, whose business success enabled him, during his retirement, to donate $10 million per year
- A life insurance professional whose ambition is to help structure his client's affairs so that cumulatively he will be able to facilitate a total of $100 million worth of donations during his career

> *Set a goal to give away $1 million, $10 million or $100 million.*

- A family business that marked its 100th anniversary by donating $100 million to a charitable foundation that is now administered by members of the family's third generation

CHARITABLE GIVING AS ADULTS

In 1988, Dad invited my siblings and me to sit on the board of the family foundation that he and Mom had established. We initially considered including our spouses in the meetings but then decided to start with just the six of us. We reasoned that we already had enough relational challenges to overcome, without prematurely adding additional family members.

Mom recommended that we adopt the name "The Larkspur Foundation," using the name of one of her favourite flowers. Dad was not that keen on the idea, but as siblings we reasoned that he had been able to get his own way in the business for almost five decades, so surely Mom could have her preference on this one. This was the first decision we had to make as a foundation board. We had trouble convincing Dad of this, but eventually we persuaded him by reminding him that it was "Mom's turn" to have her preference.

When it came to making donation decisions, we found it difficult to reach agreement because we had different values and priorities.

SHARING AUTHORITY BETWEEN GENERATIONS

For example, one day Dad indicated that he wanted to make a sizeable gift to The Salvation Army. In contrast, my brother, Chuck, wanted to target the funds to support music and the arts. The discussion at the board table soon became tense. Trying to assist, my sister Helen pointed out that the money was really Dad's anyway, so he should do whatever he wanted with it. However, Chuck responded by questioning "If Dad is going to do whatever he wants with the money, then why were we invited to the meeting?" The discussion was difficult because there was a legitimate question of who had the power and authority to make decisions. All six of us were board members. Did Mom and Dad still have the authority or not?

For simplicity, and to avoid arguments like this, some families resolve to let Dad and Mom make virtually all charitable decisions until they die. Then, after their parents are gone, the kids assume responsibility for all charitable decisions. This way of transitioning decision-making authority is illustrated in the attached diagram. It is certainly simple, but it also creates a very abrupt transition. (See figure 9.)

Figure 9. Abrupt Transition of Authority and Responsibility

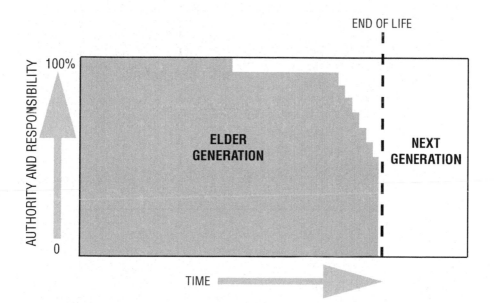

INCREMENTAL TRANSITION OF POWER AND AUTHORITY

One option we considered for our foundation was an incremental transition of power and authority. With this plan, the four of us siblings would be granted authority to determine a portion of the annual donations budget. Initially, we considered each having jurisdiction over 5% of the annual budget, for a total of 20% of our giving. This would have left Mom and Dad with responsibility for 80%. However, after discussing this as a family it was agreed that each sibling would assume responsibility for 12.5% of the annual charitable giving for a total of 50% among the four siblings. We did this mostly because Mom and Dad were, by this time, in their mid-70s, and they wanted us to be more involved in the affairs of the foundation. Subsequently, when Mom and Dad died, we (their children) assumed responsibility for 100% of the foundations activities. In hindsight, had we been able to do more planning in advance, we might have had a more gradual transition of authority and responsibility, perhaps in several increments.

Figure10. Incremental Transition of Authority and Responsibility

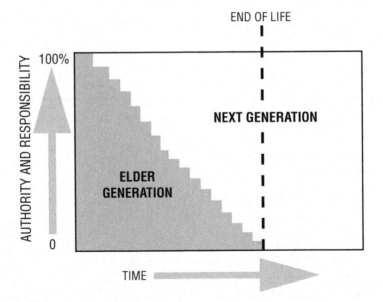

SHARING POWER AND AUTHORITY:

The transition of authority from one generation to another is likely to be smoother and more effective if done gradually. In addition, it is possible to simultaneously pursue a strategy of sharing power (as illustrated by figure 11). This approach provides for a partial transition of authority while at the same time some elements of decision-making are shared. In practice, this requires both generations to listen to one another to either compromise or collaborate. To achieve this, the elder generation will need to voluntarily relinquish some authority to the next generation. This approach is what I call the "messy middle."

Figure 11. Shared Authority and Responsibility, including the Messy Middle

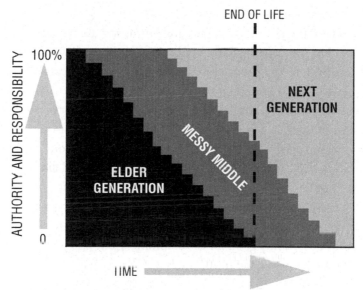

I recommend that families embrace this "messy" zone so that they can learn the art of compromise, develop their ability to share power and learn to really listen empathetically to one another. Philanthropy is an ideal environment to explore this kind of joint decision-making and the sharing of power. This is because the dollars involved are typically less than those involved in the business, and the decisions involved do not affect careers or lifestyles of those involved. By engaging in charitable giving activities together, families can develop the essential skills of compromise and collaboration.

MAKING A DIFFERENCE

In addition, families who engage in philanthropy together have an opportunity to make a difference in the world by using their financial resources to help others. Joan

Charitable giving as a family provides a venue for learning the skills necessary for collaborating in business.

215

Kroc, widow of McDonald's Corp. founder Ray A. Kroc, had a significant challenge when deciding how to wisely distribute the vast fortune that her husband had left her. After careful consideration, she elected to donate $1 billion to The Salvation Army. At the time, this was the largest charitable gift in history. She chose The Salvation Army because of the work that they were doing in inner-city communities, and she was confident that they would be good stewards of the money. Her decision would have been endorsed by management guru Peter Drucker, who once observed that The Salvation Army is one of the most efficient organizations in the history of the world.

Dick Meyers, the president of our family firm, was also an advocate of charitable giving. He was a particularly big fan of The United Way, as an effective way of giving back to the community within which we had earned our success. Because The United Way supports such a broad range of charities, including health, education and a variety of other causes, it is easy for everyone to get on board and support their efforts. In our business, we also discovered that The United Way campaign was a wonderfully unifying time for our staff each year. The posters, guest speakers and promotional activities created almost a pep rally atmosphere. Adding to the momentum, most of our senior executives and board members donated personally and many of our management team gave of their time to canvass other companies for contributions. Campaigning for The United Way proved to be not only good for the community but also good for morale. In fact, you could say it was good for business.

THINKING BEYOND OURSELVES

In order to think philanthropically, an individual must think beyond himself or herself. This begins with a person's attitude. Obviously, some people give away money primarily for the tax relief that it affords, while others do it for the prestige that can come through making a large public gift. These are legitimate motivations, but the most important reason for giving is to help those in need.

As he neared the end of his life, a former client of mine had accumulated a very substantial fortune and definitely had more than he needed. Yet he had no plan for the vast resources he had amassed. There was also more money than his children or grandchildren could ever need. As a result, he began to worry about leaving them too much. What would he do with all of the money? In the end, he decided to make a modest gesture towards charity. He left the bulk of the estate for the benefit of his great grandchildren and beyond. In contrast, a good friend of mine has chosen to emphasize charitable work, and so his estate plan specifies that two dollars will go to charity for every dollar that goes to his children.

Obviously, how much anyone gives to charity is a personal decision. There are no right answers regarding what percentage should be given to heirs or how much should go to charity. However, for most people the pendulum could swing a long way in the opposite direction before they would be giving away too much. Locally and internationally, there are many people in need. Unfortunately, those who own and run family companies are sometimes guilty of overindulging their families and neglecting the rest of the world. Are these families blind, or are they just not thinking? Perhaps it is a little of both.

> *When we give to charity, we not only help those we don't know, we also help those we love the most, our children.*

Most family business owners can afford to shift priorities substantially. By deciding to give more to charity, businesses can help to make the world a better place. As an added benefit, fewer taxes will be paid, and families will not need to worry quite as much about their offspring being spoiled by the money that is left to them.

REASONS TO GIVE MONEY AWAY

When a family business is successful, its owners will be able to start accumulating wealth, which may be saved for retirement or their offspring. In addition, they will be able to purchase new cars and larger homes. They will also be able to provide quality education for the next generation and trips around the world. Some may even want to begin collecting art. Unfortunately, for most, all of these priorities seem to come before philanthropy. As a result, most family businesses can afford to move charitable giving higher up on their priority list.

In my associations in the business community, the main reasons that people tend to be involved in philanthropy are:

- To defer tax
- To diminish their guilt over having too much
- Because a friend twists their arm
- To help a cause that has been of personal benefit (for example, a recovering alcoholic giving to AA, or a cancer survivor giving to cancer research)

These reasons are not wrong. However, there are other reasons for giving to charity.

> *Our assets shouldn't all be simply given to our children.*

One reason is so that we do not destroy or corrode the character of our children. All too often, entrepreneurs unwittingly overindulge their children and swamp them with capital. This simply serves to retard their growth as human beings and to blunt their initiative in life. In essence, the financial capital accumulated by the elder generation can end up eroding the human and social capital in the family. By giving to charity, we can help those whom we may never meet, but in addition, we may also indirectly help those who are closest to us, our children.

When I published my first book, my wife, Alison, suggested that all proceeds of sales be donated to Barnabas Family Ministries (an organization dedicated to the preservation of healthy families). Similarly, other authors have chosen to give all their royalties away, as a means of curbing their own appetites and at the same time helping others. A great example of this is Rick Warren, whose best-selling book *The Purpose Driven Life* has touched millions. One hundred percent of the book royalties have been given away to charity.

MONEY IS NEUTRAL

In their excellent book *Financially Intelligent Parent*, John and Eileen Gallo assert that money is neutral; in other words, it is neither good nor bad on its own accord. Rather, what a person chooses to do with it can be good or bad, and how someone thinks about it may be wise or unwise.[91] A family business owner can choose to hoard money like Scrooge or share it with the Tiny Tims of this world. Therefore, money is a tool, which can be used for noble or ignoble purposes. It can also be spent on lifestyle, given to our children or spent to bless others. Those who have been fortunate enough to create or inherit wealth will recognize that it provides a great opportunity to not only help their children but also help others. Those who have enough for the needs of their family can afford to think beyond themselves and should encourage their children to do the same.

GIVING IS AN ATTITUDE TOWARDS LIFE WORTH CULTIVATING

A friend of mine has extended the principle of giving away a tenth of her income to donating a tenth of her other resources as well. This includes her time

---

[91.] John Gallo and Eileen Gallo, *The Financially Intelligent Parent: 8 Steps to Raising Successful, Generous, Responsible Children* (New York: New American Library/Penguin Group, 2005).

and skills. She tries to give at least 10% of her time, and often gives much more, to helping others in concrete ways. As she develops skills in the area of marketing and design, she also "tithes" her skills by giving pro bono help to a local charity. She has even applied this principle to include 10% of her social relationships by befriending those who are socially disadvantaged or ostracized. This change in lifestyle was at first calculated but over the years has become customary. For example, over lunch, she was telling a friend about her "discovery" of the health benefits of vitamin E oil and how it has improved her skin and hair. Realizing the bottle had about 15% remaining, she handed it to her friend and said, "Give it a try." This may be a trivial example, but it clearly demonstrates the mindset she has cultivated. This approach to life has made "charitable giving" a natural, ongoing element of her *daily* life, rather than a one-time, isolated act at year-end.

CONCLUSION

For many years, Bono, the lead singer of U2, has challenged wealthy nations to annually set aside approximately 1% of their gross national product to bring an end to world hunger.[92] Around the world, many young people wear white armbands as a symbol of their solidarity with this cause. Unfortunately, the self-centredness and self-indulgence of the developed world have resulted in very few countries signing up to meet his challenge.

However, those of us who are privileged to be a part of business families can play an important role in making a difference in the world. We have the capacity to do an enormous amount to improve our neighbourhoods, our countries and our world. As Bono has encouraged the developed countries, I would like to encourage all family business owners to become active philanthropically and to teach the next generation to do the same. For some of us, this can be done by establishing tax-effective charitable foundations. We can also use life insurance structures and other mechanisms to extend our capacity to help others.

Bill Gates has pledged to give billions to charity,[93] and Warren Buffett has al-

---

[92] "The specific goal for G8 countries like Canada is to invoke a commitment of 0.7% of their GNP towards foreign aid." (Miriam Booy, Heidi Gulbrandsen, Elizabeth Kim and Mark Witten, "Bono as a Person of Faith" (Langley: Trinity Western University, 2005), http://www.david-kilgour.com/mp/Bono%20as%20Person%20of%20Faith.htm#_edn-ref47.)

[93] Sophie Borland, "Bill Gates Pledges to Leave His £30billion Fortune to Charity... Rather than His Children" (Mountain View: MailOnline, 2008), http://www.dailymail.co.uk/news/article-1027878/Bill-Gates-pledges-58-billion-fortune-charity--children.html.

ready given away $42 billion.[94] These are two of the most intelligent and success-ful business executives the world has ever seen. They might be on to something. Prudent parents would be wise to consider following their example.

---

[94]. "Warren Buffett Donated $42 Million In Stock To Mystery Charities" (Huff Poste Impact Canada, 2012), http://www.huffingtonpost.com/2012/01/26/warren-buffett-42-million_n_1234571.html.

CHAPTER 18

DISCOVERING MY LIFE'S CALLING

TITANS OF HISTORY

Our calling in life may best be thought of as our destiny. Before we were born, our heritage, our unique place in history and our DNA were all predetermined, and they all provide a context for our calling. For example, Nelson Mandela's calling was undoubtedly to play a leadership role in the ending of apartheid in South Africa. Similarly, Sir Winston Churchill's calling was to champion the cause of freedom against the threat of Nazi Germany. Their unique gifts and talents intersected with a moment in time, and they fulfilled their heroic destinies.

Two similarly extraordinary leaders, who like Mandela and Churchill have inspired me, are William Wilberforce and Alexander Solzhenitsyn. Both men experienced an irresistible calling.

William Wilberforce spent most of his life working to bring an end to the slave trade in England. He describes his sense of calling by saying "God Almighty has set before me two great objects; the suppression of the slave trade and the reformation of his manners."[95] As a young man, he felt the call of God to make a difference in the world, and he did just that. In fact, he devoted almost 50 years to his campaign to rid Britain of the scourge of slavery. Just before his death, a bill was passed that officially outlawed the slave trade. He sensed a calling, and his response changed his life, as well as his country and our world.

[95.] William Wilberforce, "Journal, Sunday, October 28, 1787" (London: Trinity Forum Curriculum).

Aleksandr Solzhenitsyn, winner of the Nobel Peace Prize, felt compelled to speak for those who had suffered and died in the Russian Gulag. In his book *The Oak and the Calf: Sketches of Literary Life in the Soviet Union*, he describes the cost of this call. "I could have enjoyed myself so much, breathing the fresh air, resting, stretching my cramped limbs, but my duty to the dead permitted no such self-indulgence. They are dead. You are alive: Do your duty. The world must know *all about it!*"[96] When he was released from prison and living in the USA, he devoted 18 hours per day to writing down what had happened in his homeland under the oppressive Communist government's rule. So influential were his writings that some would later argue that he was perhaps the single most influential person in the ultimate collapse of the Communist regime in Russia. He sensed a call from God to speak for those who could not, and he responded. His words changed the future.

WHAT IS YOUR CALLING?

Not many of us will have the opportunity to radically change the face of a nation or have a prominent role on the world stage. However, each of has been born into a unique place and time in history, and we each have a family and a heritage that were given to us at birth. Our DNA is unique, and our skills and abilities are ours alone. Our education, our nationality and our upbringing all combine to make us one of a kind. This complex blend of inputs creates for each of us a unique set of opportunities. If we find what we are ideally suited to do, we may be said to have discovered our calling.

From age ten, when Dad first spoke to me about one day becoming president of our family company, I thought my path was more or less set. However, when Alison and I got married and went on our honeymoon to Hawaii, we discussed what I should do upon graduation. I had one year left before I would finish my degree, and we

> *If we find what we are "ideally suited to do," we probably have discovered our calling.*

prayed that God would make it clear if I should join the family firm. The very next morning, Uncle Bob phoned, stating, "I would like you to come and work for our family company for the summer, and then, when you graduate, join the business full-time." Couldn't be clearer, could it? I had asked for a sign and surrendered to God's will. Then my uncle phoned. Working in our family business seemed to be my calling.

---

[96] Aleksandr Isaevich Solzhenitsyn, *The Oak and the Calf: Sketches of Literary Life in The Soviet Union* (New York: Harper & Row, 1980), 219.

THE TROUBLE BEGINS

During my final term at university, we were given assignments in groups of three. We were asked to identify a company that we could interview to determine a problem and then develop a recommended solution. Key to the process was digging deep to find the root problem before developing alternatives or recommendations. Our group chose BC Millwork Products as the company we were going to examine. It was one of the smallest operating subsidiaries of The Bentall Group. From a distance, it seemed that this business was not achieving its potential. As we interviewed people from the firm, it became apparent that this might be due to a lack of marketing expertise. However, as we looked deeper still, there were other problems, including a lack of corporate direction and a lack of management depth. Over time, we drafted several different problem definitions, each leading us to a deeper understanding of the company. After 13 separate problem definitions, we settled on what we felt was the root problem. We concluded, without much knowledge of the company or its leadership, that the main problem was Uncle Bob, who was, at the time, president of the parent company. We got an A on our paper, but when I graduated from business school, I had developed a very poor opinion of Uncle Bob. As naive undergrads, we assumed that we knew better than my uncle, who was an experienced veteran of 30 years in business.

Upon graduation, I was given a full-time position in our millwork division and then over the next ten years I worked in Toronto, Calgary, Winnipeg and Orange County, California, before returning to Vancouver in 1986. As time passed, I found it very difficult to get along with Uncle Bob. This is mostly because I was critical of his leadership and had mistakenly assumed that it was my duty to point out his imperfections. As just one of 11 cousins, my ownership stake in the company was less than 10%, yet somehow I wrongly believed that being an owner gave me the right to recklessly criticize my uncle and agitate for change.

To make matters worse, one of our senior executives confidentially told me that he believed that Uncle Bob was an impediment to our company's progress, and he recommended we seek to find him work elsewhere. In other words, this manager wanted to have Bob removed from the company. I consulted my dad and asked for his help in dealing with the situation. I will never forget his response. As we walked across the plaza between Bentall Two and Bentall Three office towers in downtown Vancouver, my dad said, "This company can go to hell in a handbasket, but I will never fight against my brothers!" This statement was particularly forceful, in that I had never before heard my dad swear, not even once, during my first 27 years of life. Clearly, he wanted me to know he would *never* take up arms against his brothers. (In later years, he proved to be a man of his word, for he refused to battle them in spite of all the challenging things that would eventually come his way.)

When I asked Dad what he thought I should do with my concerns, he encouraged me to speak up about them. He invited me to get them out in the open so we could deal with them. Dad was not a political person, and although he was personally reluctant to create controversy, he believed that if I had a problem, there was nothing we couldn't talk through.

About the same time, we had a respected management consultant interview all our senior managers. His goal was to assist my dad and uncle in determining how to work together more collaboratively. As a result of his intervention, our VP of finance left the company and a temporary truce was established. However, the consultant noted that the company was 75 years old and needed to adapt if it was going to continue to prosper. In addition, he noted that we needed a "defecation disturber" to shake things up a bit. From what he had heard, I was playing this role, as a catalyst for innovation and change. He believed that it was important for me to "keep at it" in this regard. I now realize that at that stage in my career, I should have been primarily in a learning mode. I should have been focused on learning how to be a good follower, and I should have been willing to submit to my uncle's authority. Instead, armed with my critical mind, critical spirit and freshly-minted business degree and encouraged by our consultant, I assumed that I was the answer to all our company's problems.

> *Right beside a critical mind lived a critical spirit.*

Without realizing the chaos I was creating, I had been radicalized into a rabid, insubordinate iconoclast. Nothing was sacred for me, and I began charging about the company, tilting at windmills.

No wonder my uncle began building a file documenting all the trouble I was causing. Eventually he would use this information to buttress the decision to terminate my employment. Sadly, this happened just when it appeared that I was on the verge of being able to take a senior vice president's role and become a legitimate candidate to succeed him as the company president. In hindsight, I now see that

> *I forfeited my opportunity to lead largely because of my insubordination and my critical spirit.*

224

I forfeited my chance to lead because of my critical spirit. You could say that I brought the house of cards down on myself. Subsequently I got a second chance, and for eight years I was privileged to serve as the president of Dominion Construction. However, when this too came to an abrupt end, I found myself asking what I was supposed to do with the rest my life.

A VISIT TO THE ABBEY

As I was wrestling with this, my two best friends, Carson Pue and Bob Kuhn, invited me on a 24-hour prayer retreat at a remote monastery in Mission, BC. I was intrigued and wanted to join them, but I wondered what would we do for 24 hours. Uncertain and sceptical, I decided to join them. We walked and we talked; we napped and we ate; we read and we wrote in our journals. We also prayed that God would make it clear what He wanted for each of us in our lives.

It was during this memorable experience that I decided to sell my shares in our family construction company. However, this was simply a decision to stop doing what I had previously thought I would spend the rest of my life doing. It didn't clarify what I should do in the future. At the abbey, I essentially decided to get off the path that I had been on, even though I didn't know what I was going to do next. I had prayed, but hadn't heard a call from God, at least not yet.

LOSING MY IDENTITY

Shortly after that experience, I met with my brother-in-law to advise him that I wanted to sell my shares in the company to him and my sister Mary. I assumed that he would want to choose someone else to run the company, given that I was no longer going to be an owner. Although he initially asked me to stay, I told Phil that I was willing to leave the business at any time if he wanted to bring in someone new. After a few months, I was asked to step down as president. My career with Dominion was over.

Phil and I met on a Saturday afternoon, and I went to clean out my office later that night. My secretary came downtown to help me, as did my wife, Alison, and her brother, Dean. We took pictures off the wall and packed up my personal belongings. We filled several cardboard boxes with books and knickknacks off the shelves. It was deathly quiet and a bit eerie, almost surreal.

In downtown Vancouver, there are not a lot of people in office buildings late on a Saturday night. Even the commercial cleaners had long since finished their work and locked up for the night. I wanted to cry but for some reason couldn't.

I had come to the end of the line. Granddad was president of Dominion for 40 years. Dad had worked there for 50 years. I had only made it for 20.

The next day was Sunday. In the morning, as I walked up the stone steps outside First Baptist Church, I came face to face with a heritage plaque on the wall, just to the left of the main entrance. It noted my grandfather's role in helping to rebuild the historic building after a major fire decades earlier. It also mentioned that Dominion Construction, our family company, had performed the work. On previous Sundays, I barely noticed the plaque. However, when I occasionally noted it, the words provided a link between my history and the origins of our church and our family. Now I felt like I had been cut off from my roots. Not just professionally, but personally as well. That morning, as I stood up to sing a hymn and to bring worship to God, I no longer knew who I was. It felt like I was no longer my grandfather's progeny, no longer a part of our family. It felt strangely like half of my face had been erased. Without my title, who was I?

In retrospect, I am grateful for these experiences, because they eventually led me to discover what I believe is my true calling. Out of this crucible of pain has emerged a new career that is more fulfilling and also better suited to my talents and skills. The hurt that I had endured may have come at least, in part, because I had never seriously considered any career other than with our family business.

WHAT SHOULD I DO NEXT?

After leaving Dominion, I had no idea what I was going to do next. So I decided to take a one year sabbatical, during which I planned to complete a book I was writing. I also wanted to devote more time to my pursuit of a national water-ski championship. It took several years, but eventually both of these goals were achieved. It was a privilege and a great opportunity for me to be able to pursue these two important lifelong dreams. The process was stimulating and revitalizing.

However, I had barely launched my sabbatical when I was induced to take on a new and exciting role. Much to my surprise, I was asked to head up the venue planning for the Vancouver/Whistler bid to host the 2010 Olympics. I was very happy to be able to engage in such a challenging project, which utilized my skills and experience. I was thrilled and privileged to be an integral part of such a landmark success.

After the domestic bid was successful, the bid committee needed a CEO to lead the international bid. I applied for the job and was one of six candidates interviewed. When someone else was selected, I was crushed. The way I saw things, I had now failed in my attempt to run The Bentall Group, then Dominion Construction and now the Olympic bid. Like a batter who had swung and missed for the third time, I felt like a loser.

MAYBE YOU SHOULD BE A TEACHER

Around this time, my sister Mary said to me, "David, now you can do what God always intended you to do with your life." I asked her, "What do you think that is?" And she replied, "Maybe you should be a teacher."

By way of background, you should know that both my sister and my wife had been elementary school teachers. So when I heard my sister's words, I misinterpreted her to be saying "You wanted to run Bentall, then Dominion and then the Olympic bid; none of those worked out. You're hopeless as an executive. So instead you should become an elementary school teacher."

This is not what she said, but this is how I internalized her comments. I was so insulted by what I "heard" that I was actually "miffed" for several years. I thought it was presumptuous of Mary to think that she knew what God had in mind for me, and as someone with more than 20 years of management experience, I thought I was too important to "just be a teacher." For a long time I brooded over her comments. I was not only offended; I was hurt.

Later that year, I was at a water-skiing tournament in Toronto. My back was sore, and so I arranged for a massage. The therapist asked me what I did for a living. When I explained the potpourri of things I had been doing since the Olympic bid ended, he startled me with the words "I knew you were a teacher!" He then observed, "You haven't stopped teaching me since you lay down." I was stunned. Why would both my little sister and a massage therapist from Toronto have come to the same conclusion?

> *Long before I recognized it, others knew that I should become a teacher.*

A couple of months later, I was down in California at another water-ski tournament, when a skier approached me. He explained that he was having problems with his water ski. He then asked me to help with the adjustments to his fin. I didn't know this athlete very well, and I was not that interested in helping him. However, when he came up and asked for my assistance, I did the best I could to help him out. Standing in the sun, all of us were getting thirsty, and one of the other guys asked if a couple of us could go and buy some water for the group. Driving to the convenience store, a brother of one of the skiers said to me, "So what do you do for a living?" I didn't want to talk about it, so I asked what he did. I found out that he was a teacher. Curious, I asked him, "Why would any-body want to be a teacher?" He said, "I love being a teacher because of the op-portunities I get to influence people's lives. Why do you want to know?" That's when I confessed to him that my sister had said I should be a teacher and that I wasn't buying it.

He then explained how he had watched me helping the other skier on the beach with his fin. He had been so inspired that he said, "On Monday morning when I go back into my high school classroom in LA, I want to engage with my students with the same kind of passion you displayed when you engaged with that guy on the beach."

I was surprised! Everyone was suggesting that I should be a teacher. I was getting the message, and for the first time I allowed myself to accept the idea that perhaps God was sending me a message. Maybe my calling was to teach.

MY SISTER MARY WAS RIGHT

Since that day, the majority of my time has been devoted to teaching and advising others regarding the dynamics of family business. In addition, several things have happened to confirm to me that my little sister was right. Consider the following opportunities that have come my way that utilize my skills and abilities as a teacher:

- The UBC invited me to teach an undergrad course on family business suc-cession each year.
- The Business Family Centre retains me several times every year to teach weekend workshops for families in business.[97]
- The Directors Education Program regularly asks me to co-instruct a gov-ernance workshop for them with Dr. Nancy Langton.[98]
- The UBC Sauder Business School employed me to annually teach an MBA course entitled "Working in the Family Business."
- Several times each year, I have been invited to teach seminars for profes-sional advisors as part of the Family Advisors Program at UBC.[99]
- As an advisor, I have been engaged by over 55 different families to assist them with their succession planning.
- As an executive life coach, I regularly work with numerous business leaders, mentoring and supporting them in their careers.

[97.] The Roadmap Course is usually taught in partnership with Wendy Sage-Hayward.

[98.] Dr. Langton is a widely published author and a member of the faculty at the Sauder Business School at UBC.

[99.] I co-facilitate these seminars with Ruth Steverlynck.

With all this happening to me, I now see the wisdom of my sister's perspective. Every day I have the honour of being involved in other people's lives, helping them and teaching them. I am so grateful for the opportunity I have to serve others in this way.

The transition from corporate executive to teacher has taken me several years. However, I must acknowledge that I am much more fulfilled now than I ever was at Dominion. To be honest, I am a bit sad that our family company just celebrated its 100th anniversary and none of our family was involved in any way. However, I would not trade my life today for the life I had before as an executive in a construction company. I recognize that I have now found my life calling, or should I say, my calling has found me.

A couple of years ago, our son sent me an email with his observations on my new website. He said, "It's cool that you're doing such a unique and necessary job" (referring to my coaching, teaching and speaking). He then went on to say, "It seems like you're more in your element now than you were at Dominion. Not that you didn't do a good job there. But maybe this is your calling and the 20 years before were just leading up to it."

I think Jon got it right. I also think my sister Mary got it right. My calling is to be a teacher, and the years that I spent at Dominion were primarily just to prepare me for the opportunities that I now have before me.

Just like there are no two snowflakes alike and no two fingerprints alike, each and every human being is a unique and special creation. Some of us are gifted musically and others athletically. Some people are gifted relationally, and some are more naturally gifted in business. We may be able to hone our God-given gifts through education and experience, but at birth we all have unique and special attributes that make us who we are.

Rather than simply following in the footsteps of generations that have gone before, we owe it to ourselves to explore our own uniqueness. For some, this may lead to a career in the family business. However, for some their calling may be quite different.

When we are gifted in a special way, this is an indication of what our destiny may be. If we are tall, we ought to take advantage of our height. If we have a studious mind, we ought to be studying something. In other words, our DNA gives us clues as to what our creator intended for us to do with our lives. As a result, we should all pay attention to our uniqueness, and then we will be more likely to discover our life calling.

The most important thing is to build our lives around our natural gifts and talents, and not to build our lives around the business that may be associated with our family.

CONCLUSION

For years, I personally resisted the fact that I had been uniquely gifted to teach. I had other plans for my life and other dreams. I wanted to be a leader and aspired to have the command of a company. I "looked down" on teachers and didn't value them the same way I valued business executives. Because I was proud and judgmental, I regarded myself as too important to simply be a teacher.

Our DNA gives us a clue as to what our Creator intended for us to do with our lives.

As a result, it took humility to look in the mirror to see myself accurately, and it took courage to listen to those around me who were encouraging me to teach. Thankfully, they were able to discern the unique and special way I have been put together and they were able to help me uncover my life's calling. When I finally accepted my uniqueness and teaching gifts, I was able to discover an amazing and gratifying career.

CHAPTER 19

LEAVING A LEGACY

When I was young boy, just 12 years old, I was induced to make my first charitable donation when a diminutive man by the name of Dr. Ben Gullison explained how a mere $20 could give to another human being the priceless gift of sight. How could I not help? Every year since, for the past 30 years, I have supported his work through the organization he created, Operation Eyesight International.[100]

Several years ago, when I attended the memorial service for this remarkable man, I was astonished to learn that as a result of his efforts over 500,000 people had been given the gift of sight. "Dr. Ben," as he was affectionately known, was hardly a fundraiser, yet during his lifetime his leadership had resulted in over $50 million dollars in donations for this work. Dr. Gullison died many years ago, but the work he started is still thriving. His name will forever be associated with the gift of sight for the blind. He was a man who made his life count; he was a man who left a legacy.

THE LEGACY OF THE BENTALL NAME

When Bentall Real Estate merged with Penreal Advisors in the late 1990s, one of the first decisions they had to make was what to name the new combined enterprise. When I spoke to the company's chairman at the time, he said they elected to go with the name Bentall because the reputation of our family

---

[100.] Information about this organization is available at http://www.operationeyesight.ca.

and company were very positive. I believe that Granddad, Dad and Uncle Bob were all instrumental in establishing this enduring legacy. Their heritage is multi-faceted and includes many elements, including, business, community and family components.

A LEGACY OF HOW TO DO BUSINESS

After graduating with his engineering degree, Granddad's first job was as a draftsman in an engineering office. One day, in spite of his best efforts, his supervisor put his hand on young Charles' shoulder and said, "I guess, Son, you just won't do." With those words, my granddad was fired.

He and I never talked about this incident, but my father relayed the story to me. This event had a lasting impact on both my granddad and my dad. As a result of that painful experience, my granddad was always determined to prove that he was "good enough." Consequently, over his extended career, Granddad established a legacy of industriousness and hard work. In short, he became an exemplary "man of industry."

This legacy lives on in the lives of his great-grandchildren. After our son, Jon, spent his first week working on a residential framing crew, I asked his supervisor if he had gotten his money's worth from our teenage boy. His boss told me that he expected a young man with the last name Bentall probably wouldn't know how to work. However, he said that he had never met anyone who could work as hard! I think Granddad would approve.

As a young man, I was hired for several summers by Dominion Construction as a carpenter's helper. One of the first assignments I was given involved being part of a small crew doing repairs at our parents' summer cottage. Near the water's edge, there is a long pier leading to our dock. Underneath the pier, the ocean tides and wave action had eroded one of the footings.

His supervisor said he had never met anyone who could work as hard.

I was instructed to build a small rectangular form so we could pour a new concrete base to support one of the pilings. The surface I was working on was very uneven—partially sand, partially rock, with a gradual slope. I found it difficult to make the form square, even though I worked at it for several hours. At the end of the day, it still looked cockeyed. When my boss took a look at my work he said that the rough form looked "good enough." I protested and asked if he would help me to square it up a bit better. Recognizing how hard I had tried, he said, "Don't worry about it. It's underneath the pier, and no one will ever notice it."

I explained that I still thought we should redo the form. After all, it might have been under the dock, but I knew my dad would see it. In fact, I suspected that the first thing Dad would do when he arrived at the cottage would be to check out the work that I had done. We would have to do it right. My foreman finally agreed, and with his help, I trued up the form to make it square. That weekend, as I had anticipated, my dad carefully inspected our work, and I'm glad we took the extra time to do it correctly.

Like Dad, Granddad was also a stickler for quality. Apparently, he once walked on a job site and noticed one of the crew mixing concrete in a wheelbarrow. Observing that there might not be enough cement in the mixture, he simply opened an extra bag and poured in some more just for good measure. Granddad didn't believe in cutting corners.

As president of Dominion Construction from 1915 to 1955, Granddad didn't believe it was necessary to have formal legal contracts with our clients. If he gave you his word, you could rely on him to follow through, and he expected the same of our customers. Over time, the construction business became more susceptible to litigation, and signed written agreements became ubiquitous. Naturally, our company eventually adopted the industry norms for contractual arrangements. However, it always irked Granddad that we would waste time and money having lawyers document our obligations in a formal contract. As my dad explained, "When Granddad shook your hand and guaranteed to build something for you by a certain date, at an agreed-upon cost, you didn't need a contract to ensure that he would follow through." Unfortunately, in today's world, this brand of integrity is becoming very rare.

Granddad's word was his bond.

My dad knew many people, but he didn't just build a network for business purposes. Instead, he built genuine friendships, and these provided opportunities to serve others. Bill Sauder is a great example. Over the years, he became Dad's good friend and closest business associate. His company, Sauder Industries, was one of the first tenants of The Bentall Centre in the heart of downtown Vancouver. Today, they occupy the 33rd and 34th floors atop Tower Four, with a commanding view of the inner harbour. For many years, Dad and Bill served on the board of TD Bank at the same time, and the two of them would often make the cross-Canada trip to monthly board meetings together.

Bill once commented that my dad was "the best salesman I have ever met." This was a puzzle to me, because Dad had taught me that salespersons were not to be trusted. However, as I pondered this apparent inconsistency, I came to realize that my dad never saw himself as a salesperson. Rather, he saw himself as someone whose primary role was to understand what people wanted and needed. Then he would set about to help them by building or leasing them a project that would satisfy their requirements. No wonder people like Bill Sauder kept coming back to Dad to satisfy their real estate and construction needs. Dad wasn't after a fast deal or a quick buck. Instead, he was looking for genuine relationships and always looking for ways to professionally satisfy the needs of others.

A LEGACY OF PERSONAL CHARACTER

A person of integrity is someone who is incorruptible and honest, someone who firmly adheres to a moral code. These words are an accurate picture of both my dad and my granddad. My dad expected moral behaviour from himself and from everyone in our family. So did Granddad. In fact, Granddad's high moral expectations for his children and grandchildren were perhaps, for some, a bit daunting. However for me, they were inspiring. I viewed his unwavering commitment to integrity as something of a moral compass for my life. I didn't always measure up to his benchmark, but he provided a clear standard by which I could judge all my actions.

THIS CENTRE IS NAMED IN HONOUR OF
CHARLES BENTALL
1882 ~ 1974
A MAN OF INDUSTRY AND INTEGRITY

Charles Bentall reflecting pool, Bentall Centre Plaza, Vancouver, December 1977.

The word "integrity" has the same root as the mathematical term, integer (a number that is indivisible). Hence, *Webster's Dictionary* states that integrity is the "quality or state of being complete or undivided." Granddad was like that. His life was not compartmentalized or divided. He was the same honest, God-fearing man on Friday afternoons as he was on a Sunday morning at church. He was a man who honoured commitments, including his marriage vows, for life. He lived an exemplary life, a life of true integrity.

A MAN OF FAITH

At his core, Granddad was a devout, Bible-believing, Christian gentleman. He was never showy or pushy about his faith, but he was a man with firm convictions who trusted God with his whole life. He recognized that the sovereign Lord who created the world was in charge of it still, and he sought to bring his whole life into submission to his understanding of God and how He intended us to live.

When he left England and sailed by boat to Canada, he undoubtedly had both high hopes and great uncertainty regarding the future. Upon his departure, his mother read to him from Psalm 121. In part, it reads,

> I lift up my eyes to the hills–
> where does my help come from?
> My help comes from the LORD,
> the Maker of heaven and earth…
> The LORD will keep you from all harm–
> he will watch over your life;
> the LORD watch over your coming and going
> both now and forevermore.[101]

This psalm became something of a beacon for his life with its truth, illuminating every step he took. More importantly, it reminded him that God superintends all of life and is watching over us every hour of every day. Granddad believed that we don't need to worry about what others think of us; we only need to consider God's opinion. As Oz Guinness puts it, "We only need to satisfy an audience of One."

101. THE HOLY BIBLE, NEW INTERNATIONAL VERSION, NIV. Copyright © 1973, 1978, 1984 by Biblica, Inc.™ Used by permission. All rights reserved worldwide.

Granddad's faith was personal, but it has also had a lasting impact within our family. One of his three boys served as a pastor for his entire working life, and today, two of his grandchildren are involved in full-time ministry. My cousin Rob Bentall together with his wife, Kathy, founded Barnabas Family Ministries over 20 years ago, and they are dedicated to "strengthening and encouraging families." Similarly, another cousin, Laura Nelson, now serves as senior pastor at Olivet Baptist Church. Many other members of the Bentall clan would profess a deep and abiding faith in God. Granddad left us a legacy of faith.

> *"We only need to satisfy an audience of One."*

A LEGACY OF GENEROSITY

Granddad attended the Vancouver chapter of the Kiwanis Club on a weekly basis for decades and continued to do so well into his 80s. He made business contacts through this organization, but at its heart the Kiwanis Club is dedicated to "giving back to the community." That is why Granddad loved the organization so much. He was generous, but he was not philanthropic in order to be admired, or even to be noticed. He genuinely cared about the people in his community and that is why he did what he could do in order to make a difference. He was also a founding member of the Better Business Bureau in Vancouver, again displaying his concern for the community in which he lived.

As Granddad noticed people aging around him, he realized that providing housing for them in their sunset years was a priority that needed to be addressed. As a volunteer, Charles Bentall spearheaded an initiative to create Beulah Gardens. Today this seniors' complex houses over 300 residents on a beautiful campus in East Vancouver, BC.

In the 1920s, a group of church leaders was looking for property where they could establish a conference centre. They found an ideal parcel of land on Keats Island. It was a beautiful forested area with abundant waterfront, just 30 miles from downtown Vancouver. Unfortunately, they couldn't afford the $25,000 required to purchase the 300 acres. Hearing of this need, Granddad organized a small group of business people who each invested $5,000 to buy the property. They then sold 99-year leases for the development of summer cottages and donated all the land for camping purposes. Over the past 80 years, thousands of young people's lives have been impacted positively by Keats Camps.

THE LEGACY OF A LOVING FAMILY

In the summertime while I was growing up, our family spent much time at Keats Island, because Granddad had a summer cottage that overlooked the Pacific Ocean. During his retirement years, he would rock gently in his swivel rocker that afforded him a bird's-eye view of the main dock, as he gazed out his picture window. From this front row seat, he could keep an eye on who was coming and going to the island and vicariously enjoy our generation's activities and water sports.

Whenever I visited Granddad, he would extend his arms to me, as he did to all the grandchildren, offering a warm embrace. We loved his generous affection, and he gave big, strong hugs. However, he also insisted on rubbing his sandpaper-like chin against our cheeks. He had such a coarse beard that even though he shaved daily, he was able to give us a gentle scratch whenever we popped in for a visit. It was his playful way of telling us how much we were loved.

He also encouraged us, as his grandchildren, to be financially prudent. I remember being surprised when it was explained to me that if I saved $90 towards the purchase of a Canada Savings Bond, he would add the last $10 so I could purchase $100 worth. He made the same offer to all 11 of his grandchildren. This generous gesture was more about love than it was about financial planning.

FINISHING WELL

In the book *Healthy at 100*, author John Robbins explores several regions of the world where the life expectancy far exceeds that which we currently anticipate in North America.[102] One could argue that if we simply choose to live wisely and eat healthily, our life expectancy may approach 100 years of age, rather than the 65 years that was commonly anticipated during my granddad's generation. But, what are we going to do with an extra 35 years?

In regions of the world like the island of Okinawa in Japan where there are many centenarians, there is a radically different view of aging. If someone says, "You look old today," it is a compliment. The elders in

> *In Okinawa, Japan, if someone says, "You look old today," it's a compliment.*

this community are generally revered and respected. As I age, one of my goals is to be more respectful of those who are older than me and more attentive to their

---

[102] John Robbins, *Healthy at 100: The Scientifically Proven Secrets of the World's Healthiest and Longest-Lived Peoples* (New York: Ballantine Books, 2006).

wisdom and knowledge. At the same time, I also want to be generous by sharing any insights that I may have accumulated along the way.

Sadly, in North America we tend to discard our elders, letting them wither away in old folks' homes, or, if they are fortunate, they may move south where they can spend their golden years golfing. Thankfully, as my dad aged we were able to successfully remain involved in his life, and vice versa.

When my sisters and I bought Dominion Construction, Dad was in his mid-70s. Rather than isolating him from our business affairs, we invited him to chair our board of directors, and we established an office for him in our new premises. Although he no longer had day-to-day management responsibilities, we still included him in many meetings and other activities. At the same time, he and Mom acquired a property in Palm Springs, where they spent the months of November, February and March each year. They were not alone there but were surrounded by their extended family and good friends, who would come and visit for one or two weeks at a time. Dad was always eager to return to Vancouver for our board meetings.

I respected my dad a great deal, but I also felt deeply for him. He had endured severe disappointment because of the breakdown in his relationships with his two brothers. I wanted to do something to help ease the pain and to honour him for all he had done for me and the rest of our family. I wondered how I could I assist.

One day, while reflecting on this, I realized that during his career the most important thing for Dad, every day, had been who he was going to have lunch with that day. Whether he was meeting with a past or potential client, the mayor or members of the staff, Dad made the most of every opportunity to meet people during the noon hour. He would learn; he would laugh; he would build relationships. This was done either in our executive dining room at the top of Bentall Three or in the stately environment provided by the legendary Vancouver Club in the heart of the city. As Dad aged, I wanted to help ensure that his lunchtime experiences remained positive.

Consequently, in 1998 I made a personal promise, just between God and me, that I would have lunch with my dad at least two or three times a week for the rest of his life. For almost 10 years I enjoyed the fruit of this private pact. At first, most of our lunches were with Dad's friends and business associates. Over time, as Dad's capacity began to wane, I had the

For 10 years, I was able to honour my dad by having lunch with him at least twice per week.

privilege of introducing him to our new clients and business associates. Dad was held in such high esteem within our community that he was always welcome, regardless of the company or the topic of conversation.

Through this simple gesture and his involvement on our board, Dad was able to quietly offer mentoring advice and support as long as his health permitted. Sometimes he would come and sit for a while in a management meeting, and then he would quietly slip out when he got tired. Regardless, he was always welcome. If I was to prescribe a graceful and gradual exit from a business, I can't think of a much better way of doing things.

Shortly after celebrating his 75th birthday, Dad began to experience some early symptoms of Alzheimer's disease. He survived another nine years, but before the next decade was over, he was gone. When Mom passed away at age 80, my dad was alone, and the confusion and debilitating effects of his disease were relatively well advanced. My wife, Alison, and I, together with our four children, decided to move in and live with Dad. Alison's mom had modelled this for us when she invited her dad to live in her home during his declining years. Perhaps this is why our eldest daughter, Christy, suggested that we move in and help look after Dad. I am thrilled that my loving and servant-hearted wife agreed to the plan.

Near the end, we needed to have round-the-clock nursing care for Dad. This included a team of four, and ultimately we put a hospital bed in his bedroom. With the exception of his last two weeks, Dad was able to stay in his home and gracefully "age in place." I am so glad we were able to do this for Dad, and I believe this was the best decision I ever made in my life. Bob Lee, former chancellor of UBC, stated, in reflecting on our living arrangements, "You would have made a good Chinese boy, David; that's how we do it." I can think of no finer compliment.

Looking to the future, some members of our generation may need to work longer than we might have anticipated just to avoid becoming dependent on the government, our family or others. However, regardless of our financial circumstances, I believe we should aspire to making the last several decades of our life "the mentoring years" rather than "the retirement years."

Across North America, there is an assumption that 65 is the appropriate age for retirement. Some people are fortunate enough to achieve "Freedom 55." Yet, somehow, deep in our psyche, most of us believe that it is our right to live in the lap of luxury once we've achieved retirement age. However, these arbitrary benchmarks are now out of date.

Age 65 as a retirement age can allegedly be traced to post-World War I Germany. At that time, returning war veterans were having difficulty finding work, in part because most of the jobs were held by those who had been too old to join the armed forces. In order to resolve this problem, it was decided that a mandatory retirement age should be created. After examining the actuarial tables, it was determined that the life expectancy of a male in 1919 was 65 years of age. Consequently it was decided that those who were holding a job at this age should be required to step aside to make room for returning soldiers. In other words, if you weren't dead you should retire.

I propose we recover this idea that retirement and death should be linked. In other words, we should seek to remain active and productive until we die, rather than pursuing a life of leisure once we have reached a certain age. The standard approach to retirement can lead to a selfish, self-centred approach to life. It also tends to put off "real living" until one's career is over. By way of contrast, I think we should savour every day as a gift, enjoying each precious day, rather than waiting until we hit a certain age to start living.

Some people might be offended by my bold statement that we should rethink retirement. However, having observed Dad's last ten years, I think he modelled a better way. He was able to visit the office almost every day during his final 10 years of life. He didn't meddle or interfere, but he enjoyed being around and watching while our generation exercised full authority to run the business. Dad was welcomed and honoured during this time instead of being cast aside.

> *Dad retired after 50 years with the company, but he was welcome in the office every day, right up until a few months before he died.*

As I age, I want to spend more time in Palm Springs, and I don't want to be required to go to the office every day. However, rather than seeking a self-indulgent phase of life where I play tennis and sit by the pool for months on end, I want to find ways to give back and remain active. I hope to stay physically active, eat wisely and read broadly. But, most importantly, I want to be able to offer the next generation mentoring and coaching.

In his excellent book *Family Wealth*, James E. Hughes recommends that we use our wealth to help develop the next generation's intellectual and social capital.[103] In addition I would suggest that we should also use our golden years to

---

[103]. James E. Hughes Jr., *Family Wealth—Keeping it in the Family: How Family Members and Their Advisers Preserve Human, Intellectual and Financial Assets for Generations* (New York: Bloomberg Press, 2004).

teach and guide. To accomplish this, we will need to give to our successors our time—not just our money.

THE LEGACY OF ALFRED NOBEL

Alfred Nobel was a gifted chemist and industrialist who invented dynamite. "When his will was made known after his death…in 1896, and when it was disclosed that he had established a special peace prize, this immediately created a great international sensation. The name Nobel had been connected with explosives and with inventions useful to the art of making war, but certainly not with questions related to peace."[104]

However, as his will clearly attests, Alfred wanted to make a difference in the world for peace and was actually concerned that some of his inventions were being used for the purposes of war. No one knows all of his motivations. But before he died, he decided that a prize should be given "to the person who shall have done the most or the *Our legacy is created by how we live each day.* best work for fraternity between nations, for the abolition or reduction of standing armies and for the holding and promotion of peace congresses."[105] When he had written these words, he informed Bertha von Suttner, the author of the famous anti-war novel *Lay Down Your Arms*, of his decision. She expressed her delight, saying, "Whether I am around then or not does not matter; what we have given, you and I, is going to live on."[106] She was right—what they gave has lived on.

Alfred Nobel is not famous for the company he built or for the 355 patents that he registered. He is not remembered for his brilliance as the inventor of dynamite but as someone who promoted world peace.

CREATING A LEGACY

When as individuals we walk on the beach, we all leave footprints in the sand. Those who walk behind us can see the marks we leave in our path. Similarly, in our lives, the way we live each day creates a record of how we have lived. When the waves roll onto the beach, our footprints are washed away forever. Not so for our legacy in life. How we live our lives will be remembered for years to come by those who knew us, by those we touched, and by what we did for others. This will become our legacy.

---

[104] Sven Tägil, "Alfred Nobel's Thoughts about War and Peace," Nobelprize.org., http://www.nobelprize.org/alfred_nobel/biographical/articles/tagil/.
[105] Ibid.
[106] Ibid.

If we build a business, we may leave a legacy of industriousness. If we serve, we may leave a legacy of service. If we love, we can leave a legacy of love. Our legacy will not be created tomorrow; it is created by how we live today.

CONCLUSION

When each of us dies, we may be remembered for a short time for our business achievements. However, if we want to have a legacy that is longer lasting and of true significance, we need to do more than just build a business:

Dr. Ben Gullison left a legacy of sight restored for the blind.

William Wilberforce left a legacy of freed slaves.

Alfred Nobel left a legacy of peace.

My grandad left a legacy of industry and faith.

My dad left a legacy of integrity and hard work.

What will my legacy be?

What will be yours?

PART III

LEARNING FROM OTHER *Business* FAMILIES

ENTREPRENEUR WILLINGLY SURRENDERS POWER

SUBMITS KEY DECISION-MAKING TO GUIDANCE OF THE BOARD

Peter Armstrong on dedicated engine.

Armstrong Family, Rocky Mountaineer, Vancouver, British Columbia

In 1990, a British Columbia entrepreneur by the name of Peter Armstrong began one of the most successful business makeovers in Canadian history. He had just purchased a money-losing Crown corporation named Via Rail, and his plan was to transform it into a world class service-oriented enterprise.

Unfortunately, the company bled a lot of red ink during its first years, and Peter was forced to recapitalize the company. Several far-sighted investors were willing to support his dream, but with a catch—those who put up significant sums of money also wanted a seat on the board of directors.

No entrepreneur likes being told what to do, but Peter had no choice, and he reluctantly accepted a new governance structure for his fledgling corporation. A few years later, the business began to take off, and it wasn't long before all of the "angel investors" had been repaid. Now that he controlled 90% of the stock, Peter was free to disband the board. Yet, to the surprise of almost everyone, he didn't.

When asked why, Peter said, "They are there to protect me from myself. I also recognize that not all of my ideas should get approved, and even those that may get approved after discussion and debate are made better by the brain trust that we have been fortunate enough to assemble."

It would be unfair to try to put a value on the contribution of Peter's board because, in his words, "their advice is priceless." As a result, Peter is willing to pay for this advice, and he annually invests a significant amount of money in board fees, travel and disbursements. Most private companies would opt to save the money or pay it out in dividends. Peter bucks this trend and is convinced that the money is well spent.

Since it is a private company, it would be inappropriate to reveal how much Peter pays his board members. However, to provide a general idea how much Peter appreciates their input, he confirmed to me that the annual cost of his board is more than three times the annual salary I used to earn as president of our $300 million per year construction company.

Peter clearly believes his board is invaluable, and he is prepared to back

that premise with cash, saying, "I would rather lose the argument in the board room than the business in the marketplace."

For those who might cringe at the idea of surrendering control to a group of outsiders, Peter smiles and states, "As the owner of the company, I always have a silver bullet." By this he means he has the power to fire the board of directors at any time. He hasn't, and likely won't ever, take such drastic action, as he would find it extremely difficult to get another group of capable directors to join him in the future.

In 2010, Rocky Mountaineer celebrated a milestone anniversary of 20 successful years. Today, this family-owned business has grown to become the largest privately-owned passenger rail service in North America, and it has now welcomed over one million guests on board. In 2009, the World Travel Awards recognized the company as the provider of the world's leading travel experience by train. Peter would be the first to say that his board of directors deserves at least some of the credit for this extraordinary success.[107]

[107.] An independent board of directors can "play an invaluable role in the success of a family business" and "serve as a catalyst to the continuity planning process of a family business." (Jennifer M. Pendergast, John L. Ward and Stephanie Brun De Pontet, *Building a Successful Family Business Board* (New York: Palgrave Macmillan, 2011), 25, 54.)

PATRIARCH DISCOVERS SECOND CAREER

STUDIES "FAMILY" IN BUSINESS

Carlo Inc. annual meeting group photo, (Stockholders, board of directors, management and family members).

Bachechi Family, Carlo Inc., Albuquerque, New Mexico

Carlo Bachechi built a successful real estate company in the years between 1953 and 1980. His son, Victor, now serves as the company's fifth president and chairman of the board. The company's core holdings are industrial and office buildings, and it is headquartered in Albuquerque, New Mexico, but also owns and manages properties in Sydney, Australia, and Vancouver, BC. Vic has a notable and exemplary approach to family business. Foundational to his philosophy is his belief that "managing the family side of a family business is like a second career." When I asked him what he meant by this, he explained that "planning for and managing family related issues can take as much time as running the business itself." Consequently, in addition to his leadership responsibilities with the company, he has devoted himself for the past 15 years to studying best practices for family businesses.

In spite of some resistance, he has been diligent in applying the lessons he has learned. Early on, when he contemplated creating a board of directors with outside independent members, his corporate attorney scoffed at the idea, saying, "That's the dumbest thing I've ever heard!" A dozen years later, this same friend and advisor bears witness to the wisdom of Vic's decision as he has seen first-hand the many benefits the independent board has brought to the company. Rather than giving up control to outsiders, as his attorney worried would happen, the company has gained the perspective and support of knowledgeable, competent professionals. Their advice and input has helped the business to grow steadily and continue to prosper. The board's existence has also been reassuring for some of the company's major tenants as well as for vendors, employees, stockholders and family members, because, as Vic explains, "Our board is charged with the responsibility to make sure this company is around long after I am gone."

Vic also led the effort to develop a clear and concise corporate constitution that serves to inspire and unify the clan. One of my favourite sections is their statement of values. It reads as follows:

"LOVE GOOD, DO RIGHT, RESIST GREED AND LIVE HUMBLY, PATIENTLY AND WITH GOOD HUMOR."

(The complete Carlo Inc. corporate constitution can be found in part IV,

kindly reprinted with permission of their board.)

Ironically, one of the defining moments in the company's history was also a time of great challenge. Prior to their deaths, two of Vic's siblings placed their ownership interests (which approximated 50% of the company stock) in two family trusts. Both trusts named Vic as the sole voting trustee, and the grantors' wishes were that the family business would remain intact, with Vic leading the business. Unfortunately, the beneficiaries of the two trusts were not happy with this structure.

The shareholders' agreement that was in place at the time provided some guidance for dealing with this situation, but it was not comprehensive. The parties contemplated litigation. However, they were dissuaded from this course of action, in part because the time and cost would have been excessive.

Instead of a legal battle, the family chose to mediate, and appointed a retired federal judge to assist. For most of two days, the parties negotiated the terms of an agreement for the dissatisfied parties to be bought out by the company. Vic was in one room, advised by his trust attorney; the company's independent directors and their attorney were in a second room. In a third room were the dissident family members and their legal team. The mediator cycled among the rooms, searching for an agreement. In the end, Vic said, "We got an agreement that everyone could live with, and we all accepted the deal because the level of dissatisfaction was equally shared amongst all the parties."

He added, "No one was happy, but we avoided a long and costly legal fight, and we also avoided the company being broken up. We endured, we learned, we grew and got through it." Consequently, to avoid this kind of situation in the future, Vic is highly motivated to include, involve and educate members of the family related to Carlo Inc.

Since that time, the family has been very active in integrating the next generation into ownership of the family business through the following steps:

All members of the family are invited to attend the company's annual shareholders' meeting, regardless of age.

Once they reach 18 years of age, all family stockholders are asked to read the company shareholders' agreement. If they are ready and want to take the next step, they are then given the opportunity to formally sign the agreement.

All new signatories are toasted with champagne, and their ownership is celebrated happily by the family, board and shareholders.

In Vancouver, where they have been active for over 40 years, the Bachechi family invited another family to become shareholders. This was done for two primary reasons: because of a longstanding business relationship and to demonstrate the family's ongoing commitment to the Vancouver marketplace. Rather than view this shift as a step away from family business, the company owners have decided to include the children of their new investor on the same basis as their own kids. It's a bit like the new shareholders are new siblings in the family, and Rob and Melissa Fiorvento, together with their offspring, have now essentially become "part of the family." Perhaps the most unique and creative initiative that Vic has instituted is the annual "All Age Family Gatherings." To put a new twist on shareholders' meetings, the company invites all stockholders and their families to attend a short retreat each year. Not only are the shareholders' offspring included, but also the children of their executive management team, the board, the executive team, the company's advisors and the shareholders, together with their spouses. The cross-pollination of ideas that occurs is remarkable.

Last year, the group went on an Alaskan cruise, and in 2011 they met in San Diego. The agenda included age-group-appropriate activities and educational presentations (usually with an outside speaker), all designed to help the participants learn about the business and to develop their potential. The agenda also included the annual shareholders' meeting, the annual board meeting, a family council meeting and a charitable foundation meeting. In a non-threatening environment, board members, company officers and advisors are able to get acquainted with the successor generation, and vice versa. The executives and future company owners are able to develop relationships in a relaxed fashion.

By shunning outdated taboos about how stockholders, management and board members should interact, the family has created a culture of inclusion and a penchant for transparency. All of this helps foster trust and mutual understanding.[108] Board members are able to get to know the next generation of owners by meeting them informally during the annual retreat. Likewise, years before next generation shareholders are asked to vote on a slate of directors to oversee the company, they are given the opportunity to know something about the role of a director, in part by spending time with the incumbents.

In addition to the annual shareholder retreat, a family meeting was planned for California in 2012. This event focused on the development and formalization of a family council. There was also a discussion of charitable giving, making grants in each market in which the company operates and the role of the family foundation. Vic notes that it takes both time and money to invest in these gatherings. However, he is convinced that the relationships built through these get-togethers will pay dividends for generations to come. I believe he is right!

[108.] Such activities as family trips, family annual retreats and family annual meetings are good opportunities for family members to get together to know each other and build trust.

LOOKING OUT LEADS TO EXCELLENCE WITHIN

NON-FAMILY TALENT KEY TO LONG-TERM SUCCESS

Keith and Ryan Beedie, in front of SFU's Beedie School of Business, Burnaby, BC.

Beedie Family, the Beedie Group,
Burnaby, British Columbia

As a young man, Keith Beedie left high school to take a job at Boeing and at the age of 18 joined the Royal Canadian Air Force. After leaving the RCAF, by a fluke Keith bumped into a school chum who needed help in a very small woodworking shop. Keith joined up with Fred Banbury, and in about 3 months they outgrew the shop. They bought a lot for $190 in Vancouver and built a 1,200 sq. ft. shop, doing all the work themselves at the age of 19. A year later they sold the shop and Keith

started his own construction company building houses, learning how to build as he went along.

Keith is now 85 years old, and he has seen his small company morph into a real estate and construction enterprise, specializing in warehouse development. The Beedie Group is now the largest industrial landlord in British Columbia, owning 8.4 million square feet of space.

Keith built his business the old-fashioned way, by working hard, being honest and being dedicated to fulfilling his promises to clients (such as com-

251

pleting new projects on time and on budget). Over the years, all of Keith's children from his first marriage have worked in the family business, but, for one reason or another, none of them have made it a long-term career. Ryan, Keith's only child from his second marriage, has now been with the company for over 15 years. At his mother's urging, he completed his MBA before joining the family company, and this may have helped him to develop a long-term working relationship with his dad.

When Ryan first joined the business, the market value of its assets was $160 million. Today, just 10 years after he was named president, assets of the firm are worth over one billion dollars.

From the outset, Ryan focused on growth, largely by building connections for the company. He typically spends 50% of his time outside of the office, meeting with clients and partners. In fact, Keith agreed to make Ryan president of the company when he was only in his mid-30s in an effort to give him "more clout in the eyes of clients and those outside of the firm." Keith now says that the relationships Ryan built outside the company have been important in growing the company, but "The real key is that he has hired excellent people with expertise in every field."[109] It's often difficult for family firms to realize the need to professionalize their management ranks, but it has obviously been a successful formula for the Beedie Group.

Keith looks at it from a very practical perspective, saying, "Whenever I ask our staff what they think we should do, 99% of the time they are right and I'm wrong. We pay them well, so we might as well take their advice!"

Although none of Keith's other children are involved in the company on a day-to-day basis, they all benefit from the success that Ryan is creating for the family.

Families in business can learn several lessons from Keith and Ryan Beedie's success. Consider the following observations:

---

[109]. "Non-family executives enable your business to grow ... business growth requires a larger, deeper pool of qualified management talent than any one family can realistically produce ... good, well-chosen and wisely-managed non-family executives help your company keep its competitive edge." (Craig E. Aronoff and John L. Ward, *More than Family* (New York: Palgrave Macmillan, 2011), 4.)

1. An advanced degree in business, especially an MBA, can help accelerate both career development and company growth.

2. Offering the title of president to a successor while they are still under the tutelage of their parents' generation can have many positive benefits for the company, without undermining the authority of their elders.

3. Sharing "the spoils" from a company's success with those family members not involved in the business can go a long way to helping keep peace in the family.

4. Once a company has achieved a measure of success, attracting and retaining professional managers can help family businesses to continue on a growth trajectory.

RETIREMENT NEEDS FULLY FUNDED

NEXT GENERATION FREED TO RUN THE BUSINESS

From left to right: Ben, Murray, Jason & Dan Berstein.
Murray is now able to spend more time traveling with his wife, Marie, because
he and his three sons developed a plan to fully fund his retirement
independent of the family firm.

Berstein Family, Nixon Uniform Service and Medical Wear, New Castle, Delaware

Murray Berstein is the chairman of the board of Nixon Uniform Service and Medical Wear. The company is headquartered in New Castle, Delaware, and his three sons, Ben, Dan and Jason, all work in the business, making it a true family affair. Murray says the family enterprise is dedicated to growth and "instills an atmosphere that provides the company's associates with challenge and opportunities for advancement."

But his motivation in growing the business was "to build a company that would be large enough to both attract my three sons and provide for their families." The firm has been on a steady path of increasing sales and profits for the last decade, even though it has pro-actively sold significant parts of the business on two separate occasions.

How do growth and selling assets go hand in hand?

The first selling off of assets was done to accommodate the desires that he and his brother each had for more independence. Through the sale, each of the brothers acquired a component of the original company that they had grown together, and it was done without any acrimony between parties. This transaction was completed in 1997, and since then both of the brothers' companies have continued to prosper and enjoy success.

The second asset disposition occurred as Murray was approaching his 65th birthday, and his family advisor had suggested that it would be prudent for Murray to be financially independent of the family business during his retirement years. "Best practice" would suggest that such planning occur much earlier and that funds set aside for retirement be invested outside of the family business.

This type of retirement planning is typically a 20 to 30 year process, which ideally should be initiated when the retiring owner is around 40 years of age. By starting early, the retiring owner is then able to become independent of the company by the time he is in his sixties. This approach also ensures that any burden on the company to fund such a plan is minimized.

By not relying on the company for retirement funds, Murray and his wife are able to enjoy peace of mind during their retirement years, and, more importantly, the next generation will have the freedom to lead the organization into the future without concerns about funding the retirement of their elders.

If such a plan weren't in place, Murray's son Jason, who is now president of the firm, says, "I wouldn't blame the retiring generation for being conservative. If I was worried about my retirement, I wouldn't be inclined to let the next generation take the risks that are necessary to be successful over the long term."

Unfortunately, no plans had been put in place earlier in Murray's career to provide for his independent retirement fund. However, before Murray shared his desire for financial independence, his sons and their executive team proposed that the company sell a non-strategic division of the business.

They identified one segment of the company that was profitable and marketable but not essential to their long-term growth. By selling this division, the company would be better able to focus its attention on a specialized market where they believed there was more potential for future growth. As an added bonus, the sale provided the company with the liquidity that was necessary to contribute towards Murray's retirement.

Selling the family business should typically be avoided and considered only as a strategy of last resort. However, as the Bersteins' experience shows, there are times when it is tactically wise to sell a profitable division of the company. Most entrepreneurial owners don't think about creating a fund for retirement independent of the business; instead, they view their business as their retirement plan. Others may have the wisdom to realize they should have some money invested outside the company yet fail to do so decades before retirement.

The Berstein's family experience illustrates how families in business can experience numerous benefits if they plan in advance to create an effective strategy for funding the retirement of the elder generation, and how ideally these funds should be held outside the family enterprise.

MIDDLE SON
APPOINTED PRESIDENT

FAMILY UNITY MAINTAINED

Members of the Bornstein family enjoy a break during a recent board meeting, held at the Bellingham Golf and Country Club. Pictured here, from left to right: Kyle Bornstein (shareholder and board member); Andrew Bornstein (shareholder, board member and director of acquisition; Jay Bornstein (chairman of the board, recently retired as CEO); Colin Bornstein (shareholder, board member and CEO).

Bornstein Family, Bornstein Seafoods, Bellingham, Washington

Jay Bornstein is the second-generation owner of his family's fish processing business, Bornstein Seafoods, Inc., in Bellingham, Washington. At age 62, he began to think seriously about his plan to retire at 65 and quickly realized that he needed to select a successor to run the business—and he needed to do it soon! However, with three grown sons working in the business, he feared that it would be hard on family relationships if he picked one of the boys to "rule over the others." He then reviewed the skills and experience of the rest of his management team, and it soon became clear that there was no natural successor from within the family or the company. Facing challenging economic times and tough competition, he also realized that it was not financially feasible to recruit a hired gun to come on board and take over the ship.

Sharyn, Jay's wife, suggested that the easiest way to avoid a family squabble was to sell the company. This was a sensible idea on one level, but Jay's commitment to the industry and his heritage, as well as his deep emotional bonds with Bornstein Seafoods, meant that he would rather have cut off his right arm than sell the company.

Kyle, the eldest son, worked for the business during the summers while going to school and then joined the firm full-time upon graduation. After working with the company for many years, he started his own business buying and selling fish. Eight years later, he continues to do this very successfully.

The middle son, Colin, had been with the family company for almost 20 years and was now a senior sales manager. He worked hard and played an important role in the business. But he was primarily a sales guy, and he didn't appear to possess the skills or experience to run the whole business.

The youngest son, Andrew, had just graduated with his MBA and was contemplating a career with the company. He was intelligent and well educated, but his interests lay more in real estate development than fish processing. Even if he was willing to join the firm, he definitely lacked the experience to be put in charge.

Rather than trying to rush to a solution, the family decided to be methodical and collaborative in dealing with succession. Over a three-year period, the family took the following steps:

1. They began to have regular family meetings to discuss issues and build unity.
2. They developed a clear, strategic direction for the company in collaboration with the whole management team (including family and non-family members).
3. They recruited, with the assistance of an independent consultant, three independent advisory board members and delegated to them the task of choosing a successor.

The advisory board invited the three sons and all members of the management team to apply for the president's job.

Kyle and Andrew decided to support Colin in his application. Rich, one of the senior managers, also applied for the position. After interviewing both candidates, the board recommended that Colin be appointed as president, on the condition that Rich serve as senior vice president to assist Colin with operations and finance. The family unanimously endorsed this proposal.

Kyle has been invited to sit on the board of advisors and is paid for this role on a similar basis as the independent directors, while Andrew has been given a critical new role as operations manager.

It has only been about 18 months since Colin took over the top job, but so far the company is flourishing and everyone seems to be happy with the new arrangement. A formal retirement party was recently held for Jay, and it proved to be a joyful occasion for the whole family. In addition, Kyle, Colin and Andrew have all signed an agreement to become equal partners to buy the portion of the company that they don't already own.

Looking back, some people might think Colin got the best deal by getting the top job in the family business. That's certainly one way to look at it. However, now that his brothers combined will eventually own 66.66% of the business, they could end up exercising majority control. You might say Colin has the toughest assignment, as he will now be working for his brothers!

SPOUSES CHERISHED

LEGACY OF LOVE AND INCLUSIVENESS

Dewey and Dina DeVries with their children, spouses and grandchildren gathered around them at a family retreat.

Devries, Newton Omniplex Industrial Centre, Surrey, British Columbia

There are six children in the DeVries family, which makes it a rather large family by today's standards. It grew even larger as each of the children got married, and Dina and Dewey DeVries were determined to treat their children's spouses as equals. Philosophically and practically, they wanted their decisions and actions to reflect that they now had 12 children.

Two actions in particular reflect their commitment to this ideal:

1. The family holding company, created for the benefit of their offspring, is called R 12, in a reference to "our 12" children. This label is more than a token gesture as it appears on legal documents. Most importantly, it reflects the true heart of generosity that is lovingly extended to all 12 individuals.

2. When addressing any of the married couples in conversation, the "married in" member of the family gets first billing. For example, the eldest son, DJ, and his wife, Hea-

ther, are referred to as Heather and DJ.

I was deeply moved and inspired by the depth of love and mutual respect that was evident when I first facilitated a family meeting with Dina and Dewey and their adult children. When I got home that night, I told my wife, Alison, that I had now seen what I hoped our family might one day be like. The spark that created the warmth that burns at the heart of this family is the love that Dina and Dewey have for each other. This love is extended consistently to all of their children and, in turn, to their marriage partners.

The DeVries family is not perfect; no family is. However, if one measures the success of a family by the amount of love shown to its members, this family ranks near the top of the heap. It is also no wonder that the family has enjoyed success in business since "relationships are the language of family business."[110]

To help build relationships and family unity, the DeVries clan has an annual family retreat, which is mostly about food, fun and the grandkids. Last year, they went to a conference centre for five days where they erected a Christmas tree, exchanged gifts and cooked a turkey to feed 35 people!

In a further expression of unselfish love, the elder generation has set the following financial priorities:

1. Charitable giving (largely focused on gospel ministries and helping the poor).
2. Providing for their children and grandchildren.

As a result of these priorities, Dewey and his wife have a very modest lifestyle. Their financial resources, which are now considerable, are primarily used for the benefit of others.

[110.] Edwin A. Hoover and Colette Lombard Hoover, *Getting Along in Family Business: The Relationship Intelligence Handbook* (New York: Routledge, 1999), 13.

FAMILY SHARES POWER
TEAMS UP WITH NON-FAMILY EXECUTIVES

From left to right: Richard Bracken, chairman of Royal Canadian Securities Limited; Ashleigh Everett, president of Royal Canadian Securities Limited and chairman of Royal Canadian Properties Limited; Bruce Hamilton, president of Royal Canadian Properties Limited, at Royal Canadian's boardroom, in the Cargill Building in Winnipeg, MB.

Everett Family, Royal Canadian Properties Limited., Winnipeg, Manitoba

The Honourable Douglas Everett served Canada as a senator for over 25 years. Prior to his appointment, he served as CEO of the family business, which now has interests in service stations, real estate and retail. The enterprise includes such well-known companies as Domo Gas, Corpell's Water and Royal Canadian Properties.

This amazing family from Winnipeg has done a remarkable job of including both family and non-family executives in senior company roles. How they have accomplished this is a testament to the wisdom of their balanced approach to family business.

One example of this is how they have structured the senior leadership of Royal Canadian Properties (RCP). Ashleigh Everett is chairman of RCP, but Bruce Hamilton, with over 25 years' experience, serves as president and presides over the day-to-day affairs of this business. Consequently, they effectively share power and authority, and their teamwork allows for non-family and family influence to be shared. My siblings and I have had a ringside seat to observe the interplay between these two executives, because our family has partnered with RCP in the ownership of the Cargill Building in Winnipeg for over 20 years.

Obviously, Ashleigh represents the family and is the senior person on the organization chart. However, she has given responsibility and authority to Bruce for all day-to-day management decision-making. He also has all of the property management and leasing staff report to him directly. In this role, he is accorded both the respect and compensation any senior executive would expect in a well-run organization.

Earlier on in her career, Ashleigh spent eight years with Scotiabank in Toronto. During much of that time, Richard Bracken served as both the chairman and CEO of RCP. When Ashleigh returned to Winnipeg, she was initially appointed president, working under Richard's guidance and mentorship (another example of how the Everetts have had a partnership between family and non-family executives in leadership). At the time, Bruce Hamilton was her principle lieutenant, and he carried the title of vice-president. Over time, as Bruce and Ashleigh learned the ropes, they were able to free Richard up to focus more of his attention on holding company matters.

Each of these executives holds themselves to a high standard of performance. They are all highly competent, articulate and dedicated. In addition, there is a great deal of mutual respect and genuine collaboration between all the team members, and this integration seems to be the key for this family (and any family) to make a great team out of family and non-family members.

In addition, the Everett family has been able to find elegant ways of providing separate territory or "turf" for family members, enabling siblings to work in different areas of the company where they won't step on one another's toes.

For example, Ashleigh's brother, Douglas, was promoted to president of Domo Gas in 1999, and he has been running that company ever since. Ashleigh's husband, Stuart, had previously occupied the role of Domo president, until he was asked to head up the $300 million Canadian Museum for Human Rights for the federal government. From 1993 to 2005, Ashleigh's sister Sarah was president of Bowring, the high-end retail chain. Finally, Ashleigh's younger sister, Kate, is president of Corpell's Water, a company acquired in 2009.

All too often, families in business suffer from destructive jealousies and power struggles between family and non-family managers or rivalry between siblings. Yet the Everett family has virtually eliminated these problems through wise guidance and unity in the executive team. It is no wonder that Douglas Everett was asked to provide wisdom and guidance to our country as a senator.

LEAVING LEADS TO STRONG RETURN

Successor Gains Experience Working Elsewhere

Karen Flavelle, chief executive officer of Purdy's Chocolates.

Charles Flavelle, chairman of Purdy's Chocolates (and one of the founding members of Cafe Vancouver).

Flavelle Family, Purdy's Chocolates, Vancouver, BC

Purdy's Chocolates has a sterling reputation for delicious chocolate, both for personal consumption and for gift giving. Charles Flavelle is very proud of the reputation that this successful family-owned business bears.

The Flavelle offspring were never encouraged to join Purdy's, as Charles did not want to parachute his kids in over long-term employees.[111] Instead, Charles and his wife, Lucile, encouraged their children to find the vocation that was right for each of them:

• Karen was interested in business, so she took a bachelor of commerce degree at Queen's University and went into marketing.

• Scott found his passion as a professional mountain guide.

• Alix had gained a master's degree in forestry and was intent on doing what she could to save the world's forests.

• The youngest, Keith, pursued his interests in carpentry and boat building.

As a result, they all set off on their own paths.

Then everything changed when Keith died while climbing Mount Logan in April of 1986.

About this time, the family had become involved with CAFE—the Canadian Association of Family Enterprise. The combination of Keith's death and the recognition of the need to pass a business from one generation to the next caused Charles to realize that mortality happens and there comes a time to step aside.

But what was the future to be?

1. Transfer leadership within the family?
2. Sell the company?
3. Continue to operate the company with a professional manager from outside the family?

A sale of the company would be neat and clean, but Charles did not want to let long-time employees down. Similarly, operating with a professional manager did not seem to be a practical solution for the long term.

CAFE's recommendation of holding family meetings was the start of a solution for the Flavelles. In the fall of 1986, still raw from the death of Keith, the family met to discuss the future of the business and the choices that each of the three siblings were making.

Scott and Alix each chose to carry on with their professions. Karen, the one with the interest in business and who had marketing expertise, requested that the business not be sold even though, at that time, she did not see herself running it.

Karen was intelligent, hard-working and the consummate professional. She had accomplished a lot in building her own legacy, including the following:
– An undergraduate degree in business
– Two years working and traveling in Japan and Asia
– Five years in packaged goods marketing experience at General Mills
– One year of new product consulting in London, England

In 1988, at age 31, Karen was continuing to build her career 3,000 miles away from home. When she returned to Canada from England, she analyzed her strengths and interests in order to start the search for the next stage of her career. She realized that a medium-sized retail company was exactly what she was looking for, and called her father. Karen suggested there needed to be a firm plan in place before she could uproot her husband from his successful career and for her to take the leap. Her husband wanted to stay in Ontario for at least five years. Charles wanted to make sure that Purdy's continued to provide a secure place of work for long-time employees. They both agreed that the five-year time span gave Karen and Charles time to work out a plan of transition that would meet both their needs.

This led to protracted discussions, which lasted nearly six years, during which Karen worked at Swiss Chalet in retail marketing and gave birth to three children. However, with the assistance of a skilled intermediary, an agreement was finally reached for Karen to join the family firm as executive vice-president just before her dad turned 65.

She had also negotiated an agreement that assured her of two essential terms:

1. Her appointment as president was guaranteed to occur within two years, provided she was competent.
2. She would have an option to buy the company.

Most would-be successors in family firms nod politely when it is suggested that they work outside the family company for five or ten years. "That may be OK for somebody else, but it's just not right for me" is a typical response. It may be insecurity or a lack of role models, but I continue to be astonished that many people are unable to see the benefits afforded by this kind of career path.

Based on her experience, Karen discards the conventional opinion that suggests two to five years "working outside" as ideal. She maintains that ten years is more appropriate, and their family employment policy now requires that any member of her family who aspires to the CEO's office must have a minimum of ten years' external work experience plus the appropriate business education. In addition, they must have also earned at least one merit promotion, thereby demonstrating their ability to add value in an objective external environment.

Since coming to Purdy's, Karen has done a great job leading the company and continuing its successful growth in sales and profits. She has championed the company's expansion into Ontario, where they've established 10 new stores. I sincerely doubt that she would have had the courage to make this happen had she joined the company without any outside experience. Her success story is a beacon of light for all family business owners and would-be successors. Why would anyone want to take a different path?

[111.] "To offer employment in the family business to the heir right out of school is a bad idea ... a son (or daughter) should learn about business elsewhere where he (or she) can make mistakes and not embarrass his (or her) father and where his (or her) early uncertainties and ignorance won't cast doubt on his (or her) ability as a manager in the years to come." (Leon Danco, *Beyond Survival: A Guide for Business Owners and Their Families* (Edmonton: Predictable Futures, 2003), 152.)

CEO SHARES DECISION-MAKING AUTHORITY

Succession becomes a non-event

Ken Finch, chairman of the board and ex-president, and Robert Foord, current president, in front of Kal Tire Store in Vernon, BC.

Foord family, Kal Tire, Vernon, British Columbia

When Tom Foord retired as president and CEO of Kal Tire, the leadership transition to his son-in-law, Ken Finch, went so smoothly, there was scarcely a ripple. Similarly, the transition from Ken to Tom's son, Robert, was accomplished without acrimony. How could this have happened? After all, management succession in a family business is fraught with challenges, and the corporate landscape is littered with examples of those who failed to succeed in succession. But Tom Foord

seemed surprised at the notion that there should have been any problems.

Ken says that Tom is responsible for the ease of the transition noting, "Tom has been generous in sharing decision-making with the rest of the management team, so when he formally stepped down as CEO, the rest of us had already become quite accustomed to exercising both the responsibility and authority necessary to provide effective leadership for the company."

Unlike the characteristic autocratic entrepreneur, Tom was a consensus builder, and he trained his family and non-family management team members by giving them ample opportunity to participate in major decisions. In essence, the company was led by a team rather than by one man.

This culture of collaborative decision-making was still very much in evidence when Robert succeeded his brother-in-law as CEO. Rather than try to hold on to power, Ken was willing to give it away, even though he was still a relatively young man. Like Tom, he could have waited until he was 80 years of age before retiring, but instead he was willing to step aside at age 65 to make room for Robert.

In order to assist with the succession planning process, the Foord family has also invested significantly in the development of good governance. Initially, they began by creating an advisory board. Over time, this was replaced by a fully functioning legal board for the family holding company.

More recently, the shareholders of Kal Tire adopted a two-tier board structure. At the holding company level, all family shareholders are welcomed at the board table, where they are joined by independent professional board members. Today there are five family members on the board and two independent directors. Below the holding company is an operating company that conducts the day-to-day business of Kal Tire. Providing oversight to the operating company is a separate board called the partnership board. All of these board members are selected based on their knowledge and expertise. Selection criteria and competency requirements are clearly spelled out and agreed to by the shareholders. These are available for anyone who may aspire to be elected. Currently, this board is comprised of two family members (Ken Finch and Robert Foord), two Kal Tire executives and four independent members. By observing the Foord family, there are several key strategies that can be noted. These could effectively be applied to the management succession process in virtually any family business:

1. Collaborative decision-making
2. Willingly giving up power and authority
3. Investing in good governance, tailored to suit the family and its business interests

In order to adopt strategies like this, the family leadership requires maturity, self-confidence and humility. Clearly, Tom and Ken have these traits in abundance.

PRUDENT LIFESTYLE FACILITATES GROWTH

MODEST DIVIDENDS MAXIMIZE REINVESTMENT

Paul Higgins Jr. on the left, co-chief executive officer; Michael Higgins on the right, co-chief executive officer, at their head office in Mississauga, Ontario.

Higgins Family, Mother Parkers Tea and Coffee, Mississauga, Ontario

Mother Parkers Tea and Coffee will soon celebrate its 100th anniversary. Founded by Grandpa Higgins in 1912, the business now resides in the hands of Paul and Michael Higgins, two members of the third generation who each own 50% of the shares. The two brothers joined the company on the exact same day 38 years ago, and they were both mentored by their dad for 20 years before taking over management responsibilities in 1994.

According to Michael, "Dad modelled a very modest lifestyle. His priority was always reinvesting in the business, rather than spending money on himself.[112] Paul adds, "As a rule of thumb, we endeavour to annually reinvest an amount equal to the depreciation recorded in our financial statements."

As a result, dividends to the family have always been modest, and available funds have helped the company to continuously expand, to keep pace with the competition and to employ the latest in technology. By plowing earnings back into the company, Mother Parkers has been able to avoid becoming overly dependent on debt. Consequently, whenever the economy hit a rough patch, they were able to weather the storm. This approach has allowed the company to continually be early adopters of technology. In 2000, the company made a huge capital investment in a new state-of-the-art plant in Fort Worth, Texas. Not only is this facility the most modern coffee roasting plant in North America, but it also won *Food Engineering* magazine's Plant of the Year award in 2001. Consequently Mother Parkers has been able to capture some outstanding new customer accounts, including 7-11, Walmart and Dunkin' Donuts.

Michael and Paul are 50-50 partners and serve as co-CEOs of the family enterprise. How can they comfortably share power and authority? Paul says, "We both recognize that the most important thing is to make decisions that are in the best interests of our 650 employees. Therefore, we each try to park our egos at the door and operate with humility."

Michael adds, "We have complementary strengths; Paul is better with business operations and financial matters. He is also a bit more hard-nosed than me, and sometimes we need that. I take the lead in the areas of marketing, sales and human resource management. I could be described as the more sensitive one, and so I think we make a good team. Outside of the business we're best friends, and we make this work because we typically don't talk about business once we leave the office."

When asked how they make decisions as co-CEOs, Paul noted, "We collaborate on everything. We also believe that in business, typically there is no right or wrong way to do something. However if one of us is passionate about a specific direction, the other one will usually defer."

As an example, when planning to build a new office and warehouse in Toronto years ago, Michael wanted to locate the facilities across the street from the company's existing plant. Paul thought this was too expensive and instead recommended a location near the airport. Michael felt passionate about having all of their operations

---

112. "The availability of unrealistic amounts of riches in a family business tends to intensify quarrels over shares and distributions ... living modestly can contribute to family concord because it maintains a perspective regarding basic values and it ensures that the family's good works in the community will be continued by future generations." (William T. O'Hara, *Centuries of Success: Lessons From the World's Most Enduring Family Businesses* (Avon: Adams Media Corporation, 2003), 181.)

together, even if it cost more money. After some considerable debate, Paul deferred to Michael—not because he agreed with him, but out of respect for him as a partner. In hindsight, both say they are happy with the decision.

In the 1950s, Paul and Michael's father acquired sole ownership of the business by buying out his two brothers as the ownership transitioned from G1 to G2. This "pruning of the ownership tree" resulted in a simplified ownership structure and helped resolve some of the challenging family dynamics they were facing at that time. Similarly, when transitioning to G3, it was agreed that the three siblings who are not involved in management would also be content to not be involved in ownership. Therefore, Michael and Paul's three sisters are neither owners nor involved in management of the firm.

However, in order to provide for everyone fairly, their dad provided equally for all five siblings and left them each sufficient financial resources that all of them could live well without any money from the business.

Today, two of Paul's three children work in the business. The family has adopted clear guidelines governing their employment, and policies ensure that they must produce results if they wish to remain in the firm. No plans have yet been put in place for the future ownership of the business, but, given the thoughtful approach of the Higgins family, the fourth generation will likely be able to continue the legacy of success as well as continue the culture of reinvesting and reinvigorating the enterprise, as have the generations before them.

FOUNDATION
FOSTERS UNITY

FAMILY MEMBERS CREATE SHARED VISION

*Ivey family at the 1995 naming of the Richard Ivey School of Business,
London, ON. (Photography by Ross Breadner.)*

*Ivey Family, Ivey Foundation, Toronto,
Ontario*

Richard W. Ivey is a third-genera-
tion member of a prominent Canadian
family. The business school at Western
University in London, Ontario, carries
the family name and has a worldwide
reputation for high quality education.
Trained as a lawyer, Richard is secre-
tary-treasurer of the family charitable
organization, the Ivey Foundation.
Established almost 65 years ago, it is
among the oldest in the country and
has given away an average of over 1
million dollars per year. Today, with
assets of approximately 70 million dollars, it is an extraordinary example of
unified family philanthropy and an inspiration to all wealthy families.

Together, Richard's grandfather
(Richard G.) and father (Richard M.
or Dick) established a company that,
at one time, included 13 businesses
in Canada, the United States, the
United Kingdom and Europe. The initial plan was to pass the company on
to Richard and his three sisters, Jennifer, Roz and Suzanne. However, in
1984 the family made the decision to
sell most of the company's businesses

and instead provide each of the three daughters with their proportionate share of the estate in cash. Eleven of the businesses were sold, and Richard, as his share of the estate, took over the remaining two—Livingston Group, a North American-wide logistics company (which was sold in 2000), and a small local real estate company known as Ivest Properties Ltd. Today, through that real estate company, Richard and his partners constitute Canada's largest developer and manager of student housing.

As the family's succession plan was being implemented, Dick and his wife, Beryl, determined that "if there wasn't going to be an ongoing family business, the family foundation should be the vehicle through which the family remained together."[113] Consequently, when the last of the corporate holdings were sold in 1990, an additional $20 million was placed in the foundation, and Richard's sisters were invited to join him and his parents on the foundation board. Over the next 10 years, the six of them worked together on their philanthropic endeavours. The sharing of power and responsibility between generations, with everybody "feeling their way," as Richard recalls, was a challenging but ultimately bonding process. In 1998, Roz succeeded her father as chair of the foundation, and in 2000, both Dick and Beryl retired as board members.

Prior to the third generation's involvement, Dick and Beryl made all the decisions, and the foundation supported a broad spectrum of charitable causes, including health care, the arts, education, the environment and community services, primarily in London and throughout southwestern Ontario. In 1990, the foundation hired its first professional staff member, and over the next two years the family had a series of retreats to seek consensus regarding the focus of their charitable giving. Their first five-year family plan focused on two major areas: biodiversity in forest-dominated ecosystems and environmental education. The foundation's second five-year plan continued with the forest biodiversity program and replaced environmental education with a new program called Tele-triage in health care.

In 2002, the foundation narrowed its focus even further to a single program called Conserving Canada's Forests. With four full-time staff now administering the foundation, the family has truly professionalized its charitable work. Approximately 50% of the organization's effort is focused on preserving pristine forests, while the other 50% relates to encouraging forestry companies to adopt standards that will ensure the sustainable management of Canada's forests. Over the past 10 years, through the assistance of the Ivey Foundation and others, the area of Canadian forests protected by certified, sustainable management practices has grown from 2 million to almost 45 million hectares.

Richard believes that his parents taught him and his siblings about philanthropy through their own example. As he says, "They set amazing examples of the importance of giving of one's time and money to important causes, but there were no dining room lectures about the importance of giving back to the community. Mom and Dad just lived it, so we learned mostly by osmosis." As children, they met a number of interesting people seeking the foundation's support. For example, Richard fondly remembers meeting Dr. Christiaan Barnard, the famous doctor from South Africa who performed the world's first heart transplant. Richard was invited to join the foundation's board at the tender age of 24, and he said this definitely assisted him in realizing the importance of business families giving back to the communities in which they earn their living.

So, has the foundation served to unify the family as Richard's parents had hoped? Richard says, "The process of developing five-year plans for the foundation was key, because it was through that process that we were able to develop a consensus regarding the focus of the foundation. That shared vision, more than anything, has been a strong, unifying force and source of great satisfaction for our family."

[113.] "[A] family foundation helps to hold the family together … and can prevent a rift from occurring." (Randel S. Carlock and John L. Ward, *When Family Businesses Are Best: The Parallel Planning Process for Family Harmony and Business Success* (New York: Palgrave Macmillan, 2010), 222.)

YOUNGER BROTHER REJOINS FAMILY FIRM

A COMPANY NOW OWNED BY HIS ELDER SIBLING

Greg and Todd Kuykendall (standing in front of the water ski lake where they regularly train together).

Kuykendall, Kuykendall Hearing Aid Center, Enid, Oklahoma

Greg and Todd Kuykendall are brothers who work for the successful hearing aid supply company that their father started. They never dreamed that they would be working together, yet they are—both men are in or nearing their fifties and next year will mark their twelfth year of collaboration. Fortunately, the two have an extraordinary relationship. They get along extremely well, both on and off the job, and are both highly accomplished competitive water skiers who train together regularly.[114]

Greg joined his dad's business straight out of college, but his younger brother, Todd, took a very different route. Todd first went to a seminary to begin studying for a master's degree in theology. Prior to completing this, he joined the family business for five years. Still drawn powerfully to a life of service, he then left the hearing aid business and spent seven years working with the Fellowship of Christian Athletes (during which time he was finally able to complete his degree). Family and friends assumed that he had found his niche in life and wouldn't return to the hearing aid business. When their father retired, it seemed natural for him to sell the business to Greg.

But after a 10-year career as a pastor and youth worker, Todd realized that he needed to earn a better living to provide for his growing family. So he returned to the family firm. He was warmly welcomed by Greg. Both of them are glad to be working together again. Todd is paid a market salary for his role and works under the direction of his older brother. According to Greg, "Todd works hard and has done a great job running one of the company's key divisions." What is remarkable and unique about their relationship is that Greg granted Todd a "right of first refusal" should an attractive offer ever be received for the company. This would provide Todd with a means of securing long-term job security if Greg ever decided to sell the business. In addition, if there is such a sale, Todd will receive one-half of the proceeds.

Greg is so committed to these promises that both of these generous terms have been put into legally enforceable documents. Why did Greg extend such generosity to his brother? He offers three reasons:

1. I did nothing to deserve the whole business. Even though I bought it from Dad, it was more like a gift.

2. I am not rich, but I have plenty. I am content with what I have and don't need more.

3. Todd is my brother, and I want him and his family to be financially secure.

The only major difference in their current financial situation is that Greg has accumulated a more substantial industry pension as a result of his longer tenure in the business and his long-standing ownership stake in the company.

All family business owners can learn some key lessons from the Kuykendalls:

1. Career plans can change radically over time, and being flexible is important.

2. Even after a business is sold, adjustments can be made to accommodate changing circumstances.

3. If you really want to confirm your intentions, it is helpful to do so in writing (so others can count on you and you won't be tempted to go back on your promise).

4. Brotherly love and an unselfish attitude are far too rare in business, but they are beautiful to behold.

[114.] "Harmony in the family is the basis for success in any undertaking" (Chinese proverb).

BREAKING THROUGH THE GLASS CEILING

DAUGHTERS PREPARE TO SUCCEED THEIR FATHER

*From left to right: Rebecca Legge (vice president of sales, Canada Wide Media),
Peter Legge (CEO/chairman/ publisher, Canada Wide Media) and Samantha Legge
(vice president/publisher, Canada Wide Media) at the BC Business Best Companies
event in Vancouver, November 2011.*

Legge Family, Canada Wide Media Limited, Burnaby, British Columbia

A recent survey of family businesses in the United States revealed that more than 30% believe that the next CEO of their company may be a woman.[115] At family-owned Canada Wide Media, the odds are much higher. Peter Legge, the chairman, CEO and founder, has no sons, and two of his three daughters not only work in the company but are dedicated to proving they are capable contributors and not just "Daddy's little girls." They are now so accomplished that Samantha ("Sam") is a vice-president and publisher of several magazines, while her younger sister Rebecca ("Bec") is vice-president of sales.

Canada Wide Media has met with great success and is now western Canada's largest independent magazine publisher. It owns numerous well-respected brands, including *BC Business Magazine* and *TV Week*. I remember being startled when I first heard Sam address her father as Peter. It struck me as overly formal and awkward, but I soon learned that this was a reflection of the professionalism with which both Sam and Bec conduct themselves. Rather than expecting special treatment because they are family members, these wise young women have taken the following steps to prove themselves in the eyes of their father and, even more importantly, in the eyes of the board and other company employees:

MANAGEMENT SUCCESSION

1. Sam worked outside the family company for more than five years. Over that time, she gained relevant work experience, developed her skills and increased her self-confidence.
2. Each of the girls served an apprenticeship in the company, gaining knowledge and experience working in virtually all departments.
3 During their early days with the company, they focused on listening and learning, rather than trying to exert authority beyond what they had been given.
4. Respectful and adoring of their father, they have not presumed to displace him but rather have sought to serve him as the CEO of the company.

5. For as long as Peter wants to remain at the helm, the girls are content to let him be the boss. This has avoided an intergenerational power struggle and made it easier for Peter to give more authority to the girls.
6. Most remarkably, Sam and Bec display a rare combination of self-confidence and humility. Their confidence permits them to take on whatever tasks they are assigned, while their humility prevents them from being presumptuous. This combination is very rare in potential successors to family businesses; far too many have a toxic combination of insecurity and arrogance. The former attitude is often rooted in insufficient work experience in the "real" world, while the latter commonly stems from an entitlement mentality or an inflated sense of one's own importance.

Each sister took a very different career path. Sam, who worked in multiple divisions of the company, is more of a generalist and has been mentored by the current non-family president of the company.

In contrast, Bec started at the very bottom (according to Peter) and

---

[115.] MassMutual Financial Group, "American Family Business Survey" (Springfield: Massachusetts Mutual Life Insurance Company, 2007), 5.

has specialized in sales for the past 10 years.

The 21st century will undoubtedly see many women rising to positions of senior leadership in family companies, if they follow the wise and professional approach that Samantha and Rebecca have taken.[116] All would-be successors, both men and women alike, can learn from these two classy ladies.

OWNERSHIP SUCCESSION

Succession in management is an ongoing process at this company, as is succession in ownership. Peter started planning for the transition of ownership to his children 15 years ago when he owned 75% of the company and his long-time partner owned 25%. The first step in the ownership succession process took place when Peter's partner retired and agreed to sell all of his shares to the Legge family. Peter arranged for the ultimate transfer of these shares to his daughters, along with an additional 5% of the company shares he already owned. This enabled Peter's three daughters (Sam, Bec and Amanda) to collectively acquire a 30% ownership

stake in the business. Amanda is an elementary school teacher who has no plans to work in the company. Nonetheless, Peter wanted to ensure she was not disadvantaged by her career choice and gave her the same number of shares as Bec and Sam.

In the future, when Peter is ready to retire, the company will commit to an enhanced pension sufficient to enable him to retire and travel as much as his heart desires. At that time, the remaining shares will be transferred to the girls, and they will then own 100% of the company.

Amanda, Samantha and Rebecca meet regularly to talk as owners. They discuss the performance of the company, their expectations and their dreams for the future. The Legge sisters are deeply loved by their dad and are making him very proud by working hard and adding value to the company. They are also being patient and respectful as they wisely wait for their turn to lead.

---

116. "We have moved into an era where primogeniture is loosening its grip and, in a departure from the past, daughters can take over no matter the industry." (Ann M. Dugan, Sharon P. Krone, Kelly LeCouvie, Jennifer M. Pendergast, Denise H. Kenyon-Rouvinez, and Amy M. Schuman, *A Woman's Place: the Crucial Roles of Women in Family Business* (New York: Palgrave Macmillan, 2010), 19.)

ENTREPRENEURIAL SIBLINGS SHARE PROFITS

ESTABLISH AUTONOMY, ACCOUNTABILITY AND TRUST

Stuart McLaughlin is all smiles as Grouse Mountain Skyride soars overhead.

Stuart McLaughlin, Grouse Mountain Resorts Ltd., Vancouver BC.

Bruce McLaughlin is a legendary Canadian entrepreneur. As a young man, he launched his illustrious career by acquiring a small resort in the town of Halliburton, just north of Toronto, Ontario. During the summer months, he expanded his operations by building more cottages on the property, and he spent the winter months building more rowboats for summer rental. Over time, he began building houses, which he reasoned were simply larger cottages. Soon after, he was buying land and

developing real estate. One of his most insightful moves was to assemble vast tracts of land west of Toronto in the area that is now known as Mississauga. A true visionary, Bruce expanded across Canada and throughout North America. Today, his five children have diverse holdings in Ontario, British Columbia and Texas. Three of his children, Julie, Joanne and Stuart, remain in business together, each responsible for their own division. Joanne manages the real estate development arm and two golf course projects in Ontario. Julie is responsible for all operations in Texas, which include a golf course project and a recreational property development company. Stuart resides in Vancouver, where he oversees the operations of Grouse Mountain, a water company and other investments.

All three are equal partners, and virtually all of their investments are held through a single holding company. They each have an equal voice at the boardroom table, and any major decisions, new investments or capital expenditures must be agreed to by all. If one partner is not in favour of a new project, it won't proceed. In short, they operate by consensus.

They also make a priority of meeting face to face numerous times throughout the year. Obviously, family Christmas celebrations and other festive occasions provide an excuse to get the clan together. In addition, when their travels take them to a common city, they schedule time to discuss their business interests and ensure they can stay on the same wavelength. They work hard to keep family and business in balance.

To avoid any potential controversy, many years ago the three decided on a policy of equal compensation. This includes equality regarding salaries, benefits and any dividends paid. They also decided to pay themselves less than market compensation, so they can place a priority in reinvesting in the corporation to ensure its long-term growth.

This is something they learned from their dad, who always emphasized the importance of long-term sustainability. The traditional view of real estate holds that it is all about location, location and location. In contrast, Bruce taught his children that the only three things that matter are staying power, staying power and staying power.

All three siblings bring unique gifts and talents to the company. Joanne is the artistic, creative one, while Stuart, like his dad, is a bit of a dreamer with an analytical nature. Julie is the one who is research oriented and more methodical in her work.

Despite their differences in personality and geography, Stuart believes they all get along well, saying, "We are all really different, but what makes it work is a combination of autonomy, accountability and trust."

Autonomy is assured, as each sibling has the freedom to run his or her own operations without interference from the others. Day-to-day operational decisions are the sole jurisdiction of each sibling within his or her sphere of influence.

Accountability stems from regular monthly and quarterly reporting, which is provided to all partners. In addition, all three siblings are in communication with one another multiple times per month, if not weekly.

Trust is the glue that holds it all together. As partners, they don't second-guess each other; nor are they constantly looking over one another's shoulders. Rather than looking for opportunity to check up on each other, these siblings have created a culture where they seek one another's advice and input. All siblings who want to work together successfully could benefit by following the strategies of this entrepreneurial trio.

FAMILY MAKES CONSENSUS WORK

AS DOES BILLION-DOLLAR CORPORATION

Front, left to right: Brenda McLean, vice-chair; David McLean, chairman. Back, left to right: Sacha McLean, vice chairman and chief executive officer, Blackcomb Aviation; Jason McLean, president and chief executive officer, The McLean Group of Companies; at their head office in Vancouver, BC. (Photography by John Hollander.)

McLean Family, McLean Group, Vancouver, British Columbia

David McLean is known across Canada for his exemplary track record as chairman of the board of CN Rail. He was first elected to this position in 1994, shortly before CN transitioned from a Crown corporation to a private company in November of 1995. Annually re-elected for the past 17 years, he has overseen the transformation of this enterprise into a corporate powerhouse with a market capitalization of over $33 billion. Bill Gates, through

his investment company, is the largest shareholder in CN and owns approximately 10% of the company's shares.

A lawyer by profession, David has focused much of his business career on real estate acquisition and development, for both clients and his own holdings. He has done this through the McLean Group, a family-owned business he established in 1972 in partnership with his wife, Brenda. Today, he remains chairman of the board of the McLean Group, which is also served by Brenda, who is vice-chair, and their sons, Jason and Sacha, who have transitioned to leadership roles.

Sacha and Jason have added new energy to the company in keeping with the enterprising spirit exemplified by their father. Under their leadership, the company has expanded into numerous new ventures, such as Vancouver Film Studios and Blackcomb Aviation. Sacha, a commercial pilot, has translated his love of flying into a helicopter and jet charter and aircraft management company serving corporations and private citizens throughout the Pacific Northwest. Always in search of new opportunities, Sacha pushes the envelope and looks for growth.

Jason, a lawyer, is responsible for consolidating and managing the myriad of details (and entrepreneurial challenges) created by his brother and his father. Brenda, an advocate for health and education through the family's philanthropic foundation, provides balance and investment guidance to the three optimists, who need to be reined in on occasion.

Despite his strong personal track record for leadership, David has strategically made room for both sons, who exercise a growing influence over the firm's operations. David is willing to step back and let his sons take on leadership roles, saying, "I don't believe in retirement, but I do believe in changing gears."

When I asked Jason and Sacha for their perspectives on the management succession process at the McLean Group, each of them had insightful comments. Sacha wisely observed that "when it comes to both growth and succession, structure is your friend. My brother, Jason, has worked hard to bring organizational discipline and structure to all of our businesses. This is critical as we prepare for the future."

Jason said, "The key is to be fully committed to the success of your brother. I know I am prepared to do whatever it takes to ensure Sacha succeeds, and I know he feels the same way about me. Together, this ensures we will continue to get along just fine."

In 2010, Jason was appointed president and CEO of the McLean Group, and Sacha was appointed CEO of Blackcomb Aviation. Jason also serves as Blackcomb Aviation's chairman. Both Jason and Sacha have been successful in their leadership roles in the company. But, even more importantly, they are getting along well as brothers. With the kind of teamwork they display, I am confident the McLean Group is in good hands for the future. No wonder their father, David, trusts them to lead.

In addition to clearly defined leadership roles, this family relies on the McLean family council to help keep everyone informed and to foster family unity. David is the chair, and the council includes five additional members: his wife, Brenda, his two sons,

Sacha's wife, Melanie, and Jason's wife, AJ. Melanie is a naturopathic physician in a private practice setting, while AJ recently joined the business and is responsible for the real estate brokerage function within the company. All family members are committed to attending regularly scheduled family council meetings. Some family businesses are afraid to involve or inform spouses. Not so with the McLean clan. According to Melanie, it is a reflection of the many ways in which "this family is welcoming, warm, loving and inclusive."

OFFSPRING LEARN BY OWNING

FAMILY CREATES COMPANY FOR UNITY AND EDUCATION

Paul and Donna Melnuk.

Melnuk Family, FTL Capital LLC, St. Louis, Missouri

Paul Melnuk is the managing partner of FTL Capital LLC, a merchant banking and investment firm headquartered in St. Louis. Educated as a CA, he was formerly president and CEO of Thermadyne Holdings Corporation, Bracknell Corporation, Barrick Gold Corporation and Clark USA Inc. With such extensive experience in big business, Paul swore he would "never go into business with my kids!"

Fortunately, Paul recently changed his tune. In order to provide for his family and to teach them about business, Paul and his wife, Donna, decided to establish a real estate investment company for their four children to own and manage.[117] They acquired 12 properties initially and are continuing to expand.

The Melnuks weren't content to just give their kids money. Instead, they decided to set up a business for their four children to own and run together. They also elected to not allocate each of their children an equal number of shares in the new company. Instead, they followed a unique strategy to gift their children a percentage of the company based on their expectations of how much each child could contribute to the company. This resulted in the following distribution.

> Kevin (the youngest child; currently enrolled in an MBA program): 32.5%
> Jillian (oldest child; mother and creative director of a web-design business): 27.5%
> Andrew (oldest son; a new father who is employed in a not-for-profit organization serving special needs adults while studying to become a CA): 22.5%
> Bryan (currently in the US Navy but detached from the family and not involved in management of the business): 17.5%

Other significant guidelines for the distribution of shares include:

a) Annual review of siblings' contributions to the business, with the potential for a redistribution of shares as approved by Paul and Donna.
b) No distributions of profit to any offspring unless he or she has healthy relationships with the family.
c) No participation in management by any sibling without healthy relationships with the family.
d) Admission into the management is only with the unanimous agreement of Paul, Donna and all three siblings.

LESSONS LEARNED:

All families in business can learn some important lessons from the Melnuk family's experience and creative approach:

1. Even those who say "I will never go into business with my kids" often end up doing just that. Consequently, family members and advisors need to be prepared for this possibility.
2. Distribution of shares to offspring can be done in ways that are not equal, yet may still be fair.
3. Putting the responsibility for decision-making squarely on the shoulders of the next generation encourages and invites them to learn joint decision-making.
4. Requiring consensus in decision-making can assist in helping siblings learn the art of collaboration.
5. Those with problems can be lovingly and wisely provided for, as long as guidelines for their protection can be put in place. These can be designed to encourage them to become healthy and restore healthy relationships with the family.

---

117. "The best way to protect the future of the business and enhance its continuity in the family is to prepare the next generation of owners for their roles and responsibilities." (Craig E. Aronoff and John L. Ward, *Family Business Ownership: How To Be an Effective Shareholder* (Marietta: Family Enterprise Publishers, 2002), 36.)

FAMILY VALUES LIVE ON

CONTINUED BY NEW OWNERSHIP

Correct Craft employees on a service project with Missionary Ventures, building bunk beds for the families living along the "tracks" in Guatemala. On bed (left to right) Ken Meloon, chairman of the board, Luis Riviera. Around the bed (left to right), Rebecca Wolfe, Joe Pikel, Thomas Bates, Tammy Eddy, Jose Cortez, Reg Ullmann, Chris Little, Dustin Abel, Ron Nace, Bill Yeargin, president/CEO, and Amanda Yeargin. Kneeling on the floor, Rolando, owner of the house (bunk bed construction site).

Meloon Family, Correct Craft (Ski Nautique Boats), Orlando, Florida

In the world of high-performance water-skiing and wake-boarding, there is one name that for over 50 years has stood above all others: Nautique. The brand is legendary as a pioneer in the design and construction of world class tow boats. Founded and owned by members of the Meloon family for five generations, Correct Craft has established a reputation for quality and performance that would be envied by any company in any industry.

In addition to the numerous accolades they have received within the industry, they are well-known for the moral and ethical framework that serves as the foundation underlying everything the company does.

Bill Yeargin is the president and CEO of Correct Craft. He notes that the Meloon family legacy is a result of an amazing commitment to manufacturing and service excellence. This dedication to superior corporate performance is matched by their commitment to their employees and their desire to make the world a better place. These foundational values are also reflected in their enduring tradition for charitable giving and community service.

As an example, Correct Craft's Orlando, Florida, factory shuts down for one week each year. For the past five years, all company employees have been invited to utilize this downtime by participating in a homebuilding project or some other group charitable project. No one is obliged to sign up, but as an incentive to would-be volunteers the company contributes about $1,000 in cash for each employee. These funds are given in support of the chosen charity and to defray travel costs (which may be incurred for out of country or out of state service). Last year, over 30 Correct Craft employees traveled to serve those living in Ethiopia and to an Apache reservation in Arizona. Other recent trips have been to Mexico, Guatemala and Nicaragua.

A few years ago, the company was sold to provide liquidity for the members of the third through fifth generations of the Meloon family. But the family in Indiana that now owns Correct Craft has very similar values to the Meloons. In fact, rather than shifting away from its roots and historical values under new ownership, the company is even more dedicated to living out its historic values and to putting its Christian beliefs into action through volunteer and philanthropic efforts.

Although it is sad to see members of the Meloon family give up ownership in this legendary company, at the same time it is exciting to see that their values are still being lived out by those in leadership today.[118]

This enduring legacy of philanthropy and exemplary citizenship serves as a reminder to all of us that the values of a founding family can, and often do, remain cornerstones for a company, even when the family is no longer involved. Correct Craft's story should inspire us all to live out our values, to teach them to those who would follow us and to use our corporate influence to make a difference in the world.

[118.] "Family values are far more important than the market value of the business." (Marshall B. Paisner, *Sustaining the Family Business* (Cranbrook: Basic Books, 2000), 13.)

PRESIDENT PURSUES PASSION

COO SHARES THE LOAD

Dave Miller pursuing his water ski passion. Dave set a 55 km world record (scoring four buoys at 10.25 m) at the 2009 Big Dawg Stop in Covington, Louisiana.

Miller Family, Fix Auto (Autobody and Repair), Abbotsford, British Columbia

Most successful entrepreneurs derive an enormous amount of pleasure from their work. As a result, their identity is often inextricably linked to the enterprise that they have built, and when they approach what might be traditionally thought of as the retirement years, they find the idea of "letting go" almost impossible.[119]

Wisdom suggests that the best antidote to this problem is to find another passion or challenge for the would-be retiree, something meaningful into which they can pour their energies. In other words, rather than retiring *from* a company, successful retirees retire *to* something else.

Dave Miller is the owner and founder of a family-owned auto-body repair business. The company boasts six locations and one mini-storage facility and has a sterling reputation for high quality service, customer satisfaction and employee loyalty. Dave started as a tradesman working on the shop floor, first as a body man and later as a painter. (In the trade, he was known as a tin banger.) He now has professional managers in place at each of his auto-body dealerships and, last year, appointed a chief operating officer to run the business day to day.

This is particularly surprising because Dave Miller is a man who has a more than average need to be in control. But he stepped back from day-to-day operations even before his 50th birthday, which he celebrated this year.

Dave explains that the only reason he has been able to hand the reins over is that he has had another all-consuming passion into which he has been able to pour his energy. This other endeavour has steadily drawn him away from his operational responsibilities and enabled him to learn to delegate the management of "his baby" to others.

This is the key: Dave is an accomplished competitive water skier. In 1999, he won gold medals at the provincial, western Canadian, and national level in slalom. In 2006, he finished first in his division at the senior world waterski championships in South Africa. In 2009, he set a new world record at 34 miles an hour, and in 2010 he became known as the top water skier over the age of 35 when he won the Big Dawg finals in Miami, Florida. Over the past two decades, he has traveled the globe pursuing his passion. At the same time, his business has continued to flourish. Slowly but surely, he has been learning the art of "letting go."

[119.] "CEOs who lack other interests are the most likely to have trouble later, when succession is complete…CEOs who enjoy the most success in passing on the business tend to begin exploring post-retirement endeavours as early as their late forties or early fifties." (Craig E. Aronoff, Stephen L. McClure, and John L. Ward, *Family Business Succession: The Final Test of Greatness* (New York: Family Business Consulting Group, 2003), 14-16.)

6 DECADES OF CO-PRESIDENTS

SHARED LEADERSHIP WORKS IN FAMILY BUSINESS

John Nordstrom, Jack McMillan, Jim Nordstrom, Bruce Nordstrom.

Nordstrom Family, Nordstrom, Seattle, Washington

In 1901, John W. Nordstrom and Carl Wallin opened a shoe store in Seattle, Washington, named Wallin and Nordstrom. Over a century later, that shoe company is known as Nordstrom Inc., operates 117 Nordstrom stores across 30 states, and has annual sales of more than $9.3 billion. In addition to its Nordstrom stores, the company operates 104 Nordstrom Rack stores, two Jeffrey Boutiques, one treasure and bond store and a website for Internet sales (Nordstrom.com). In 1971,

the company went public to fund its growth and provide liquidity for members of the second generation, as they were moving into retirement.

Traditional wisdom in business circles suggests that "someone needs to be in charge, and therefore a corporation needs to have a single leader." But the Nordstrom family has successfully bucked this trend for more than 80 years.

In the 1920s, John's three boys, Everett, Elmer and Lloyd, joined the business. In 1931, the boys took over management responsibility for the fledgling firm and, although they had no formal titles, functioned as co-presidents. The three brothers had lunch together every day, in part because their dad wanted to limit their outside activities and keep them focused on the job of growing the company. But these regular meals together also helped to unify the family leadership. These three men continued to work together and share leadership as the company grew steadily over the next three decades.

In 1968, the mantle of leadership was ready to be transitioned to the third generation. By this time, Elmer's two sons, Jim and John, were working in the company, as was Everett's son, Bruce. Lloyd had three daughters but no sons, and so his brothers agreed that he could bring his son-in-law Jack McMillan into the company. Having seen how the second generation had successfully shared power and management authority, the four members of the third generation decided to operate as co-presidents, and this was obviously a successful formula for the next 31 years as the company expanded and flourished under their direction.[120]

Jack says shared leadership worked for the four members of his generation because of two things: the simple tradition of having lunch together daily and a culture of collaboration that was deeply rooted in the company's operations. According to Jack, "Unless the four of us were unanimous about a given strategy or decision, we didn't proceed." He then added, "Because we spent so much time together, and because we knew each other and the business so well, reaching decisions by consensus didn't seem that difficult. It almost happened by osmosis."

Things changed somewhat when the company went public. In order to satisfy their board and their new shareholders, each of them had a stint as president and then as co-chair of the board. However, in practice, they still functioned as a team (with the four of them essentially sharing the office of president).

When people object to the concept of shared leadership, Jack is quick to point out that our society idolizes the lone gunman and the solitary leader, but "Jesus created a leadership team with 12 disciples, and the organization they established has lasted a lot longer than Nordstrom." Therefore, "We shouldn't be surprised that shared leadership works. As long as there is mutual respect and collaboration, a team has the potential to outperform an individual every time."

Since 2000, Blake, Peter and Erik Nordstrom, three members of the fourth generation, have successfully shared the company leadership. Their continued success makes it clear that sharing power and authority continues to work well four generations later.

With their success, Nordstrom has now enjoyed an amazing and exemplary track record with three separate sibling teams. The first one lasted for 37 years and the second for 31 years. The current team is at 11 years and counting.

Today, the public company board has 11 members; 8 are independent members and 3 are members of the Nordstrom family.

Most people know Nordstrom for its legendary customer service that goes back to John W. Nordstrom's days of carrying a large inventory to serve the diverse tastes of every customer in town. The third generation really stepped up the company's commitment to service when, back in 1971, the leadership team was trying to decide what their new focus should be for the year and someone suggested customer service. According to Jack, "That's been our focus ever since."

In a family business, subjective judgments, clouded by family loyalties, can impair business decisions. At Nordstrom, the company is run by objective standards, and emotions aren't permitted to play much of a role. Consequently, the Nordstrom family has been able to harness the loyalty and intelligence of an enterprising and competitive family. No wonder they have been able to drive this retail giant forward for over a century.

Some people say that shared leadership can't work, and there may not be a lot of companies who have been successful with this strategy. But for the past eight decades, Nordstrom has proven not only that it can be done but also that it is integral to the outstanding business results that they have enjoyed.

[120.] "Egalitarian sibling partnerships are a delicate dance … the key is the fit between the overall family style and sibling history and the ownership structure that is chosen … Most experts on organizational governance would argue against shared ownership. And yet, in some family businesses it works." (Kevin Gersick, *Generation to Generation: Life Cycles of the Family Business* (Boston: Harvard Business Press, 1997), 44.)

DAD LETS GO OF REINS
REVELS IN SON'S SUCCESS

Harry Rosen and Larry Rosen. (photography by Christopher Wahl)

Rosen Family, Harry Rosen Inc., Toronto, Ontario

Harry Rosen has developed a sterling reputation in Canada by providing customers with outstanding service and quality men's clothing. In many ways, it is without peer in the clothing industry. It consists of over 700 employees, and annual sales are over $250 million. The company is Canada's largest upscale retailer for men and has captured approximately 40% of the quality menswear market.

The Rosen family has also done an extremely fine job with succession. When he turned 69, Harry transitioned the role of CEO to his eldest son, Larry.[121] Eleven years later, and having just recently celebrated his 80th birthday, Harry still carries the title of executive chairman, but he has no day-to-day management responsibilities. Since appointing his son as CEO, Harry has wisely avoided the temptation to interfere with his son's leadership. However, he has been available to provide Larry with support and advice when appropriate. The firm is 100% family owned but has a loyal and capable management team that is not dependent on Harry or Larry. "We have a talented executive group here that can run the company according to our values and standards," says Larry. "This is too big and sophisticated a business to be run like a family fiefdom."

I first met Larry when interviewing him for the Family Business Forum through the Sauder Business School at UBC. He was impressive, articulate and confident, and both he and Harry should be proud of how seamlessly they achieved management succession. Their intergenerational transition was effective because their approach to management succession was thoughtful and wise. Note the following key steps to their success:

1. Larry obtained a law degree and MBA. He practised corporate law in Toronto before joining the company full-time at the age of 29.
2. When he joined the company, Larry started on the bottom rung, as a buyer.
3. Learning all aspects of the business along the way, it took Larry 15 years to ascend to the top job.

4. Harry retired as chairman and chief executive officer before his 70th birthday. (Note that he stayed past the traditional retirement age but didn't overstay his welcome, as so many founders are tempted to do.)
5. Larry was not put in a position of ultimate authority until his mid-40s. By this time, he had developed the maturity and experience necessary to be respected as a leader by non-family employees. At the same time, he was still young enough to have lots of energy and decades of opportunity in front of him.
6. After appointing Larry as CEO, Harry has remained interested and involved, continuing to visit stores and hold workshops for employees in the tailoring division.
7. Larry worked hard, earned his credentials and waited patiently for his father to be comfortable before the baton was passed.

Harry summarized it all by saying, "As a founder, your greatest achievement may not be what you did but that you were able to give what you did some permanence through transition. Really great organizations don't die with the founder. They continue for generations."

[121.] "Communication with the family about succession should begin as soon as possible, ideally before any candidates have been identified." (Aronoff, McClure, and Ward, *Family Business Succession,* 51.)

HEALTHY COMPETITION CREATES UNITY

SPAWNS EXCELLENCE AMONGST COUSINS

Simpson Seeds is in good hands with these six cousins all working together: (from left to right) Elyce Simpson Fraser (trader), Jamie Simpson (farm and facility operations), Tyler Simpson (trader), Nolan Simpson (IT), Trevor Simpson (farm and facility operations), Nicole Allport (accounting and seed development), in front of their new main office building, Moose Jaw, SK.

Simpson Family, Simpson Seeds Inc., Moose Jaw, Saskatchewan

Textbooks on family business often cover cousin consortiums as a natural evolution from a sibling partnership stage in a family business. However, in the vast majority of cases, by the time the family business gets to the cousin stage, the number of family members working in the business is far outweighed by the number who own shares. In essence, it's typical for a family business to move more towards a broadly dispersed group of owners while a diminishing number of family members are employed. This is not the case for the Simpson family from Moose Jaw, Saskatchewan, who own and manage Simpson Seeds Incorporated.

Tom, Greg and John are three enterprising brothers who began their careers working on their father's farm. Over three decades ago, they incorporated the company to begin value-added processing in agribusiness, principally focused on lentils. Today, the three boys have a total of nine off-spring; six of the cousins are employed full-time in the family business. I've had the privilege of working with this family on a professional basis for over four years and have noted numerous positive attributes of how they conduct their business affairs.

This cousin consortium works well, in part because of the following:

1. Healthy Competition: Years ago, a well-known book, *The Inner Game of Tennis*, presented the surprising notion that we should wish our competition to play well; only then can we be pushed to achieve our own best performance. In other words, without the stimulus of a competent competitor, none of us can reach deep inside for the focus and effort necessary to become, or do, our best. Healthy competition has played a positive role amongst the six cousins working together in Simpson Seeds. As one member of the family takes on more responsibility and excels in his role, others are challenged and stimulated to "pick up their game." As a result, the business, the family and the individuals all benefit.

2. A Commitment to the Whole: For competition to be healthy and not destructive, there needs to be a commitment to the whole. This essential precondition involves a commitment to always doing what is best for the organization and the family

(rather than simply seeking personal advancement in one's own career). Tom and John have modelled this for the family by allowing Greg, the natural salesman, to serve as company president, while Tom looks after the farm, and John takes care of production and equipment. The latter roles aren't as glamorous and don't come with worldwide travel to sell their products, but Tom and John have willingly done their part, for the benefit of the whole.

3. Branch Agnosticism: In a family with many branches, it's natural to have a stronger allegiance to your parents, your siblings and your branch of the family. Within Simpson Seeds, all the cousins emphasize the Simpson clan rather than their own branch of the family. If any family member is talking about family, they refer to the entire Simpson clan as "the family."

4. Mentoring by Uncles: Within the Simpson Seeds organization, it is typical for cousins to work for their uncles and to be mentored by them. Examples include Jamie, who has been mentored by his Uncle Tom to manage the farm, Trevor, who has been mentored by his Uncle John in his role as production manager for the red lentil processing plant, and Tyler, who is being mentored by Uncle Greg in his role as a grain trader.

COLLABORATING SIBLINGS THRIVE

INDEPENDENT PROPERTIES ENDS CONFUSION

*L.J., Laura, George and Jane at a family team event at
Thunderbird Show Park, Langley, BC.*

*Tidball Family, Thunderbird Show Park,
Langley, British Columbia.*

George Tidball is a legendary
entrepreneur from Vancouver who
brought McDonald's to western Canada and founded the Keg restaurants.
Perhaps all of this was to be expected
from this brilliant graduate of the Harvard business school.

But George is quick to point
out that it was his wife, Diane's, idea
to purchase the master franchise for
McDonald's. He also explains that he
started the Keg because he didn't want

to have to change out of his jeans in
order to get a good steak.

George and Diane have four children. The eldest, Stephen, runs his
own construction company and is co-
owner of three Keg restaurants. Kathy,
the eldest daughter, is a schoolteacher
and, while Diane's health is failing,
functions as the glue that helps keep
the Tidball clan together. Jane, a CMA
by training, is president and CEO of
Thunderbird Show Park, which Diane
created. This park spurred her younger
daughter, Laura's, passion for horse-

back riding, and she is now a two-time Olympian who has her own business in partnership with her husband, Brent, called Thunderbird Show Stables.

A few years ago, Thunderbird Show Stables and Thunderbird Show Park operated on the same property. Initially this made sense, given that the show park was devoted to hosting riding competitions and the stables were dedicated to training competitive horses and riders. Unfortunately, two operations owned by Tidball family members, bearing the name "Thunderbird," dedicated to competitive riding and operating on the same property created considerable confusion. As an advisor to the family, it was my privilege to help the family develop a plan to rectify this problem. After much discussion, Laura and Brent made a strategic decision to re-establish their business at a new location a few miles away. This move, which initially felt like we were tearing the family apart, has actually done the exact opposite. Now that the two operations are truly independent, there is less confusion, less tension and less conflict.

Laura and Brent's company (Thunderbird Stables) is still Thunderbird Show Park's biggest customer, and the two operations enjoy many synergies when hosting a major event. However, each now has clear lines of authority with their staff and a clear separation of operations and costs. As a result, both enterprises are thriving.

They say that "fences make good neighbours." If so, perhaps it can also be said that "separate properties make good siblings."

PART IV

BEST *Practices* AND TOOLS

BEST PRACTICES FOR FAMILY BUSINESS, AS OBSERVED IN THE BERSTEIN FAMILY

Ben, Dan and Jason Berstein all work for their family business, Nixon Uniform Service and Medical Wear, with their father and company founder, Murray. The brothers are all still in their 30s, and yet the family has been working diligently together on their succession plan for over 10 years. This means they started succession planning in earnest when all members of the next generation were only in their 20s.

Jason, the eldest, serves as the president of the company. His brother Dan is general manager, and Ben, the youngest, is a regional sales manager.

In order to develop a strong partnership, the brothers meet together every other week as business partners. When they get together, they talk about ways to improve the company, as well as how they are each doing as associates, partners and brothers. They also discuss career development and family business matters.

Perhaps most importantly, in their roles as shareholders and managers, they provide one another with feedback and coaching. When I asked them how they learned to give and receive coaching, Ben explained that all senior executives in their company have received formal training on how to provide and accept feedback.

One of the other major benefits of these regular meetings is that they provide a forum where the three brothers are able to plan and prepare for the future. Topics that they have addressed together include ownership succession, insurance needs and family/business relations.

When they are not in their partnership meetings, Jason is senior to Ben and Dan on the organization chart, and his brothers respect his management responsibility to lead the company. Day to day, the shareholders and other managers know that they must follow the organization's chain of command.

However, the shareholders also know if they disagree with anything that is happening in the company, they will be able to discuss it at their next shareholders' meeting. This provides a safe and regular forum for concerns to be discussed. Being able to talk about issues regularly keeps communication lines open and relationships healthy.

The more I spoke with these three brothers, the more impressed I was with the outstanding job they have done working together. The brothers take turns preparing the shareholders' meeting agenda and chairing the meetings. By rotating the chairperson every meeting, they are learning to share responsibility and to develop their leadership skills. By meeting together regularly and by communicating openly, they have also fostered a culture of interdependence.

From my perspective, this family has done many things that could be appropriately termed "best practice" for a family in business. They began about 10 years ago, when Dad asked the brothers to interview and select a knowledgeable family business advisor to help educate and guide the family through the ownership and leadership transition process.[122]

It is significant that Murray gave his sons the opportunity to recruit and select who they wanted to work with, because by doing the research themselves they learned quite a bit about the process they were about to embark upon. Perhaps even more importantly, because it was their choice who they would work with, they have been more committed to making a success of the working relationship.

With the assistance of their advisor, for the past 10 years the Berstein family has held an annual two-day planning retreat. The first day, which is not attended by spouses, is a shareholders' meeting, and it is focused on business issues. The second day is a family council meeting, which spouses are invited to attend. Here, they discuss family business practices and actively participate in topical discussions like philanthropy and the development of a family mission statement as a framework for the function of the family.

During the retreat, the shareholders also develop goals and objectives for management. These are stated in general terms; most important for this family is the target long-term growth rate.

[122.] After interviewing several potential advisors, they chose to work with Steve McClure, of the Family Business Consulting Group.

Following these annual shareholders' meetings, a formal strategic planning process is triggered within the company, involving the senior management team. This ultimately incorporates financial and budgetary planning, operational planning and workforce planning for the company. After several years of trial and error, they have developed a well-established planning process. It follows a cycle that begins in April and cascades through the organization, culminating in February, just in time to begin the cycle for the next year.

Overseeing the business, the family elected a board of directors that includes five independent members. The board was initially formed by Murray, with individuals who could advise him as he was starting the process of succession planning.

To help him figure out how to set up the board, Murray asked his youngest son to do some research. Ben came home with a stack of books on boards. Murray used John Ward's *Creating Effective Boards for Private Enterprises* as his handbook while building the board. He found it not only educated him, but it also gave him a step-by-step process for identifying and recruiting qualified candidates.

The board is responsible for approving and overseeing management's strategic plan and executive and family-employee compensation and reviewing business performance. It also provides support and advice to the family and executive team. More recently, now that the three brothers are co-owners, they are working with their father to select new directors who will help guide the business in the future.

The original board selected by Murray included people whom he trusted to help him choose who would succeed him and become the next leader of the company. In addition, almost 10 years in advance, the family discussed how they would like the president to be selected.

The leadership selection process included the role of the family, management and the board and the development of an ideal candidate profile. By having these discussions long before a decision was needed, the family could take the time to get educated on their alternatives, in an unemotional, unhurried atmosphere.

With the guidance of their family business advisor, the family, including the matriarch and patriarch, discussed whether or not they wanted to have a single leader or shared leadership for the company. After carefully considering how most successful non-family companies are led, they decided that they would like to select a "single leader." However, given that the three siblings were potentially going to become equal owners, they decided on what their advisor termed a "first amongst equals" strategy for leadership (reflecting both their plans for equal ownership and their desire to have one of the brothers serve as president).

Around the same time, the family also confirmed their intentions for the business to be eventually owned equally by the three young men. Later in the process, Murray explained that he would be willing to transfer ownership to his sons and provide them with the freedom to lead the organization, provided that he was able to achieve the financial freedom necessary to retire independent of the business. To accomplish this, the family worked with the management team to put together a financial plan to facilitate the ownership succession in a manner that would not disrupt the business.

Murray demonstrated considerable foresight in this regard. Typically, business owners build a business with a plan to eventually sell it or pass it on to the next generation. Murray did something quite unique and insightful. While his dream was always to pass the business on to his sons, he was aware that one component of the business would be more logically sold. Rather than choosing between the two traditional paths (build to sell or build to bequeath), he developed a hybrid plan.

For several decades he grew not only the part of the business that he wanted his sons to one day own but also the segment of the company that ultimately ended up being sold to a strategic buyer. This enlightened approach ended up eventually providing some liquidity for the family, which made the intergenerational transition much easier to accomplish.

Murray was also advised that it would be helpful to the next generation if he was not dependent on the company financially during his retirement years. This, he was told, would enable him to more easily keep his "hands off" the operations, because he would no longer have a vested interest in the company's performance.

Having done this, Murray has been amazed at how fundamentally this has affected his perspective. Now that his finances are independent of the company, his attachment to the business has changed. He still cheers his sons on, from the sidelines, but he no longer feels a need to influence their play calling.

In 2007, when it finally came time to choose a new president for the company, the three brothers were asked to bring forward a recommendation for approval of the family, senior management and board of directors. Together, the brothers unanimously endorsed Jason to take over the reins of the company.

The family, senior management and board all supported the recommendation. (If the family, senior management and board had been unable to reach a consensus, a family consensus or super-majority was required, and if there was still no resolution, Murray was responsible for making the decision.)

Everyone I spoke to said that Jason is doing a good job as president. (However, he and his brothers have expressly stated that Jason doesn't necessarily have the top job "for life," and his performance will be subject to annual review by the independent board of directors.)

When I asked Ben, Dan and Jason how they had managed to be so successful in all of their succession efforts, they were quick to praise their father. They said, "Dad had the wisdom and humility to plan for his own departure. He was also not threatened by the potential loss of power." This is illustrated powerfully by the fact that Jason, as president, and Murray, as board chair, both revise their job descriptions every year, so that more authority and responsibility is transferred from father to son every 12 months.

Today, the office of CEO is vacant, giving Jason something to aspire to in the future. Murray serves as executive chair. In this role, Murray has maintained some client relationship responsibilities and occasional ongoing contact with senior management. However, Jason is responsible for all operations. When Murray stepped down as CEO, he voluntarily proposed that his own salary be reduced by 75%. This, he stated, "was to avoid placing a burden on the company, and also to reinforce the reality that he is no longer in charge of day to day operations."

When I continued to search for clues as to how they had developed such wisdom in managing their family business, all four of the men stated that the education materials provided by their family business advisor were instrumental in them being able to learn what to do in order to work effectively together and to accomplish a smooth intergenerational transition. Rather than learn by trial and error, the family has been dedicated to reading and learning how to wisely integrate family and business. They have done this in every area of family business, including executive compensation, employment policies, succession planning and corporate governance.

To provide a solid foundation upon which to build for the future, the Bersteins have invested time in clarifying several important topics. Murray said that it has been important that "We have unanimous agreement on our shared values, as well as our mission and vision." This has enabled the shareholders, board and management to maintain alignment and has provided unity of purpose and direction.

As part of their review of compensation, the family adopted a policy of market pay for market jobs. This was done so that family and non-family employees would all know that salaries would be equitable and also reflective of the level of responsibility of each individual in the company.

The Bersteins also work hard at keeping clear those items that are the responsibility of the family and those that are the responsibility of the business. They believe that it is important to be clear regarding family, board and management responsibilities in order to avoid stepping on each other's toes. If they can maintain discipline in all these areas, they believe they can have harmony in the family and success in the business.

Clearly, they are having great success in both!

TOOLS FOR HELPING FAMILIES IN BUSINESS

DEFINING CONSENSUS

Making decisions by consensus is one of the most powerful strategies a family can employ for creating and maintaining unity. However, in order to adopt this approach, some individuals may need to abandon their belief that they "know better." Others may need to step up to the plate and no longer "hide" their opinions. To some, this may sound reckless or even foolhardy.

In order for consensus decision-making to be effective, all family members need to respect and really listen to one another. However, when you think about it, this is how families ought to treat each other anyway.

In chapter 14 (Boards of Directors) and chapter 16 (Governance and Family Councils), I explain some of the reasons why I think consensus is so important for families in business. In Peter Leach's book *Family Businesses: The Essentials*, he offers the following comments regarding what consensus is all about:

> *The goal for the family's planning process is consensus, but, unhelpfully, dictionary definitions of 'consensus' do not go much further than 'agreement.' The notion is so central to developing effective communication and teamwork in family firms, and for implementing a successful family plan, that it is important to try to pin down some ingredients of what consensus adds up to in practice.*
>
> *During his time at the University of Pennsylvania's Wharton School, Peter Davis interviewed leaders of the US Quaker religious community, ask-*

ing them what consensus—obviously an important tenet for this peace-loving movement—meant to them. The main responses included:

- *an understanding of, and unity with, the ideals of the organisation that make consensus rather than majority rule preferable;*
- *an understanding of group individuals and their idiosyncrasies;*
- *a deep commitment to listening;*
- *a sense of trust in the validity of each member's contribution;*
- *an openness to learn from those who may be better informed;*
- *a conviction that individual knowledge untempered by group wisdom is often shallow;*
- *a willingness to undertake self-examination, particularly when a compromise between an individual's own point of view and the point of view of the group has the potential to lead to consensus.*[123]

[123.] Peter Leach, *Family Businesses: The Essentials* (London: Profile Books, 2007), 59.

SAMPLE FAMILY CONSTITUTION

Vic Bachechi and his family are from Albuquerque, New Mexico, and their story is featured in part III of this book. The constitution that they have created for their family business is both thoughtful and comprehensive. It is included below, with the kind permission of their board of directors.

CARLO, INC., A CORPORATE CONSTITUTION

Carlo, Inc., a New Mexico corporation founded in 1953, has developed the following corporate culture that has distinguished our past and will enrich our future:

HERITAGE AND PURPOSE

Carlo is a family-owned business created to help current and future stockholders form a financial base for their security, independence and well-being. Remember those who built; build for those to come. Without ego, entitlement or guilt, we celebrate our legacy of accomplishments and rewards, of contribution to family and community and of self-determination and sacrifice as we acknowledge, expand and advance that legacy for future generations of Carlo Stockholders.

VALUES

Love good, do right, resist greed and live humbly, patiently and with good humor. Because the business horizon is always changing and market cycles while inevitable are unpredictable, it is not possible to either represent or warrant future opportunities or financial performance, nevertheless Carlo will endeavor to achieve the following goals:

INVESTMENT AND MANAGEMENT GOALS

Invest long-term and manage a portfolio of commercial, developed, income-producing real estate, assembled in economically efficient clusters which lie in the path of progress, in at least one major metropolitan market in every economically developed region in the world. Passionately practice "walk about" management so that we know our customers and markets intimately. Manage boldly and persistently but never forget the stewardship entrusted to us by our Stockholders. Perform with operational excellence in all facets of our business. Pay market compensation to all staff. Encourage family participation based on the needs of the Company and the interest, qualifications and ability of the family member; strive to keep stockholders informed about Company operations; provide education on the best family business practices.

FINANCIAL GOALS

Average a XX% annual increase over time in the Approved Stockholder share price calculated pursuant to the Stockholder Agreement and set forth in the Triennial Business Valuation. Company debt should not exceed XX% of its assets, based on the most recent Triennial Business Valuation. Pay a XX%, per share dividend annually, using the most recent Triennial Business Valuation Approved Stockholder share price, less stockholder meeting and Family Office expenses. To donate to the Foundation of Carlo Inc., in cash or in-kind services, an amount equal to the lesser of the annual dividend paid or the maximum charitable deduction allowed by the IRS for Carlo Inc. and furthermore to provide the Foundation with the information needed to determine its market allocations.

SAMPLE FAMILY EMPLOYMENT POLICY

The following family employment policy was developed by a friend and colleague for their family business. It is well crafted and a suitable model for other families to use as a reference point in creating their own policies. This document is used with their permission, but on the condition that its authors and their family remain anonymous.

PURPOSE

The purpose of this policy is to define the procedures, process and criteria that will govern how our family's lineal descendants and/or their spouses enter and exit from the family companies' employ. Where "THE COMPANY" is repeatedly referred to in this policy statement, it extends to "THE COMPANY" shops, services, and any enterprise the family might become involved with in the future.

This employment policy is intended to remove the lack of knowledge that currently exists so that interested family members can shape their career paths accordingly.

We believe that clear, constructive communication of this policy will contribute to the long-term success of our family and "Company."

PHILOSOPHY

Our family philosophy is that each offspring as they grow to adulthood should follow the path of their passions. Through their teens and twenties, hopefully they will each find something that makes them look forward to going to work every day, a field of endeavour where they feel they can make a meaningful contribution and that fits their interests and skills. As such, it is equally possible that "THE COMPANY" is or is not a fit for them. There is no interest on my behalf to see offspring in the business if it is not the right thing for them.

This policy has been developed because we, as a family, subscribe to the following principals:

1. We must raise strong, self-sufficient children. Our children will be happiest with themselves and the world around them when they are strong, independent individuals. It is for their own benefit that we have set high standards for them to meet if they hope to be employed by "THE COMPANY." Our company cannot be a haven for the weak, or an easy way out of the question, "what will I do for a living?"

2. We must protect and preserve our employees' jobs. "THE COMPANY" employs hundreds of people, who depend on the company for economic exist-

ence. We depend on our employees to run our business. In turn, we owe them an allegiance beyond a paycheque. Their jobs, and ours, will be most secure when we maintain high standards for hiring employees, be they family or non-family.

3. We must be fair to qualified family members wishing to have a career at "THE COMPANY." Just as it is unfair to the family member and the company to hire unqualified family members, it is also unfair to ignore the talents of qualified family members in employment decisions. If a family member and non-family member apply for the same position, both being equal in experience, qualifications, education, and recommendations, we should hire the family member.

While it may be easier, and less complicated, at times, to hire a non-family member, if we do so we are using reverse discrimination. Just as it is proper and right to the family member and the business to set high standards for employment, it is also proper and right to give family members equal opportunity.

It is the policy of this company to search out and employ, at all levels, individuals who have the ability to manage vertical and horizontal relationships, who show evidence of ability and willingness to take initiative, who exhibit self-confidence and high self-esteem, and who are both independent and responsible in managing their lives and their jobs.

We subscribe to the philosophy that the opportunity to be employed in our company must be earned; it is not a birthright. Our business succeeds best when professional competence is the criterion for entrance to employment. Further, high-level competence must be supported by a sustained performance record. We believe that family members who cannot meet these standards will be happiest when employed elsewhere.

GENERAL CONDITIONS

1. Family members must meet the same criteria for hiring as non-family applicants.
2. Family members are expected to meet the same level of performance required of non-family employees. Like non-family employees, they will be subject to performance reviews and to the same rules regarding firing.
3. As a general principle, family members will be supervised by non-family members.
4. Compensation will be at "fair market value" for the position held.
5. Family members are eligible for temporary, seasonal employment, with "sea-

sonal" defined as four months or less per year. Family members may be re-employed for temporary employment each year on an as-needed basis.

6. No family member may be employed in a permanent entry-level position (that is, a position that requires no previous experience or training).

7. Family members seeking permanent employment must meet one of the following requirements:

- Earn a two-year degree from an accredited college, and work twelve years for a company other than "THE COMPANY." Three of the twelve years of outside employment must be with the same company. The qualifications are, at minimum, a mid-level management position.

- Earn a four-year degree from an accredited college, and work ten years for a company other than "THE COMPANY." Three years with the same company will be required.

- Earn an advanced degree (master's, etc.) from an accredited college and work at least ten years for an outside company. Again, three years must be with the same company.

In addition to the above requirements, the qualifications achieved and capabilities developed must be on a par with—at a minimum—a mid-level manager that "THE COMPANY" would hire from the outside.

It is preferable that the family member gain outside experience in the field they desire employment in within the family business. The recommendations and comments of a family member's supervisors while working for an outside company will weigh heavily in the decision to hire that family member. It is our view that if a family member is not a valued employee elsewhere, then it is not likely that he or she will be happy or useful in "THE COMPANY."

APPLYING FOR A POSITION

Family members must make their interest known in writing to the president/chief executive officer of "THE COMPANY." When a position becomes available, only family members who have expressed an interest in employment in writing will be informed of the opportunity. They may then complete the normal application forms and submit the application for appropriate processing and consideration.

SUCCESSION

The size of our company necessitates our reliance on non-family professionals. These industry leaders bring fresh ideas into our business and thus renewal to our family and to our business. To provide incentive for these employees to excel and to aspire to the highest position their ability will allow, it is possible, and probable, that the position of president of the company will be held by non-family employees. We encourage all employees to strive for excellence in their work. Promotions at all levels of the business will only be given to employees—family or non-family—who demonstrate excellence.

A family member may rise to presidency if he/she has shown competence as a leader, as defined by the results he/she has achieved as reviewed by his/her supervisors, if the position is available. If the position is not available, the family member will have to wait until it is. If more than one family member is interested in the position and competent, the decision of the president and the board will be final.

As president or in any other position, the family member has the responsibility to act in the best interests of "THE COMPANY" and its employees, whatever difficult decisions that will entail. The president will be responsible to either the chair or the trustees or a board of advisors.

WE, the undersigned, agree with the spirit and intent of the provisions set forth in this document.

WE agree this document represents the best interests of both "THE COMPANY" and the family members to whom it applies.

NAME:_____

NAME:_____

NAME:_____

NAME:_____

Signed this _____ day of _____, 20__

SAMPLE AGENDA FOR AN INITIAL FAMILY MEETING

The following is a standard outline that may be used for an initial family meeting. This agenda assumes that individual interviews have been conducted with all family members prior to meeting together as a group.

1) Ice breaker (10 min.)

Every meeting should start with an opportunity for all family members to "check in" and "become present." By ensuring that everyone speaks, all participants are reminded that their voice matters. Because a family meeting is an inclusive gathering, everyone should have an equal say. (This is the family's first opportunity to practice good communication by all speaking up and by all listening respectfully.)

2) Review agenda (5 min.)

Even if the agenda has been circulated in advance, it is helpful to review what is coming up, both to help clarify expectations and to provide an opportunity for last minute revisions. (This is the family's first opportunity in the meeting to make a decision together: Do they agree on the agenda?)

3) Develop a family code of conduct (45 min.)

In order to create a healthy environment for open communication and joint decision-making, it is helpful for a family to develop an agreed-upon set of ground rules for how they want to conduct themselves when together for a family meeting. A well-conceived code of conduct will specify conditions that will provide for safe and productive discussions. A code of conduct should be "custom built" by each family, so that it reflects their personality and priorities. However, it will typically include statements like "be respectful, be honest, be open minded," etc. (This exercise provides the family another opportunity to practice good communication skills, by listening to each other's priorities. The family also is able to make another decision together: Do they agree with the proposed code of conduct, and are they willing to adhere to it for the remainder of the meeting?)

4) Presentation of themes (60 min.)

In working with families in business, most professional facilitators begin by interviewing each person individually, prior to meeting with everyone as a group. During this process, everyone may be asked to advise what "issues or concerns" the family should be discussing. At the first joint meeting, the facilitator is then able to provide a foundational report, which summarizes all the issues or concerns which have been raised. This report groups the topics raised into "themes," which can then be addressed by the family. (The report will usually be given formally with a PowerPoint presentation, so that everyone can hear the information at the same time and in the same way. Often, some of the themes are difficult to "put on the table," and by choosing his or her words carefully, a skilled facilitator can help a family to start dealing with the "elephants in the room.")

5) Prioritization of themes (30 min.)

Working together, the family is given an opportunity to decide, by consensus, which themes deserve priority attention. Often there will be as many as two dozen topics that warrant discussion, and so it is helpful for the family to wrestle with where to start and to seek agreement. (This is an additional opportunity for the family to practice joint decision-making.)

6) Brainstorming what to do next (20 min.)

Rather than "telling" the family what to do next, a good facilitator will enable the family to brainstorm how to proceed. The family will often know what they should do, and they just need to be invited to voice their wisdom and to act on it. (During this part of the meeting, family members have another chance to practice good communication skills, by sharing and listening, in a non-judgmental way. During a brainstorming session, all ideas should be accepted and recorded, regardless of whether they are agreed to by others.)

7) Deciding on next steps (15 min.)

Although the first meeting is essentially a time of discovery, it is also important for the family to agree on what to do next. This allows the family to see hope and to understand what they need to do in order to move forward and establish some positive momentum. A skilled facilitator will usually be able to help the family choose some clear action steps that everyone can agree on. These may include the delegation of tasks to members of the family or research to be undertaken by members of the group. (For the fourth time in the meeting, the family is able to practice joint decision-making.)

8) Next meeting date (10 min.)

While everyone is together, it is best to agree upon the next time to get together. This provides a natural "completion date" for the agreed-upon action steps and also contributes to the sense of forward momentum. (This is the fifth and final opportunity in the meeting for joint decision-making.)

9) Appreciations and difficulties (10 min.)

At the conclusion of the meeting, all family members are encouraged to express "appreciation" to one another. Everyone is invited to contribute and to be as explicit as possible in articulating what they liked about the meeting. This ritual allows everyone a few moments for reflection and an opportunity to end on a positive note, regardless of how difficult portions of the meeting may have been. If there are things that members of the family found difficult, they should also voice these briefly, so as to not "carry baggage" from the room and so that everyone can consider how to potentially do things better the next time. (This becomes the final opportunity in the meeting for the family to practice good communication, again by listening and sharing.)

SAMPLE CONFLICT RESOLUTION MECHANISMS

Families in business will have conflict; that is a reality of life. However, rather than being unprepared, families can plan ahead and determine how they want to handle disagreements when they come. The following are four creative options for families to consider.

1. THE AMULET

Four brothers in the Midwest inherited a large meat-packing business 35 years ago. On his deathbed, their father said to them, "You are each inheriting a quarter of the shares of this business. Strive to reach consensus whenever you can. However, it is very likely that there will be times when the four of you will not agree." He then produced a bolo tie with a silver and turquoise amulet that he kept under his pillow and said, "I will assign this amulet to one of you at random. And in those instances when you cannot reach consensus, the one who has the amulet should be given the right to the last word." The father paused and then said, "There is a catch, however. Whenever the authority of the amulet is invoked to settle an issue, the one imposing his will on the others must forgo the amulet and wait a turn before he is eligible to have it again."

The brothers, who instantly adopted the system, swear by it. In 35 years, the amulet has gone around twice and the brothers have managed to grow a highly successful billion-dollar company. Among the many reasons why this system seems to work so well for them are these key ones: The brothers were able to evoke the father's memory and were willing to abide by his proposal, and, from a practical standpoint, the system encourages the brother who wears the amulet to push for consensus unless he feels so strongly about an issue that he is willing to forgo his right to the last word.

2. THE WISE SWISS GENTLEMAN

Two Chilean brothers who inherited a sizeable family business from their father had been encouraged by him before his death to follow a simple procedure when they disagreed. The father had a trusted business associate living in Switzerland, a man of great experience and judgment. On those few occasions when the brothers could not agree, they were to call the father's friend in Switzerland to mediate. They follow the procedure to this day. Each brother gets on the phone and argues for his point of view. The Swiss gentleman, now in his eighties, then says, "Frederick is right" or "George is right." The brothers abide by his ruling, and that ends the disagreement. Most importantly, they have called the father's friend only three times in 30 years of working together.

3. MARTHA'S RULES

When needed, a *majority-rules-yet-a-minority-may-veto* method will be used. Decision items (proposals) that cannot be decided through simple discussion and consensus are identified, and all individuals may vote in one of four ways:

1. **For** the proposal—a vote in favour of the proposal.
2. **Against** the proposal—a vote that indicates you don't like the proposal, but you can live with it.
3. **Object** to the proposal—a vote that indicates you cannot live with this proposal.
4. **Abstain**—a vote that indicates you do not have enough information or do not want to participate in the decision.

If there are only for, against or abstain votes, then the majority rules. However, if there is only one object vote, the proposal is defeated. In such a case, three things can happen:

- The individuals who object can voice their concerns with the proposal or offer an alternative (or someone else may); the proposal can be modified, and another vote can be taken right away.
- Discussion and an alternative proposal at another date. Discussion takes the form of seeking alternatives and exploring the interests that are being served and not being served by the proposal. The objection may not be resolved during the meeting and may continue until the next scheduled meeting. However, when objecting an individual must offer an alternative proposal within a reasonable period of time.
- As a result of an honest effort, there is no change; the objection remains intact, and the proposal does not go through.

4. AUCTION ARRANGEMENTS

Excerpt: David Bentall Speech on Family Business Succession

We structured an auction that any one of the shareholders could initiate. Once triggered by a formal offer to purchase the other shareholders would then be obligated to either accept that offer within 60 days or bid back for a purchase price of at least 5% more than the previous offer. This bidding process would continue in subsequent five-day increments, with each of us offering more than the previous bid until eventually an acceptable sale price had been reached.

This auction process was designed to ensure that we would all have a long-term ownership in the business unless we were offered a price at which we would rather sell. As someone who was involved in the management of the business, this kind of arrangement was very reassuring. I knew that I would never be forced to sell without first being offered a price that was more than I would be prepared to pay for the business.

In 1998, I offered to buy the business from my siblings, and they said to me that, at the price I was offering, they would be willing to buy from me. This is how my sister, Mary, and her husband, Phil George, ended up offering to buy my shares. My older sister, Helen, then decided to also sell, and this gave Mary and Phil, through their holding company, Seacliff Holdings, the opportunity to acquire 100% of the company.

DEFINING ESTATE FREEZES AND FAMILY TRUSTS

For a family in business, two of the most common strategies for minimizing taxes are an estate freeze and a family trust. The following are a layman's definition of these important concepts.

WHAT IS AN ESTATE FREEZE?

In Canada, we do not have death taxes. When a business or family assets pass from one generation to the next at the time of death, it is considered a "deemed sale" (for tax purposes). If the assets or business are now worth more than the price paid (when acquired by the elder generation), then there will be tax owing on the increase. This is known as a capital gains tax. If a family started a new business from nothing or grew the business substantially during their lifetime, the capital gains tax owing may be significant. In cases where there has been no financial planning, the amount owing can be so overwhelming that it may even force the next generation to sell the business in order to pay the taxes.

To avoid this scenario and to defer taxes as effectively as possible, many families elect to transfer their business/assets to their offspring decades in advance of their demise. This "shelters" some of the growth in the estate by transferring it to the next generation and defers some of the capital gains taxes that would otherwise become due on their demise. One way to accomplish this is to create an "estate freeze." This mechanism essentially "freezes" the value of the estate at a point in time, so that the tax liability will stop growing during the elder generation's lifetime. To do this, the company creates two classes of shares and transfers the "growth shares" to the next generation. Any increase in value from the date of the estate freeze on will accrue to them as the owners, and not to the parents' generation.

WHAT IS A FAMILY TRUST?

Family trusts can trace their origins back to the days of lords and ladies in the British Empire. A trust was often established when a lord died, leaving infant children with significant wealth. Rather than giving an immature child/children the responsibilities of managing castles, lands and other business interests, trustees were appointed to look after these assets until the child/children became of age.

The trustees' duties were twofold: to carefully preserve the inheritance and manage the trust "assets" and to determine what "distributions" should be paid out from the trust for the care and education of the "beneficiary or beneficiaries" of the trust.

Today, trustees have the same two primary responsibilities: to manage the trust assets and to determine the trust distributions.

The obvious benefit of a trust is that it creates a vehicle whereby competent trustees can be chosen to manage wealth on behalf of those who may not yet have the age or experience to do so wisely.

Another benefit is that distributions for beneficiaries may be carefully determined so as to achieve the objectives of those who established the trust (e.g., funding a child's education).

Another key benefit of a family trust is that it functions as an effective tax deferral mechanism (similar, in some ways, to an estate freeze). When assets are transferred into a trust, they are no longer owned by an individual; they are owned by the trust. Therefore, when an individual dies, there is no "deemed sale" of assets and no capital gains tax to pay (with the exception of any assets not transferred into the trust).

Although sometimes awkward to talk about, a family trust can also be a potentially helpful shield against any fallout from a marital breakup. If a family wants to avoid having their wealth become part of a divorce settlement, it can create a family trust that specifies that only direct descendants (and not spouses) can be beneficiaries of the trust.

Typically the ancient trusts will dissolve when the beneficiary turns 21 and reaches adulthood. (This is partially why there is a 21-year rule in Canada that requires the automatic dissolution of a trust after 21 years.)

The unfortunate part of family trusts is that they can provide a means of perpetuating childhood. This can happen because if a trust provides for all the needs of an individual, he or she may never be required to take responsibility for his or her own life, including financial affairs. This can result in a permanent dependency and lack of maturation.

One of my clients cynically refers to his "ne'er-do-well" compatriots who lived off the largess of their family's trust funds in the Cayman Islands as "trustafarians."

I can think of no sadder commentary on "wealth gone wrong" than this derogatory term.

Wise families who utilize family trusts as an estate planning tool are careful to avoid creating dependencies in the next generation. However, in order to do this they are required to exercise both wisdom and diligence.

BOARD OF DIRECTORS' RECRUITMENT STRATEGY

It has been my privilege to assist numerous families to recruit boards of directors and advisory boards. The following process has been very effective in attracting excellent candidates for numerous client families.

1. Develop a board prospectus for approval of the family (summarizing background information on the company).
2. Finalize the strategic plan for the company (to ensure it is clear where you are going as a firm).
3. Develop a board expertise/needs matrix document, based on the strategic plan. (List the expertise you are looking for on the board.)
4. Hold a management meeting, to identify centres of influence (including lawyers, accountants, and business associates who could assist in the identification of potential board members).
5. Research the compensation range for directors of similar companies.
6. Phone the centres of influence, to request their assistance in identifying the desired expertise. (Send them copies of the prospectus.)
7. Develop a list of prospects and record them on the needs matrix.
8. Rank candidates, based on their expertise and company needs.
9. Discuss in a family meeting which prospects would warrant an approach.
10. Preplan calls to prospects, including careful development of questions.
11. Meet with top prospects to discuss potential. (Conduct formal interviews but do not offer them the position at the first meeting.)
12. Debrief after meetings and determine whether to proceed or not with each candidate.
13. Do reference checks.
14. Finalize compensation to be offered.
15. Draft letter of invitation to prospective board members (including a letter explaining legal structure, advisory board responsibilities, and liabilities).
16. Meet with prospects to formally offer a board position and seek agreement.
17. Prepare a board orientation package (including financial information, company history, strategic plan, and resumes for key employees, etc.).
18. Assist in the development of a board agenda for the first meeting with outsiders.
19. Return in a year, or 18 months, to do a board assessment exercise.

Based on similar assignments, it is estimated that the foregoing tasks would take approximately six to nine months to complete (not including an allowance that may need to be made for summer holidays, and assuming regular availability of the key participants).

PART V

final
THOUGHTS

LESSONS OF THE HEART

As I have wrestled with what it means to be part of a family business, I have learned many difficult lessons. The following personal reflections summarize some of the more important things I have discovered as I look back over my life. I am hopeful that these insights will be helpful to others when they find themselves in similar situations.

MONEY IS NOT WHAT WE ARE REALLY AFTER

Stephen Covey, author of *The 7 Habits of Highly Effective People*, states that we should "begin with the end in mind." In a family business, the end ought not to be simply to earn more money. There are three reasons why we should have different goals:

A) Money can't buy happiness. It won't do it for us; nor will it do so for our children.

B) Many of the most successful family companies in the world focus on their mission, rather than profits. For these companies, their positive bottom line results are a by-product, rather than the goal.[124]

C) What we all want is not more money, but rather more experiences of love and the feelings that accompany these special moments.[125]

---

[124] Danny Miller and Isabelle Le Breton-Miller, *Managing for the Long Run: Lessons in Competitive Advantage from Great Family Businesses* (Boston: Harvard Business Press Books, 2005).

[125] Jim Murphy, *Inner Excellence* (Manhattan: McGraw-Hill Professional, 2009).

In our family, there were times when we let money get in the way of relationships, and I have experienced the pain that comes from this approach. I regret that this was how we sometimes looked at things. The Beatles had it right when they sang that "money can't buy me love."

RELATIONSHIPS ARE WHAT WE REALLY WANT

My dad earned a lot of money during his career. However, he lived quite modestly and recognized that life was about relationships, not the size of his bank account. He showed us this by the way he lived, and by taking time for family and friends. His priorities were reflected in his routines; Sunday at noon, he had lunch with the family; at 6 p.m. virtually every night, he was home for family dinner; and almost every Friday evening he would have a few close friends drop in to enjoy a quiet, relaxed time, laughing and talking together. Consequently, when he died, he was a man who was rich, in terms of quality friendships. This is because during his lifetime, he invested in developing meaningful, long-lasting relationships.

INTEGRITY, VISION AND EXCELLENCE

Dad was very determined, and he worked hard. He was intent on making sure all our company's projects were done with excellence. He was also dedicated to conducting his affairs with unwavering integrity. Reflecting these principles was the development of The Bentall Centre in downtown Vancouver, perhaps his most successful venture. The complex created a lot of value for our family. However, Dad was not focused on the money. Instead, he had a vision to create an exemplary integrated office complex, reminiscent of the Rockefeller Center in New York. The financial success of this real estate project was really a by-product of his dedication to a vision.

A FAMILY BUSINESS HAS TWO BOTTOM LINES, FINANCIAL AND RELATIONAL

During the early part of my career, I focused on trying to climb the corporate ladder. I only paid attention to relationships as a means to an end. However, after my career imploded amidst all my striving, I came to realize that I had been ignoring the importance of relationships. This myopic focus on my own advancement had left me relationally bankrupt. The first place this showed up was in my home and my relationships with my wife and children. Alison and I steadily grew apart during the first seven years following our wedding. I was paying virtually no attention to her needs or the needs of our young family.

At the time, I didn't realize that I ought to measure the relational health in our family with the same dedication that I sought to measure the bottom line of the company. This would mean paying attention to family relationships and assessing how everyone was doing on a regular basis. This may sound impractical or too theoretical. But there are some simple strategies that may be employed to keep a watchful eye on how things are going in the family. In the business arena, good board governance typically calls for post-meeting assessments after each board meeting. It only takes a few minutes, but this routine enables the chair to obtain feedback on a regular basis and to respond accordingly. Similarly, it is easy to "take the pulse" in your marriage and/or family by asking a few simple questions. A good friend launched a "sea change" in our marriage when he recommended that I ask Alison three short questions, which I now recommend all men ask their wives regularly:

1. On a scale of 1 to 10, how would you rate our marriage?
2. Would you like us to move closer to 10?
3. What can I do, as your husband, to help us move closer to 10?

Similarly, when families hold a family meeting, they can make it a habit to ask for feedback from everyone in the family. This can include how things are going both individually and as a group. Armed with this information, the family can then decide what action may be needed to build its relational bottom line.

MAKE FAMILY VACATIONS A PRIORITY

At this time, I was virtually taking no holiday time and regarded this habit as exemplary. In fact, I actually considered this a "badge of honour."

Therefore, one of my first steps on the road to relational healing was when I decided to annually take the four weeks of vacation that I was entitled to. The second step was more difficult, and that was to not work during our holiday time. Instead, I decided to focus on my relationships with Alison and the children. This required me to accept that the company would be able to survive without me, at least for a week or so. My own sense of self-importance initially conspired against this, but in time I began to develop new patterns.

My executive assistant in Toronto helped me on this journey when she told me she wasn't going to call me on vacation. I told her it was "no problem" to call, because I would be thinking about work anyway. She admonished me and said that I shouldn't be thinking about work while on vacation. This simple statement challenged me to develop a new way of thinking. It has taken me many years to change, but now when I am away I can get so detached from work that I wonder why it used to be so all consuming.

Our four children are now all adults, and I can look back with fondness and recall many wonderful times spent together on vacation. At the time, it seemed like I was taking "extreme measures" by focusing on this amount of family vacation. However, as I reflect on it now, I wish I had done even more.

BEING LOVED IS MORE IMPORTANT THAN BEING RIGHT

I have always wanted to be right, and I really don't like to be wrong. However, I have discovered that being right tends to be overrated. I have been learning this in my marriage, as our relationship counsellor has been encouraging me on a quest to "be loved" by my wife, instead of trying to always "be right." This is not easy, but the more I experiment with this approach, the more convinced I am that it is a better way to live.

During the first 10 years of my career, I didn't understand that love trumps being right. Blinded by my own self-righteousness, I was a strident advocate of doing things right. Unfortunately, this created in me a very critical spirit. Ultimately, this resulted in me forfeiting my opportunity to lead our family business. This was a high price to pay in order to learn this lesson, and one which I hope others can avoid having to pay.

FORGIVENESS LEADS TO FREEDOM

One of my mentors, early in my career, was a big proponent of the philosophy that states, "Don't get mad; get even!" I don't agree with this approach. However, the reality is that most of us will be hurt or let down by someone, sometime in our career or family business. What are we going to do when this happens?

One thing that has helped me in these circumstances is to remember that as a human being, I also make mistakes. When I take time to think about this, I realize that I am probably in need of forgiveness more often than I need to forgive.

In addition, one of my closest friends once told me that when a person remains angry and doesn't forgive, they are creating a cage that holds a person captive. However, the person being held captive is not the person who is not being forgiven. Rather it is the unforgiving person who is being held in bondage. They are held in bondage by their own bitterness.

As difficult as it has been, at times, to forgive those who have hurt me in my career or in my personal life, I have tried with God's help to become a person of forgiveness.

I am thankful to have discovered the wisdom of this, because had I not learned this lesson, I could have easily been consumed by bitterness.

Instead, I am learning to be grateful. For I am a man who has been richly blessed.

CPSIA information can be obtained
at www.ICGtesting.com
Printed in the USA
LVOW01*2058080616
491630LV00002B/3/P